CW01020786

Blood and Thunder

Blood and Thunder

Rugby and Irish Life: A History

LIAM O'CALLAGHAN

SANDYCOVE

an imprint of

PENGUIN BOOKS

SANDYCOVE

UK | USA | Canada | Ireland | Australia
India | New Zealand | South Africa

Sandycove is part of the Penguin Random House group of companies
whose addresses can be found at global.penguinrandomhouse.com.

First published 2024
001

Copyright © Liam O'Callaghan, 2024

The moral right of the author has been asserted

Set in 13.5/16pt Garamond MT
Typeset by Falcon Oast Graphic Art Ltd
Printed and bound in Great Britain by Clays Ltd, Elcograf S.p.A.

Imported into the EEA by Penguin Random House Ireland, Morrison Chambers,
32 Nassau Street, Dublin DO2 YH68.

A CIP catalogue record for this book is available from the British Library

ISBN: 978–1–844–88661–6

www.greenpenguin.co.uk

For Susan

Contents

Prologue: shoulder to shoulder

'The IRFU is an all-Ireland sporting organisation which has never allowed politics to interfere with its affairs.'[1] Such was the profoundly mistaken view of the *Belfast Telegraph* in March 1995 as it welcomed the prospect of a newly commissioned anthem for the Irish rugby team.

The problem the new anthem was intended to solve had existed for a long time, and it was fundamentally political. Ireland competed in international rugby on an all-island basis. It had done so since the beginnings of international rugby in the nineteenth century, when the entire island was part of the United Kingdom, and it had continued to do so after the political partition of the island and the creation of the Irish Free State in 1922. (The national soccer team, by contrast, had split into Republic of Ireland and Northern Ireland teams after partition.) As we shall see, for a long time it was possible for Irish rugby to fudge the fact that there was no anthem corresponding to the entire island. But by the 1990s, the issue could not be avoided any longer.

The Irish Rugby Football Union's attempt to solve this problem was 'Ireland's Call'. The song was given its first airing in April 1995 amid considerable pomp. Written by Phil Coulter, a Derry native, the song was performed by the singer Andrew Strong live on *The Late Late Show*, and was simultaneously broadcast to a Northern Ireland audience on *Kelly*. Strong — a native of County Tyrone but best known for his portrayal of Dubliner Deco Cuffe in *The Commitments* — was joined on stage by groups of singers from Dublin and Portadown, and by members of the Ireland rugby squad, who looked like a group of boys reluctantly making up numbers in the school choir as they sang – or lip-synched – the words of the new song.

The early consensus among journalists and supporters was that the song – which has the 'four proud provinces of Ireland' coming together, 'shoulder to shoulder', to answer 'our country's call' – was shallow and insipid. Sean Kilfeather in the *Irish Times* described the new anthem as a 'travesty' and a 'limp attempt to nod in the direction of Irish unity'.[2] According to Con Houlihan, the song was 'appalling', and had a chorus that had to be 'heard to be disbelieved'.[3]

How had Ireland's rugby team navigated the seventy-odd years since partition without an anthem? For much of the history of international rugby, pre-match protocols were vague and inconsistent. These were put on a slightly more formal footing from 1949, when the four 'home' unions agreed that only the national anthem of the host state would be played prior to championship fixtures. This meant that 'Amhrán na bhFiann', the anthem of the twenty-six-county Irish state, was played before matches at Lansdowne Road, while 'God Save the King' was played before home fixtures in England, Scotland and Wales, and in Belfast. The key point here is that the anthems were linked to *locations* rather than *teams*. (Matters were slightly different in France, where the hosts sometimes played 'God Save the King' alongside 'La Marseillaise' – even, at times, before matches with Ireland following the creation of the Free State.) International rugby in the amateur era was not like international soccer. It was, in short, not very international at all. The Irish team rarely travelled further than

Britain and France. Ireland first visited South Africa in 1961, Australia in 1967, New Zealand in 1976 and Italy in 1995.

The anthem question became hard to ignore with the inauguration of the Rugby World Cup. At the first tournament, in New Zealand in 1987, the organizers, looking to emulate international competitions in other sports, decided that the anthems of both teams would be played before each match. Clearly 'Amhrán na bhFiann' was not a suitable anthem for a team that also represented Northern Ireland. The IRFU, thoroughly unenthusiastic about the World Cup, neglected to consider what anthem the Irish team would use. Eventually a hasty decision was made by management and players to use 'The Rose of Tralee', a politically neutral song but one clearly unsuitable for the occasion that it was chosen for. A saccharine love song featuring such lines as 'She was lovely and fair as the rose of the summer', 'The Rose of Tralee' was never going to raise the emotional pitch of the occasion.

On 25 May, Ireland played their first pool match against Wales at Wellington. While the Welsh XV and supporters lustily sang the rousing 'Hen Wlad Fy Nhadau' ('Land of My Fathers'), the Irish team huddled together nervously to the maudlin strains of 'The Rose of Tralee', played on a crackling tape recording. It was an utterly mortifying experience for the players. The *Irish Independent* described the choice of the song as 'an insipid decision'.[4] The *Irish Press* reached for the same adjective.[5] The *Cork Examiner* viewed the choice of song as proof there was 'some of the clown among the players and management team'.[6]

The IRFU deserve some sympathy, however. It was among the most testing of times for a cross-border organization. In May 1987 alone, fifteen people were killed in the Troubles. These included eight IRA volunteers ambushed by the SAS at

Loughgall while attacking the local RUC station, in one of the most high-profile incidents of the entire conflict.[7] In April, three Irish rugby internationals, Nigel Carr, David Irwin and Philip Rainey, had been injured by an IRA bomb that killed the former unionist politician Lord Justice Gibson, and his wife, just north of the border near Newry. The players had been travelling south for a training session. Carr, then rated among the best flankers in the game, was forced to retire as a result of his injuries.

The situation was made even more delicate by the backgrounds of some of the Ulster players. Jimmy McCoy, a member of the 1987 squad, was an RUC officer. Brian McCall, a member of the squad as late as 1986, was a British Army officer stationed in Germany. Both players – neither of whom ever publicly complained about standing to 'Amhrán na bhFiann' at Lansdowne Road – required a security detail while on Ireland duty.

Responding to those who viewed the playing of 'The Rose of Tralee' as an insult to 'Amhrán na bhFiann', the *Irish Times* pointed out that 'The Irish team which has gone to the World Cup is a federal team . . . One of the great strengths of rugby on this island is that it is played as an all-island sport. In its own way it has achieved some unity in Ireland . . . The unity of Ireland in sport needs to be nourished more strongly than ever. Forcing "Amhrán na bhFiann" on unwilling Northerners is not the way to do it.'[8] Mick Doyle, the coach, summed matters up more tersely: 'Our players come from two different areas of political jurisdiction and we had to play something.'[9]

After the embarrassment at Wellington, 'The Rose of Tralee' was dropped and anthems were not played before Ireland's remaining matches in the tournament. This was much to the dissatisfaction of Ireland's next opponents, Canada, whose captain snippily asserted that 'if Ireland has a difficulty, that's their problem, not ours'.[10] Anthems were somewhat less contentious at the next Rugby World Cup, in 1991. Three of Ireland's four matches were played at Lansdowne Road and one at Murrayfield, against Scotland. The usual Five Nations Championship arrangements applied: 'Amhrán na bhFiann' was played at Lansdowne Road, while no Irish anthem was played at Edinburgh. The World Cup organizers' intention that each team have an anthem had run aground on the shores of anthemless Ireland. In common with their Canadian counterparts four years earlier, Ireland's quarter-final opponents, Australia, were irked that their anthem was not played at Lansdowne Road.[11]

The IRFU's inertia was understandable. The noxious political atmosphere stemming from the Troubles hung menacingly over officials trying to manage symbolism in an all-island institution. And, despite the 'Rose of Tralee' fiasco and the diplomatic awkwardness of effectively suppressing opponents' anthems at the World Cup, the IRFU had some grounds for feeling that the status quo had served fairly well. In the face of the often poisonous political atmosphere on the island, rugby was frequently held up as a beacon of co-operation. Writing in the wake of Ireland's Triple Crown win in 1982, the *Belfast Telegraph*'s Alf McCreary wrote that 'True loyalists of a Northern red, white and blue, bought Irish tricolour rosettes . . . the police band struck up the Irish anthem. Staunch Unionists stood to attention.'[12] In 1984, before a Five Nations match against Wales at Lansdowne Road, an intrepid cameraman 'picked up prop Jim McCoy wagging an admonitory finger at his fellow Ulsterman Willie Duncan telling him to face the flag while the anthem was being played. The instruction was immediately complied with.'[13]

The anthem arrangements were a compromise solution whereby most of the compromising fell on the shoulders of the Northern players, almost all of whom were Protestant. They stood stoically for an anthem that at best did not represent them, and that at worst was antagonistic to their cultural identity. In the unionist press there were occasional suggestions that Irish rugby should be partitioned. With the playing of 'Amhrán na bhFiann' and the flying of the tricolour, one newspaper letter-writer claimed in 1980, Northern Ireland fans, officials and players were being 'swamped in Republican identity'.[14] Another correspondent, in 1988 (barely three months after the Remembrance Day bombing at Enniskillen), maintained that the unity of Irish rugby was only possible because one of the parties has 'willingly subverted all traces of its own identity in favour of the other's'.[15] In January 1993, Sammy Wilson, then a councillor and former Lord Mayor of Belfast, and later a Democratic Unionist Party (DUP) MP, called for the separation of Ireland into Northern and Southern rugby teams during an appearance on RTÉ's Pat Kenny radio show, claiming that Northern supporters suffered 'indignity' by having to stand to 'Amhrán na bhFiann', and that both hypothetical teams would be more successful than the unified one, as the anthem caused Northern players to underperform.[16] Wilson was a hardliner whose views were slightly outside the unionist mainstream, and his intervention was deemed sufficiently noteworthy to draw a barbed response from the Ulster Branch of the IRFU. Ken Reid, the Branch PRO, claimed that Wilson's views were 'nonsensical', 'insulting' and 'ignorant', and that the IRFU had 'jealously guarded its independence from political interference whenever possible'.[17] The *Belfast Telegraph*, in a measured editorial, acknowledged the contentiousness of the anthem question before poking fun at Wilson's suggestion that anthems affected performances on the field: 'If only our rugby ills could be cured by singing a different song, composers would be commissioned immediately!'[18]

Clearly, however, the IRFU could not sidestep the problem indefinitely. The direction of travel in international rugby was towards more national symbolism, not less. Rugby, now a professional sport, needed to conform with TV audience expectations of international sports competitions, where pre-match ceremonial rituals, including anthems, were the norm. There was a clear commercial imperative to all of this. In 1999, rugby's most famous pre-match ritual, the All Black haka, appeared in a television advert for Adidas as part of the New Zealand Rugby Union's sponsorship arrangement with the sportswear company. For the crowd in the stadium, the eighty minutes of action was now only part of the 'match day experience' that sport consumers now demanded. Refusing to play the anthems of visiting teams was an increasingly unsustainable position for the IRFU to maintain.

There was also some pressure from the media. Irish commentators routinely threw envious glances towards the Scottish and Welsh rugby crowds and their passionate renditions of their anthems.[19] Those nations had constitutional complexities of their own, but enjoyed a sense of national unity that simply didn't exist in Ireland and that allowed them to come up with far more satisfactory solutions to the anthem problem. Until 1975, international matches in Wales were preceded by two anthems: 'God Save the Queen', and 'Hen Wlad Fy Nhadau' ('Land of My Fathers'), which celebrates Wales's rich linguistic and literary heritage. 'God Save the Queen' routinely attracted a cacophony of boos from the Welsh crowd, and was permanently dropped in 1975, leaving

'Hen Wlad Fy Nhadau' as the sole anthem to be sung lustily by the Welsh crowd.[20] The Scots started using the rousing 'Flower of Scotland' – a song composed in the 1960s – in 1989. Though its lyrics evoked a Scottish victory over an English army at the battle of Bannockburn in 1314, it did not seem to ruffle the feathers of the unionists who played for Scotland. David Sole, later an opponent of Scottish independence, was among a group of senior players who lobbied the Scottish Rugby Union (SRU) to adopt the song as their official anthem.[21] The SRU, traditionally a stoutly unionist organization, accepted the song without any fuss. All of this was relatively low risk. When the Scots adopted 'Flower of Scotland', support for independence was a marginal political position; the Scottish National Party (SNP) was weak and factionalized. Matters were different in Ireland, where Southern Catholics and Northern Protestants did not have a shared sense of Irish nationhood and where there was a long-standing violent conflict. In that context, composing an anthem that was simultaneously rousing and inoffensive was, perhaps, an impossible task.

The immediate context for the commissioning of 'Ireland's Call' was the IRFU's decision that an anthem was needed for the 1995 World Cup. The Union were coy, only admitting in January that they had 'discussed a number of options relating to a rugby anthem' without elaborating further.[22] This was a delicate moment in the Northern Ireland peace process: the IRA and the Combined Loyalist Military Command had only recently announced ceasefires, and peace talks were underway. This was the mood music as Phil Coulter sat down to compose a new anthem for Irish rugby.

As late as February – two months before the unveiling

of 'Ireland's Call' – the IRFU would only admit that they had commissioned the song, refusing to confirm that Coulter had been given the job. Ken Reid, the IRFU president and a Northerner, told the *Evening Herald*, 'We're not talking about writing a national anthem, but you go to the World Cup and you hear the other country's songs and we felt we had nothing.' Of the new song, he continued, 'It's got to be Irish, it's got to have a call, and a rhythm, and it must be catchy, like a pop tune.'[23]

Recalling the process twenty years later, Coulter described his thinking:

> The big challenge was the imagery . . . you are trying to be all-inclusive so there were certain images and certain buzz-words that you had to stay away from . . .[.] Musically, you want a song that can be pretty instantly picked up by people in the stadium so it can't be too complicated. It had to be accessible, stirring and recognisable. Those were the boxes that had to be ticked.[24]

Coulter unwittingly failed to satisfy the first part of his brief. The final verse of the song's full version opened with the phrase 'Hearts of steel'. This was also the name of a Protestant agrarian society in eighteenth-century Ulster. Coulter's gaffe was greeted with mirth by the eagle-eyed commentators who spotted it, but Hearts of Steel was an obscure organization and the song was not revised. In any case, an abridged version of the song was performed on match days and the later verses had no salience with the public.

After making its match day debut at the 1995 Rugby World Cup in South Africa, 'Ireland's Call' – which was played after 'Amhrán na bhFiann' at home matches – struggled to gain any traction with the Lansdowne Road crowd. The PA announcer routinely felt compelled to encourage fans to sing it: 'a despairing effort to get the fans to take the song seriously', in the words of one commentator.[25] In the week leading into Ireland's home international against Wales in 1998, the team's head coach, Warren Gatland, publicly appealed to fans to sing the song that weekend. Columnist Kevin Myers captured the consensus in 1999 when he asserted that 'Ireland's Call' 'arouses no resonances in the crowd: it is an orphan-tune, unloved and unsung, and rescued from terminally embarrassing silence by a huge backing track'.[26]

It was unfortunate for the song's prospects, perhaps, that its adoption by the IRFU coincided with one of the grimmest decades in Irish rugby history. The international team's record on the field in the 1990s was abysmal. Ireland won just eight out of forty Five Nations matches played that decade and took the Wooden Spoon – for the bottom-placed team in the championship – on four occasions. On five tours in the southern hemisphere, Ireland failed to win a single Test match – not even the two they played against lowly Namibia in 1991.

'Ireland's Call' was thus caught up in the deep malaise that enveloped Irish rugby in the 1990s, and it became common among observers in the second half of the decade to hold the song partly responsible for the team's woes on the pitch. (This was clearly unfair, as the team had been terrible before the song was introduced.) Mick Doyle, a former Ireland player and coach whose efforts to avoid controversy were rarely strenuous, took his anger out on 'Ireland's Call' after a record defeat in Paris in 1996. 'Ireland, poor innocent Ireland,' he fumed, 'our decent rugby players from all parts of an island whose politicians won't even talk to each other, have now no anthem . . . unlike every other nation on earth.'[27] After an embarrassing defeat to Italy in Bologna in 1997, the *Limerick Leader* reported disdainfully that 'Before the match kicked off the players in green shirts were forced to listen to a poor version of . . . "Ireland's Call" while the Italians were fired up singing their national anthem.'[28] In October 1999, a couple of weeks before Ireland were eliminated from the World Cup by Argentina, the *Limerick Chronicle* was of the view that 'It is an utterly cringe-inducing spectacle to see fifteen reasonably capable athletes being made to stand in front of the class and go through their little turn, "Ireland's Call."'[29]

The derision heaped on 'Ireland's Call' from predominantly Southern commentators was, to some degree, rooted in complacency and insensitivity. The unionist press in Northern Ireland was more circumspect, welcoming any alternative to 'Amhrán na bhFiann'.[30] This came from a heightened appreciation, perhaps, that symbols matter in societies divided along cultural and religious lines. And symbols have the potential to be especially fraught for a rugby team whose players are drawn from the island's conflicting traditions. Rugby did not exist in splendid isolation from Irish society, culture and politics. This was a sport which, throughout its history, had to contend with war, revolution, partition, the Northern Ireland conflict, religious divisions and profound social change. In rugby terms, 'Ireland' and 'Irishness' carried different meanings for different people; and these meanings changed over time. Arriving at settled solutions on questions of symbolism, in that context, was neither trivial nor straightforward. 'Ireland's Call' might not have been the most rousing song ever written, but it was the solution to a considerable problem.

Now that the Irish were equipped with their own song, the way was clear for opponents' anthems to be played at

internationals in Dublin. Thus 'God Save the Queen' got its
first airing at Lansdowne Road for generations when England
were the visitors in February 1997. Martin Murphy, then an
IRFU administrator, told the press that the new policy had
been introduced as 'a courtesy to all visiting countries'.[31]

Rugby officials in Ireland might have been forgiven for
thinking that a potentially tricky issue had been permanently
resolved. But then, in 2006, a proposal that the PSNI and
Garda bands would play before the Ireland v. Scotland match
was scrapped when members of the PSNI band hesitated at
the idea of playing 'Amhrán na bhFiann'.[32] Not long later,
in 2007, a pre-World Cup warm-up match against Italy was
arranged for Ravenhill in Belfast. The IRFU decided that only
'Ireland's Call' and the Italian anthem would be played before
the match. This led to a backlash from unionists. Former
Irish international Trevor Ringland, a moderate unionist and
peace campaigner, was of the view that 'God Save the Queen'
should have been played along with 'Ireland's Call'; the fact
that it was not played meant, he argued, that the IRFU should
no longer include 'Amhrán na bhFiann' in the programme
at Lansdowne Road.[33] This was a reasonable point, but the
IRFU held firm, refusing to even meet Ringland and stating
that the anthems protocol for away matches would apply to
all fixtures played outside the Republic of Ireland. The Union
evidently calculated that to play 'God Save the Queen' would
have been a striking and potentially troublesome departure,
and not worth the risk.

In December 2021, an *Irish Times* poll of Republic of Ireland
citizens found that 72 per cent of respondents would 'not
accept' a new national anthem in a united Ireland. Speaking in
general terms in 2022, Andrew Trimble, a Northern Protestant
who won seventy caps for Ireland, and who expounds very

moderate political views, claimed that the Republic of Ireland was 'not ready' for unity and that those likely to campaign for unity were not willing to 'compromise'.[34]

Ultimately, Phil Coulter was successful in serving up a song that was uncomplicated and inoffensive, if short on inspiration. Though the anthem was an IRFU commission, it has been adopted by the Ireland cricket and hockey teams, which also compete on a thirty-two-county basis. A *Sunday Tribune* editorial written some years before 'Ireland's Call' was composed asserted that the government ought to do away with 'Amhrán na bhFiann' and replace it with an anthem that represented all the island's traditions, promoted mutual respect, and had no military undertones. Such a song, the *Tribune* speculated, would be 'depressingly worthy', and would thus have the merit of being played infrequently.[35] The IRFU achieved at least that much, perhaps, with 'Ireland's Call'.

1. Tom Brown's game in Ireland

It is difficult to determine with any certainty when the story of Irish rugby begins. Dublin University Football Club, founded in 1854, proudly declares itself 'The oldest rugby club in the world in continuous existence'.[1] On the surface, this claim is plausible: we know from press reports that a football club existed at Trinity College from the mid-1850s; we just cannot determine if the sport that its members then played could meaningfully be called 'rugby'. In reality, there was no such thing as rugby clubs or, indeed, soccer clubs in the 1850s. Until at least the mid-1860s, the word 'football' was an imprecise term, encompassing a range of forms of what became soccer and rugby.[2] Both handling and kicking the ball were generally permitted in all types of football, most encompassed some version of a scrum, and the basic aim in all the variants was to propel a ball of varying shapes and sizes over the opposing team's goal line. There were efforts – never successful – to codify the variants into a single unified form of football, and the division of the sport into distinct rugby and soccer codes was not firmly settled until the 1870s. Even then, clubs in Britain switched freely between codes, such was the lingering similarity between them, and it was not until 1892 that the Rugby Football Union specified that a rugby ball must be oval rather than round.[3]

The first rulebook of the Football Association (FA) – founded in 1863 – specifically permitted handling the ball, and the game it codified was one in which tries were scored;

and the Rugby code, at this stage, privileged kicking the ball over handling it. In 1868, there were forty-five football clubs in England playing under the rules of Rugby School, safely outnumbering the thirty playing the FA's variant.[4] Soccer's transformation into a commercial and cultural behemoth did not take shape until the 1880s.

So what form of football was being played at Dublin University Football Club in its earliest years? It is possible, indeed likely, as we shall see, that the young men of DUFC preferred the type of football then played at Rugby School, but it is also possible that they played a game (or games) whose rules were few and varied from match to match. We cannot accurately consider the football club at Dublin University to have been a 'rugby club' from its founding because the footballers of the 1850s simply would not have recognized such a precise categorization of their sport.

A bolder, more vivid account of the origins of the game in Ireland came from Sir Charles Burton Barrington. Born in County Limerick in 1848, Barrington grew up on his family's 10,000-acre estate at Glenstal Castle. The Barringtons were among the most influential families in Limerick and were well liked as landlords. Barrington's father, Sir Croker, had studied law at Trinity and had a busy professional career. He was Clerk of the Crown for Limerick and his law firm had been solicitors to the Great Southern and Western Railway. When he died in 1890, 'very great regret was expressed by all classes in Limerick'.[5] As was the fashion among men of his class, Sir Croker sent his sons to school in England. His eldest son, Charles, entered Rugby School in 1864, having previously attended St Columba's College in Dublin. He completed his schooling in 1866 and enrolled at Trinity College Dublin the following year, where he took an MA.

Sir Charles, who inherited his father's title in 1890, moved in fashionable circles on both sides of the Irish Sea. He was married to the daughter of an English aristocrat, and signalled his conservative and unionist leanings through membership of the Carlton Club in London and the Kildare Street Club in Dublin. He was a founding member and president of Limerick Football Club, the city's first rugby club, and also held the presidency of the Limerick Amateur Athletic and Bicycle Club. An accomplished oarsman, he was vice-president of the Limerick Boat Club. He was also deeply involved in affairs outside sport. On top of all of that, he was Provincial Grandmaster of the North Munster Freemasons, a leading member of the Limerick Branch of the Irish Unionist Alliance, and a notable figure in Limerick civic life. In 1879, he became High Sheriff for Limerick and devoted much time to various philanthropic causes in his native county.

Of all the prominent roles held by Charles Burton Barrington, the most significant from the perspective of Irish rugby came when he was elected captain of Dublin University Football Club in 1867. For it was here that Barrington, by his own account, was responsible for the introduction of rugby football to Ireland.

A detailed account of his role at DUFC survives thanks to correspondence Barrington conducted in the 1920s and 1930s with Edward McCartney Watson, then an academic at Trinity. Having arrived at the college in 1867, Barrington soon set about replacing what he considered the 'little desultory football' then played by the club with the rules of his old school, Rugby.[6] The 'Dublin University Laws of Football' were printed in January 1868. Barrington's account was charmingly homespun: he recalled that he and R. M. Wall, another club member, met in a room at Trinity College in January

1868, where 'He wrote and I dictated. Gradually and gradually as one could remember them the unwritten laws that govern the immortal Rugby game were put on paper.'[7] Rugby School, according to Barrington, 'had no written rules! . . . They were traditional, like the British Constitution or the secrets of the Free Masonry.'[8] The new DUFC rulebook was soon distributed to other Dublin clubs, and the whole initiative, by Barrington's own estimation, was a triumph: 'The Club was really a great success and did introduce the rugger game into Ireland.'[9]

Key aspects of Barrington's account were, however, farfetched. Two features of it can be disproven without difficulty. First, his claim that the Rugby School rules were unwritten was simply false. The *Laws of Football as Played at Rugby School* had been through several written versions by 1868. The latest rules were not long off the press when Barrington entered Rugby in 1864, and it is not plausible that he did not know of their existence in written form. Second, the claim that he brought the Rugby rules to Ireland is very questionable. We have no reason to doubt that he wrote the Dublin University club's first rulebook and that it was closely modelled on the Rugby equivalent. But this was not the club's first encounter with Rugby rules. In 1862, a correspondent to the English sports newspaper *The Field* informed readers that 'at Trinity College Dublin and by the "Wanderers" the Rugby rules, slightly modified, have been adopted . . . and, as many of the Irish schools have begun to play by them, there is every likelihood of their becoming universal in Ireland'.[10] In 1865, and with Barrington still firmly ensconced at Rugby School, the *Dublin Daily Express* carried an article about an upcoming match between the football and rowing clubs at Dublin University, in which it advised readers that

It is to be observed of this club that its play is conducted in accordance with established rules, such as are in force at Rugby, and in this respect it presents an example of regularity and order which we would like to see imitated by the public schools of Ireland.[11]

In 1866, press accounts of two separate matches at the college described touchdowns being followed by kicks at goal, clear features of Rugby football. It seems likely, then, that a game resembling the one played at Rugby School – possibly just the basic features of it – was adopted by DUFC from the early 1860s. The story told by Barrington – possibly true in its essence, but definitely false in some particulars – was but a modest contribution to the canon of sporting myth.

Few sporting myths are more infamously enduring than the origin story of rugby football itself. During a football match at Rugby School in Warwickshire in 1823, the story goes, a pupil named William Webb Ellis defied the rules of the game by picking up the ball and running with it. This act of rebellion was immortalized on a stone plaque erected at the school in 1900 and became the accepted version of how the game originated.

The Webb Ellis myth was first asserted by an ex-Rugby School boy, Matthew Bloxam, in 1876. He never supported his account with evidence, and the story would have remained 'an antiquarian's eccentric belief' if the Old Rugbeian Society had not set up a commission in 1895 to investigate the game's origins. The commission found nothing to substantiate Bloxam's tale, but, oddly, accepted it as the most likely explanation of the game's provenance.[12] The reality was that even if William Webb Ellis did pick up the ball in 1823, there was nothing mould-breaking about it. Many schools had their own codes of football, and handling the ball was usually permitted in these games. Various forms of 'folk' football involving kicking and handling a ball had existed in England for hundreds of years. Often violent and disorderly, these were the pastimes of peasant society. The Webb Ellis myth allowed followers of rugby to distance their 'scientific' and civilized game from these more vulgar pursuits. The myth also allowed middle-class rugby followers to draw a clear line between their sport and the working-class sports of soccer and rugby league, both of which they looked down upon. Indeed, as the Old Rugbeian commission carried out its work in 1895, the game was in the midst of a full-blown civil war. The issue of payment for play had seen the game's best clubs in the north of England part company with the staunchly amateur RFU to establish the new professional sport of rugby league. The Webb Ellis myth gave comfort to followers of rugby union in time of trauma, reaffirming the game's gentlemanly lineage.

Webb Ellis may have played no role in the development of a modern code of football, but Rugby School certainly did. In the early and middle years of the nineteenth century it became fashionable among British 'public' schools – which were in fact private, costly and exclusive – to promote games as a way of instilling moral values in boys and promoting their physical development. When the British government's Clarendon Commission examined the state of the public schools in the early 1860s, its report was especially laudatory of Rugby School. Rugby's reputation had been enhanced by the headmastership of Thomas Arnold (1828–41) who pioneered a set of ideas that would later be called 'Muscular Christianity'. School, according to this ideology, was where boys developed character and learned discipline, cooperation and leadership – key attributes for the future leaders of the Empire.

Though Arnold was no fan of sports, headmasters across England came to view rule-bound games as a useful vehicle for furthering these principles. Several variants of football were played across the public schools, but it was the Rugby code that quickly came to exemplify the link between moral values and sport. This was in no small part due to the phenomenal success of Thomas Hughes's novel *Tom Brown's Schooldays* (1857), a hugely influential portrayal of life at the school in Arnold's time. Readers were treated to exciting descriptions of football as played at Rugby, including a climactic conclusion to a House v. School match where young Tom bravely dives on the ball to prevent a certain try for the opposing team. The book gave the game played at Rugby a meaning and a set of values among readers that would become, in the words of the historian Tony Collins, 'the moral foundation for what would become rugby union football wherever the game was played'. These included 'a commitment to a masculine and anti-effeminate worldview . . . a belief in British national superiority . . . and an absolute certainty in one's own moral purpose'.[13]

Rugby produced its first written laws in 1845 and updated them periodically thereafter. But the game as played at the school remained chaotic and violent. With teams of fifty or sixty boys a side, there were very few opportunities for players to run with the ball. Instead, most of the action revolved around seemingly endless scrummages involving an indeterminate number of forwards. Unlike the modern game, scrummages had no set formation. Players stood upright and were permitted to kick each other on the shins, a practice known as 'hacking'. The object of the game was to score goals by touching the ball down beyond the opposing team's goal line and converting the resultant 'try at goal' by kicking the ball between the opposition's posts and over the bar. An unconverted try carried no value.

Rugby soon became the code of football most associated with handling and carrying the ball, and was adopted by other public schools, such as Marlborough, Cheltenham and Wellington. By the 1860s, a network of clubs playing under the Rugby rules had developed. Ex-public schoolboys, eager to continue playing their favourite code of football into adulthood, set up clubs for that purpose. The drive to standardize those rules came from these clubs' desire to play against each other.

Before past pupils of Rugby and other English public schools brought rugby to Ireland, the country had its own rich tradition of folk football stretching back hundreds of years. There was little to distinguish the Irish experience of folk football from the British one. It was a set of pastimes based on local traditions, with matches taking place on feast days and during the quieter periods of the agricultural calendar. Folk football in Ireland, as in Britain, was often viewed by the authorities with suspicion, as it could involve violence, disorder and desecration of the Sabbath. It also involved large gatherings of young men, something the British authorities were particularly anxious about, given Ireland's history of political instability and agrarian violence. As late as the 1860s, the authorities clamped down on 'football meetings' in the countryside as they assumed them to be mere cover for Fenian activity. The earliest rules of Gaelic football were vague enough to accommodate many features of older forms of the game played in the countryside. Inter-parish rural football, therefore, was largely assimilated by the GAA, which satisfied the footballing needs of the rural and small-town Catholic classes.[14]

The Anglo-Irish, by contrast, imported their favoured code of football from England. Wealthy and ambitious Irishmen, viewing Irish schools as inferior, sent their sons to school in England in considerable numbers in the nineteenth century. Some Irish institutions attempted to compete. St Columba's College was founded in Dublin in 1843 and aimed to directly emulate British public schools. A correspondent to the *Irish Times* in 1865 wrote:

> 'Tom Brown's Schooldays' has not only made many Irish boys envy the good luck of their English equals in age, but has induced many parents, who can afford it, to send their sons to [Eton, Harrow or Rugby] . . . To remedy such a state of things, it is well to have an institution like St Columba's in which Irish youths of the better class may receive an education fully equal to the English standard.[15]

Thousands of Irish boys attended English public schools in the nineteenth century and a substantial number of them were exposed to Rugby football by attending either the school itself or one that played football under its rules.

For Irish boys who returned home for university studies after completing school in England, Trinity College was by far the leading prospect. The best evidence suggests that it was here that football under Rugby rules was first played in Ireland. We know that ex-Rugby School boys (referred to as 'old Rugbeians') were members of Dublin University Football Club from its very foundation. Robert Henry Scott, an ex-Rugby boy, was secretary of the club in 1855. Among other early members of the club were four other ex-Rugby men and two ex-Cheltenham boys.[16] When, in 1856, an internal match took place between the 'Freshman classes' and the 'rest of the club', 'old Rugbeians formed the staple commodity of the Freshmen side'.[17] In 1857, DUFC held an internal match between thirteen members who had attended Rugby or Cheltenham and the best remaining thirteen of the university.[18] As we have already seen, the first direct evidence that Rugby rules were adopted by the club comes from the early 1860s. Given the numbers of old Rugbeians involved in the club prior to then, and the pride that they were known to have in the school's code of football, it seems possible that the game as played at Trinity from the beginning at least resembled the one played at Rugby. But given the fluidity of football rules at the time and the informal nature of the club's activities, great care needs to be taken in asserting when, exactly, Dublin University Football Club became a rugby club.

The few surviving match reports from the club's early history suggest that the game as played at Trinity in the 1860s was true to its public school heritage, where ad hoc arrangements could be made on such matters as numbers of players and the duration of the match. A team named 'Wanderers' played against Trinity as early as 1860. In common with the practice at public schools, where games were often played over a number of days, the match started on a Tuesday and was resumed on the following Thursday.[19] In 1867, the University XV defeated twenty players from the University rowing team. One week later, the XV had a stiffer task when they played against, and defeated, a team of thirty-three men drawn from the club's remaining players.[20]

The club used a bewildering range of criteria to form 'scratch' teams for internal matches: fair hair v. dark hair, north v. south, smokers v. non-smokers. In the case of the latter fixture in 1872, 'the lovers of the soothing weed' were said to have 'presented a poor front'.[21] To modern eyes, there was something charmingly informal about how the club ran its affairs. A fixture would be arranged and whoever turned up would play. If the teams had vastly uneven numbers, then so be it. The club's activities were also sporadic – it is clear that there were lean years with little or no football activity. In a university club the turnover of players and officials was frequent, meaning that the club's fortunes were dependent on a constant influx of new enthusiasts.

On the rare occasions when DUFC played against external opposition, compromises were made on rules, and it is clear that the club was not strictly aligned to the Rugby code. In 1867, the club played three games against the military. In the first two games, 'out of courtesy to the strangers', the college team played 'contrary to custom, by the Eton Rules'; they then won an easy victory in the third match when Rugby rules were followed.[22] Football at this time was for enjoyment alone and was mostly a private affair arranged among enthusiasts who saw no reason to advertise matches in the press. Most of the early activities of DUFC, or any other clubs that might have existed, are therefore lost to history.

Into this set-up – at best semi-formal, at worst chaotic – stepped Charles Barrington in 1867. Barrington's own account of his association with DUFC, as we have seen, was exaggerated in some key respects. He did not introduce rugby to Ireland and he did not recall from memory the 'unwritten' football rules of his old school. When the Dublin University Laws of 1868 are read alongside the 1862 Rugby School equivalent, Barrington's efforts quickly resemble a clumsily plagiarized student essay. Where the Dublin rules paraphrased their Rugby equivalents, the differences between the two versions were slight to the point of being insignificant. Six laws in Rugby's 1862 rulebook appeared word for word in Dublin University's version. Several other laws on the Dublin list were minuscule variations on those that appeared on Rugby's list. It seems very likely that Barrington had a number of rulebooks in front of him when laying down the Dublin laws. Laws 4 and 5 in Dublin University's list were paraphrased versions of laws 2 and 5 in the rules of the Blackheath Football Club in London. In 1868, DUFC hinted that their new rulebook was a synthesis of others: 'After a careful review of the rules of all clubs we have thought fit to compile a code which will . . . meet with the approbation of all.'[23]

One clear difference between the Dublin and Rugby laws was the ban placed on hacking in the Dublin rules. The practice was symbolically important in establishing the manliness of the Rugby game but it was not to every club's taste.[24] Rugby-playing schools and clubs in England routinely banned it, and clubs in particular were wary of the consequences that bloodied shins might have for professional men. For some footballers, hacking was a fundamental feature of the game and its absence was to be lamented. In April 1867, 'Old Rugbean' [sic] wrote to the *Irish Times* claiming that in his time as a footballer at school, 'all through every match of any importance we played with "hacking". Such a thing as a serious accident seldom or ever . . . [took] . . . place.'[25] This was in response to a letter to the paper from the captain of Dublin University, Arthur Dobbs, who pointed out that the college team did not practise hacking and its prohibition was a 'fundamental principle of the "Trinity" game'.[26]

The supposed dangers of rugby football caused occasional bouts of moral panic in Britain, and this may have influenced the drafting of the Dublin University rules in 1868. Dobbs's defence of rugby as played at Trinity came after an accident in a match between DUFC and the Garrison in which a military officer broke his leg. The press responded with disapproval:

> It was the opinion of many present that the accident would not have occurred had the rules of Eton, which prohibit the system of tripping and 'hacking', as it is technically termed, been adhered to. Several very serious accidents of a similar nature have taken place in the College Park, owing to the extremely rough and dangerous practices permitted by the Rugby rules, under which this match was being played.[27]

The club was probably anxious to preserve its reputation when it formally banned hacking. Specific laws against 'holding and throttling' were also included in DUFC's laws.

Barrington's rulebook may not have been conceived of in the manner that he claimed, but the very fact that it was written and shared was important. Shared rules were essential for developing a network of clubs and encouraging growth in a game. The club duly distributed the rulebook to other clubs so that potential future recruits and external opposition might become 'thoroughly acquainted with the science of the game'.[28] Barrington brought order, structure and energy to DUFC. Press coverage of the club's activities notably increased from around 1867 onwards. Whether this was due to more matches being scheduled or to a greater tendency by the club to advertise its events, it certainly denotes more energetic organization. Barrington introduced a second XV, and external teams seeking to test themselves against the first XV would only be granted that honour once they had defeated the seconds. Official colours – black and red – were adopted and a system of awarding honours caps was introduced. When members of Dublin University Football Club gathered for a meeting at the beginning of the 1868–69 season, they noted 'a marked improvement in the organisation of the club'. [29]

Charles Barrington's time in Ireland ended abruptly when his daughter Winifred was accidentally killed in an IRA ambush in 1921. The family settled in Hampshire and later offered Glenstal Castle to the Free State government as a residence for the Governor-General. The offer was declined and the castle eventually became a monastery and, fittingly, a rugby-playing school.[30] Why Barrington chose to offer such a far-fetched account of his role at DUFC is unclear. Even though he was in his eighties when he wrote his recollections, the scale of his exaggeration cannot feasibly be assigned to a frail memory. Age brought eccentricity with it, perhaps. In any case, his story followed him wherever he went, even to the sleepy corner of England where he now lived. In 1940, a local newspaper in Hampshire – where an elderly Sir Charles was now resident in the village of Curdridge – wrote a long tribute marking his imminent ninety-second birthday. Barrington, according to the paper, 'claims to have been responsible for introducing rugby into Ireland'.[31]

2. 'Against the World'

At a general meeting of Dublin University Football Club in October 1874, delegates decided to invite the other 'principal clubs' to join them in setting up a national governing body. Following a meeting of clubs in early December, the Irish Football Union (IFU) officially came into being.[1] And on Christmas Eve, operating out of the Trinity College Dublin rooms of George Hall Stack, a young law student, the IFU issued a circular to inform the press that the committee of the Union intended to select twenty Irishmen to do battle with England the following February in Ireland's first ever international rugby match. The IFU promised to select a team that was 'as representative as possible', and that would 'hold their own "against the World"'.

Rhetorically, at least, the committee were committed to inclusiveness. Selecting an international team was something that should attract 'the practical sympathy of their fellow-countrymen of all shades and degrees'.[2] The committee went on to remind the public that 'these international contests . . . have a direct and very powerful tendency to remove international asperities and to inspire the youth of either country with mutual feelings of respect and toleration'.[3] The London newspaper *Bell's Life*, getting a touch carried away, wondered if the question of Home Rule, an emergent problem in British politics, 'may be deprived of half its bitterness to the assembled thousands of Dublin by a stoutly contested scrummage' and whether 'the last traces of Fenian feeling might be lost sight of after a brilliantly-dropped goal?'[4] The questions were rooted in a stubborn reality: Irish rugby, in almost all respects, was thoroughly British.

The IFU's stated desire to select a team representing 'all Irishmen' fell at the first hurdle: it appears that the clubs of Belfast were not invited to join the Union.

In Belfast, rugby had taken root at around the same time that Barrington re-energized DUFC. In 1868, the North of Ireland Cricket Club decided to form a football team. This was common at the time in Britain: cricket clubs, looking for a winter activity for members, often turned to football. Irish boys educated at English public schools were, as in the case of DUFC, to the forefront of the new club. The inspiration behind North of Ireland Football Club (NIFC) was Edward H. Moeran, an ex-Marlborough boy. Moeran, a Dubliner and the son of a Trinity professor and clergyman, had captained both the football and cricket teams at Marlborough and brought the sporting lessons of school back to Ireland.[5]

At its inaugural meeting, NIFC adopted Rugby rules but, like DUFC, banned hacking, having deemed it suitable only for schoolboys. The club's first ever fixture, in January 1869, was an internal match between 'English public schools' and 'the World'.[6] Later in 1869, another scratch match was organized, in which a team composed of members who had been to Cheltenham, Marlborough and Bromsgrove schools took on the rest of the club.[7] Abram Combe, later a merchant in Belfast, left Rugby School in 1869 and appeared on an NIFC team list in November of the same year. The Rugby rules, as we have seen, had also been adopted by this time at Cheltenham College. Thus Herbert Lanyon, an ex-Cheltenham boy, would likely have been familiar with the game long before he lined up alongside Combe in the same match.[8] Combe, later capped for Ireland, entered Rugby School in 1866, the same year that another Belfast merchant, Thomas Gisborne Gordon, enrolled there. Gordon too played for NIFC and also received the first of his three caps for Ireland in 1877.

Why the IFU did not invite the footballers of Belfast to join the new organization remains a mystery. The Dublin committee could not claim ignorance of Belfast football. DUFC had played NIFC for the first time in 1871, and one member of the Trinity team that day, Brabazon Casement, was now a member of the IFU committee.[9] Whatever the reason for their omission, the Belfast men reacted indignantly. According to the Dublin journalist Jacques McCarthy, feelings ran high among the Northerners in the aftermath of a match at Belfast between Dublin club Wanderers and NIFC in November 1874:

> The Dublin fellows got up an Irish Football Union all to themselves, quite oblivious of the fact that they might not be considered quite competent to dictate to the whole country, or that there was such a little village as Belfast in existence. Of the latter fact, however, they were pretty sharply reminded before long at a dinner held in the Linenhall Hotel after the first match between the Wanderers and North of Ireland . . . one after another, the North men stood up and gave it very hot to the Dubliners for not inviting their co-operation.[10]

The Northern Football Union (NFU) were founded in January 1875 to further the game in the Belfast region. The NFU immediately decided to cooperate with the Dubliners in the selection of the international team, but a string of efforts by the IFU to effect a merger were rebuffed by the Belfast men.[11]

This did not bode well for the selection of Ireland's first international team, a task that preoccupied officials, North and South, in the winter of 1874–5.

England and Scotland had contested the first international rugby match in 1871. As early as 1873, unspecified 'arrangements' were said to have been in progress in Dublin to select an Irish international team. In March 1874, Richard Bell, the secretary of NIFC, hoped that a forthcoming trip by his club to Scotland might lead to 'an international match between Ireland and Scotland'.[12] Neither initiative went anywhere.

In late 1874, England's Rugby Football Union accepted a challenge issued on behalf of Ireland by Dublin University, and the match was fixed for Kennington Oval in London the following February.[13] It was the arranging of this match that prompted the formal establishment of the IFU. The first international team, comprising twenty players, was picked using an elaborate system: the IFU and the NFU elected seven men each, and the remaining six were selected from a pool of twenty-two (eleven nominated by each Union).[14] Rugby, at this juncture, was weak in Munster and effectively non-existent in Connacht. Ireland's maiden international team was composed entirely of Leinster and Ulster men.

Of the seven original committee members and office holders of the IFU, all except R. M. Peter were selected for the first Irish team. George Stack was named captain. The two most influential administrators in the NFU, Richard Bell and Abram Combe, also helped themselves to a place each on the team.[15] The selection of the first Irish rugby team, therefore, resembled a group of children picking teams for a kick-around on the schoolyard. But the available pool of players was small and the keenest committeemen were often the most enthusiastic players.

The recollections of Jacques McCarthy give us some insight into the chaotic lead-up to Ireland's first international. McCarthy was the great narrator of late-nineteenth-century Irish rugby. His columns in the Dublin newspaper *Sport* ran from the early 1880s until his illness and eventual death in 1901. With their combination of obscure analogies, hastily composed verse and long, tangential anecdotes, they often made for entertaining reading. He was a well-known character around Dublin and was mentioned in passing in Joyce's *Ulysses*. 'Father Son and Holy Ghost and Jakes McCarthy', Myles Crawford exclaims, as he attempts to inspire the youthful Stephen Dedalus in his early journalistic endeavours. McCarthy added humour and humanity to sports writing, a genre then dominated by dry description. All of this often came at the expense of factual accuracy. He was also prone to name-dropping and snobbery; his sniffy attitude to Gaelic games, in particular, provoked criticism.

He was unsparing in his summary of Ireland's first rugby international. 'I well remember the first match in 1875,' McCarthy would recall a few years later, 'when our team was about as correct a specimen of mismanagement as was ever witnessed. It could scarcely have been otherwise . . . The result of the discord in 1875 was that our disconnected executive sent a very useless team to London.'[16] The seemingly hapless Irish twenty, McCarthy wrote elsewhere, 'had never previously seen each other; the twenty a-side game was absolutely unknown in Ireland . . . Backs were put to play forward and vice versa, and the whole lot were immaculately innocent of training.'[17]

The Irish team was comfortably beaten but not disgraced in its first international match. Most of the play took place in the vicinity of the Irish line, but such was the nature of the game at the time that a determined pack of forwards – which Ireland possessed – could cause sufficient disruption to keep the scoreline respectable. In this case Ireland lost by two goals (i.e. converted tries) to nil. The efforts of Ireland's forwards drew praise, but the feeling among observers was that the Irish backs were naïve of the tactical demands of the game and deficient in its basic skills, especially drop-kicking.[18]

Ireland's fortunes did not improve in the short term. Eleven of the first twelve matches against England were lost – a draw in Dublin in 1882 the only exception. It was much the same in matches against Scotland: fourteen of the first fifteen fixtures in this series resulted in defeat for Ireland, including a six-goal hammering in the first ever match between the teams at Belfast in 1877. The *Ulster Examiner* gave an astringent summary: 'a group of beardless schoolboys, collected promiscuously from the lower forms of a preliminary school, without any idea of sustaining national honour, but merely going in for a lark, would have shown better play than our Irish "team" in the "international match"'.[19] Commentators attributed Ireland's hopelessness on the field to rancour off it. Having two unions on one island was 'a matter which has brought us into much ridicule with Englishmen', the *Cork Constitution* noted.[20]

It was the question of Munster's representation on the Ireland team that finally brought matters to a head. The game had steadily taken root among the Protestant elite in Cork and Limerick cities in the 1870s, and in 1877 Munster played Leinster for the first time in Dublin. By then, Cork FC and Limerick FC both had representatives at the IFU committee table. The Munster men were growing impatient – and would remain so for much of the near century and a half since – at their perceived lack of representation on the international team. Meanwhile the NFU, characteristically, were ignoring IFU pleas for cooperation on the question of Munster representation. The annual interprovincial fixture between Leinster and Ulster was now a trial for the international team. There was no clear mechanism, therefore, by which Munster players could stake a claim for selection.

In a gesture that had all the appearances of tokenism, two Limerick men were selected for the match against England in 1878. This drew a furious letter to the *Freeman's Journal* from Pierce Goold, the honorary secretary of Cork FC: 'The picking of this team is only another instance of the many injustices done to Cork men, although they have done all in their power to co-operate with this so-called union.'[21]

The IFU continued to pursue a merger with the NFU, going to the trouble of drawing up a 'scheme of amalgamation' in 1877 that would have seen the creation of provincial branches in Leinster, Ulster and Munster. This proposal was greeted with silence by Belfast. The IFU grew increasingly frustrated, and in October 1878 a meeting resolved that if 'the NIFU [sic] declined to take any steps in the matter [of amalgamation], the IFU should recommend the Munster clubs to form a Southern Union, in which capacity they could claim a share in the selection of the Irish XVs'.[22] A month later, the NFU relented. Richard Bell, the Northern body's secretary, attended an IFU meeting in Dublin to 'assist in the drawing up of a general scheme' for amalgamation.[23] Thus, the Irish Rugby Football Union, with branches in Leinster, Munster and Ulster, came into being at the beginning of the 1879–80 season. Munster were treated like junior partners and were welcomed into the IRFU with a swift kick in the teeth – they were awarded two committee members fewer than the other two provinces and would only gain parity when the interprovincial team drew with or defeated either Leinster or Ulster.[24]

These developments made little difference to fortunes on the pitch. We have noted Ireland's abysmal record against England and Scotland. Matters in fixtures against Wales were an unmitigated fiasco. When the teams first met at Dublin in 1882, most of the selected Irish team, including the entire Munster and Ulster contingents, cried off, and the starting XV included players not usually picked for their club teams. 'If I were among the powers that be,' Jacques McCarthy fumed, 'I should decidedly object to their receiving . . . international caps.'[25] The teams next met two years later in Cardiff. A week before the match, the IRFU were groping around Dublin looking for players willing to travel. Thirteen players made the journey; two Welshmen in Cardiff made up the 'Irish' XV. A few years later, McCarthy claimed that the 1884 team were a 'few lads over in Wales on a cheap trip at Easter' who 'took it upon themselves to play as Ireland'.[26]

If the IRFU had not yet worked out how to assemble a competitive international team, progress was being made at the grassroots. By 1884, the IRFU had twenty-six affiliated clubs, with an aggregate membership of close to 2,000. There were a further twenty-one unaffiliated clubs with over 800 members,[27] and any number of semi-formal teams that popped in and out of existence.

Leaving aside the quality – or lack thereof – of Irish teams in the early years, we must ask one simple question: what 'Ireland' did these men represent? The IFU circular issued at Christmas 1874, as we have seen, promised to unite Irishmen of all types and to heal international 'asperities'. Given the stark social, religious and political divisions of nineteenth-century Ireland, these were highly ambitious aims – and of course they were not achieved.

The IFU, in their mission statement, spoke of appealing to Irishmen of 'all shades and degrees'. But the composition of the IFU's first committee was not an encouraging portent for an organization committed to sporting inclusivity. All seven were middle-class Protestants, most of whom had attended Trinity College and all of whom had comfortable professional careers in Ireland or abroad. Of the twenty Ireland players who took the field against England at Kennington Oval in February 1875 – representing an island that was about three-quarters Catholic – we know for a fact that fifteen of them were Protestant; and it is virtually certain that the remaining five were Protestant as well. Only two of the first hundred men capped for Ireland – over a period of eight years – were Catholic. Jack Keon, a Limerick bank official from a gentry background, was the first, in 1879. Thomas St George McCarthy – a Trinity man, a founding member of the GAA, and a District Inspector in the Royal Irish Constabulary – was the second, in 1882.[28]

The dominance of Protestants among international players is hardly surprising, considering the nature of Irish rugby's grassroots at the time. Early Irish teams were drawn from a minute playing pool, which, in turn, was drawn from a fairly small but influential sector of Irish society. When those twenty men set off for Ireland's first international match in February 1875, it seems doubtful that the rural Catholic peasantry were huddled anxiously around their fireplaces awaiting news of the result from London. By extension, the game's prospects of healing international 'asperities' were for now quite limited. The type of Irishman minded to dislike England was not very likely to play rugby and was even less likely to be selected to play it for Ireland.

Until at least the mid-1880s, rugby was predominantly a Protestant pursuit in Limerick and Cork. Trinity College Dublin – the heartbeat of Irish rugby outside of Belfast – was also an overwhelmingly Protestant place. In 1871, over 90 per cent of the students enrolled there were Protestant. In the decade 1867–76, when DUFC established themselves as the citadel of Irish rugby, an average of a mere twenty-seven Catholics entered Trinity each year – not enough for two rugby teams.[29] Catholics had to defy the wishes of their own clergy to enrol there. Critics constantly cited the harmful 'atmosphere' at Trinity, as though Catholics would inhale toxic fumes if they happened to stray inside the college gates. Not that they were particularly welcome anyway: religious tests preventing Catholics and Presbyterians from holding fellowships at Trinity were removed only in the 1870s. According to a Protestant commentator in 1895, Trinity 'has never claimed to be a National University . . . the tone of the place is essentially West British . . . the Anglo-Irish College is almost emotional in its loyalty to unionism'.[30] 'Trinity', one historian has remarked, 'was a little piece of Britain that happened to be located in Ireland.'[31]

This 'little piece of Britain' was central to the fortunes of Irish rugby. Over a quarter of all Irish internationals selected before 1914 were DUFC men, including nine of the inaugural twenty. Just three clubs, DUFC and two of their offshoots, Wanderers and Lansdowne, provided over 60 per cent of Irish internationals from outside Ulster before the outbreak of the Great War. Wanderers and Trinity, one journalist remarked in 1882, 'represented the town and gown strength of the metropolis'.[32] DUFC's supremacy was also evident at club level. Credible opposition was scarce and strings of short-lived clubs came and went in Dublin in the 1870s and

1880s. When the Leinster Senior Cup was eventually inaugurated – a sign that an established network of clubs now existed – DUFC won five of the first six titles, and thirteen of the first twenty titles.

DUFC were not just a club: they were an entire footballing ecosystem. When the IFU held a general meeting in March 1875, seven clubs in addition to DUFC attended. The representatives of four of them – Engineers, Portora, Monaghan and Bray – were themselves Trinity men.[33] One of the purposes behind the foundation of Wanderers was to create a sanctuary for those no longer eligible to play for the university. The moving spirit behind the club was Richard Milliken Peter, a middle-ranking civil servant who had developed a passion for football while attending Blackheath Proprietary School – a hugely influential school in the development of rugby.[34] Former DUFC men at Wanderers were barred from playing against the college team, thus ensuring that the new club, in their early years, would not threaten Trinity's preeminence. Future Irish internationals such as Abraham Cronyn and Brabazon Casement, among several others, were simultaneously members of DUFC and Wanderers. Another founder member was the Trinity graduate John Baptist Crozier, who at the time of his death in 1920 was the Church of Ireland Primate of All Ireland.[35]

The Lansdowne club was founded, essentially, to give football a permanent presence on the grounds of the Irish Champion Athletic Club at Lansdowne Road.[36] As with Wanderers, there was considerable overlap with the membership of DUFC.[37] R. M. Peter of Wanderers became an honorary member, giving the new club some administrative experience. By 1880, Peter noted with satisfaction that Lansdowne had become 'more independent of College aid, and that the Fifteen is not a Trinity team under another name'.[38]

What we had here, then, was a small, densely interconnected scene, composed almost exclusively of privileged Protestants. The prevailing political orientation would have been unionist, though there were exceptions. Brothers Edgar and Robert Galbraith, who were among Ireland's first international twenty, were the sons of Joseph Galbraith, a professor of experimental philosophy at Trinity and Church of Ireland clergyman who was also a political radical and a supporter of Home Rule.[39] The brothers themselves attended Home Rule meetings. Another early international, Jack Myles, was the brother of Sir Thomas Myles, a Home Ruler later involved in gun-running for the Irish Volunteers.

The game in Ireland also maintained close links with English public schools. From the early 1870s, Wanderers initiated an annual match in Dublin between boys educated in England and in Ireland.[40] The great majority of Irish rugby men, even in the game's earliest years, were educated in Ireland. But the prominence of ex-public schoolboys tells us something important about how the Irish game became firmly intertwined with the social and political networks of Britain and the Empire.

This is neatly captured in the life of David Arnott. Born in Tynemouth in 1855, he was the son of John Arnott, a Scottish-born businessman who had migrated to Cork in 1837. Arnott senior became an extravagantly successful businessman: he owned the chain of drapery stores that bear his name to the present day, was involved in railways and brewing, chaired the Cork Steam Packet Company and owned both the *Irish Times* and the *Northern Whig*.[41] In 1865, his ten-year-old son

David was sent to Cheltenham College, where he would be selected for the football twenty.[42] After school, David Arnott took a commission in the Connaught Rangers before standing for Parliament in 1880, where, as a Conservative candidate, he narrowly lost in the Youghal constituency in County Cork. Though he campaigned in favour of the mainly Catholic demands of peasant proprietorship and denominational education, his defeat was attributed by one newspaper to 'priestly influence' and voter intimidation.[43] He was involved in his father's various business ventures in Cork, Belfast and Dublin before focusing his career on the *Irish Times*, where he held a directorship and worked at the paper's London office.

In rugby, as in life, Arnott was nomadic. In 1874, he played for NIFC in what was essentially a final trial for the first Ireland team. (He was not selected.) In 1875, he was both honorary secretary and captain of Lansdowne FC in Dublin,[44] and the following year he appeared on team lists for Wanderers in Dublin and again for NIFC in Belfast.[45] Arnott received a solitary cap for Ireland, in December 1875 in the second ever international against England. Originally selected as a substitute, he took his place in the team when another player withdrew.[46]

By 1898, his playing days over and now based in London, Arnott was a founding vice-president of London Irish Rugby Football Club.[47] When the club celebrated its fourth annual dinner in March 1902, Arnott presided over a lavish event attended by 110 members and guests. Then in his mid-forties, Arnott could claim to be one of the first men to have dedicated a significant proportion of his life to rugby.

After guests had offered a toast to the King and sung the national anthem – London Irish was not exactly a wellspring of Irish nationalism – Arnott got to his feet. In his speech he paid tribute to Thomas Crean and Robert Johnston, two former Irish rugby internationals who had both been awarded the Victoria Cross for their bravery on the battlefield while serving in the Boer War. Crean, a Catholic educated by the Jesuits at Clongowes, and Johnston, a Protestant who attended King William's School on the Isle of Man, were both selected to travel to South Africa in 1896 with the British Isles team (today called the British and Irish Lions), and did not return home after the tour. 'When the war broke out and men were wanted,' Arnott recalled, 'both joined the Imperial Light Horse . . . and soon showed the Irishman's true vocation was fighting.' Arnott spoke of Irish footballers' pride in 'their two countrymen, who but for their association with the great winter game might never have attained the prominence they held today'.[48] The implied links between rugby, militarism and imperialism in his speech were characteristic of the worldview that he and his fellow public school men carried through life. In July 1915, tormented by his belief that the Great War would be lost, Arnott shot himself dead at his home on the Isle of Wight.[49]

One of Arnott's colleagues at the London Irish committee table was Dr Michael Bulger. A Dublin-trained physician practising in London, Bulger, like Arnott, received one cap for Ireland, in 1888. The opposition was the New Zealand 'natives' (precursor to the modern Maori All Blacks) on their first international tour. They were the subject of unpleasant racial stereotyping, including in the Irish newspapers.[50] *Sport* carried illustrations that showed a group of strapping Maoris towering over a small but clever-looking Irishman with a large horseshoe and a shamrock attached to the back of his coat. Another illustration, after the Irish had been heavily defeated,

depicted a bare-chested Maori dressed in a grass skirt performing a celebratory dance, with a vanquished Irishman
lying helplessly on the ground.[51]

Bulger's selection for Ireland was also symbolically important. He was the product of an elite Catholic school, Blackrock
College. As we shall see, the emergence of a network of rugby-
playing Catholic schools from the 1880s was absolutely
critical in determining the future evolution of the game in
Ireland.

3. The old school tie

In March 1908 the *Church of Ireland Gazette* carried a detailed feature article discussing the social differences between the country's Catholic and Protestant populations. The author described Catholic shopkeepers and publicans – then a growing and influential class in Ireland – as money-grabbing 'philistines'. This particular class of Catholic also kept farms as well as shops, and lived 'only for making money and creature comforts', but were not brave enough to send their sons to Trinity College; in this matter, they had been 'defeated by their priests', though 'they would dearly love to see their sons associate with Protestants and playing football in the College Park'.[1]

Protestants, the author admitted, privileged games over culture and reading, but at least they played their games well. Proof of this was the Protestant devotion to rugby. 'In the matter of self-restraint we are inclined to think that no game is such valuable training as Rugby football. It is the winter pastime of all Irish Protestant schools. No game suits so well the Anglo-Irish temperament, as it gives abundant scope for the more aggressive qualities, and also calls for much endurance and patience.'[2] The crowds that assembled at Irish rugby internationals displayed 'a correctness of behaviour which is quite without a parallel anywhere else in the British Isles'. This was because the crowds were mainly composed of the middle and upper classes, while the lower classes had always refused to patronize rugby for 'political reasons'.[3]

The article gave a highly simplistic impression of Irish rugby and its social environment. There can be no doubt that the game was dominated by the social elite; but that elite, by 1908, was far from exclusively Protestant. As their relative wealth and influence grew in the late nineteenth and early twentieth centuries, Catholics developed middle-class tastes, and in sport this included a liking for rugby football. They remained generally reluctant to send their offspring to Trinity, but some did. Among these was Daniel Scanlan Bulger.

A draper from Kilrush in County Clare, at some point in the late 1870s or early 1880s Bulger relocated to Dublin, where he became a stockbroker. Clearly an ambitious man, Bulger sent his three sons to Blackrock College – at the time acquiring a reputation as one of the island's most prestigious Catholic schools – and then to Trinity. Larry Bulger won a Leinster Schools Senior Cup medal with Blackrock in the competition's inaugural year in 1887. The following year – as we saw in the preceding chapter – his brother Michael gained his only cap for Ireland, against the New Zealand 'natives'. Larry, selected for the first XV at Lansdowne while still a schoolboy, gained the first of his eight caps for Ireland in 1896 and toured South Africa with the 'British Isles' team the same year. The third brother, Dan, was also a distinguished player at Lansdowne.

For the Bulgers, rugby was a gateway to an exclusive social world. Michael and Larry both qualified as doctors and emigrated to London. Michael, as we have seen, was a founding member of London Irish rugby club, an institution that counted among its membership and patrons some of the most influential Irish people in London. Larry became president of Twickenham rugby club, and after retirement he regularly attended the Twickenham rugby ground on international match days, where he served as an honorary medic.[4] Within a generation the Bulger family had journeyed from provincial shopkeepers in the west of Ireland to the heart of professional and sporting networks in London and Dublin. Rugby was a social vehicle that enabled this journey.

Equally impressive were the Cussens of west Limerick. John Cussen farmed a substantial holding at Kilcoleman outside the town of Rathkeale. He was also a successful butter merchant, trading out of the port of Cork. He sent his son Robert (Bob) to Blackrock College, where he was captain of the first recorded rugby team at the school, before training as a solicitor. Bob established a successful practice at Newcastle West, and sent his own four sons to Blackrock, where they played on the senior rugby team, before enrolling at Trinity. Robert Jr (Bertie) and Denis starred on their school and university rugby teams. Denis captained the school team to Leinster Senior Cup success in 1918 and 1919.[5] A fast and powerful winger, he was selected for a final Irish trial match in January 1921 while still only playing for the second XV at Trinity. He scored a couple of tries in the match and was chosen to make his international debut against England barely eighteen months after leaving school. Qualifying as a doctor, he later emigrated to England. Bertie, a fine three-quarter and also a Senior Cup winner, became only the second Catholic to captain the first XV at Trinity. As they had done in school, the Cussen brothers earned major honours together on the rugby field at Trinity, winning the Bateman Cup – an All-Ireland club tournament – in 1926.

The Bulgers and Cussens were eye-catching examples of a growing trend. In late-Victorian Ireland, Catholics in increasing numbers coveted careers in business, the professions and the civil service. Elite education at one of the growing number of Catholic fee-paying schools provided a pathway to satisfying these ambitions. Educational qualifications were only part of the story, however. Of equal importance, perhaps, were social networks – and here rugby was central. The importance of this can scarcely be overstated: the adoption of rugby by Catholic schools was one of the most significant developments in the history of the Irish game. Ireland's success at the highest levels of international rugby in recent years would be unimaginable if Blackrock College and other elite Catholic schools had gravitated towards Gaelic games or association football.

Rugby in schools, of course, was more than just an instrument of social advancement. The widespread adoption of codified games in the nineteenth century by British schools stemmed from the belief among headmasters that the physical as well as the intellectual development of boys needed to be nurtured. Healthful pastimes such as football were also viewed by educators as a useful diversion from all manner of vice, thus moulding boys into morally sound Christian gentlemen. 'Let our schoolmasters recognise that a lifelong brainwork cannot be built up on flimsy bones and flabby muscles', IRFU president W. C. Neville declared in 1880.[6]

One such Dublin schoolmaster, Dr Charles Benson, had long recognized this principle. As early as 1862, the headmaster and owner of Rathmines School advertised his institution as one where 'the health of boys is carefully attended to', and, of course, where 'in winter there is a field for Foot-ball'.[7] In 1885, an article in the school's magazine described football as 'the manliest of games'. It was better to see 'a boy with his eye in a sling', from the effects of football, 'than walking up and down Grafton Street with kid gloves'.[8]

Ulster was the cradle of Irish schools rugby. From the 1860s onwards, there is evidence that the game was played at the Royal Schools at Portora, Dungannon and Armagh. These schools, set up by King James I to provide education for the planter population of Ulster, and other elite Protestant schools in Ulster struggled to compete for enrolments with English institutions. Maurice Hime, headmaster of the Monaghan Diocesan School, complained relentlessly about Irish parents enrolling their children in English schools. 'Irish boys are sent for their education, sent to their lasting injury, by parents, who for the sake of avoiding a "nasty vulgar Irish brogue" ensure to their sons a still more nasty vulgar English one.'[9]

At the Monaghan Diocesan School, football became properly organized under Rugby rules in 1869. A crude form of the game had existed there in the decades prior, with one ex-pupil recalling that the only aim of the game was to 'kick the ball from your own to the enemy's quarters if you could'.[10] The school soon started arranging fixtures with their neighbouring Royal Schools at Armagh and Dungannon. Already, rugby was becoming more than just a means of developing Christian manliness through sport. The authorities at Monaghan, for example, were eager to prepare their boys for life at Trinity, and this meant that familiarity with Rugby rules was essential.[11] The school team's first three captains, Ashley Westby, Harry Jackson and Abraham Cronyn, all received caps for Ireland, having been selected for the first XV at Trinity.[12] At Monaghan as well, at this early stage, we can see the development of an idea that would soon flourish across the elite education system: that the reputation of the school somehow rested on the quality of the football team.[13]

In November 1875, the Northern Football Union decided

to establish a schools cup competition to encourage the growth of the game. In the inaugural tournament, just four teams entered.[14] But within a decade the number of entrants expanded. In 1891, the headmaster of Methodist College (aka Methody) devoted a part of his speech at the annual prize-giving ceremony to the achievements of the school team, recently crowned Ulster champions. Dismissing the notion that the emphasis given to rugby in the school might distract boys from study, he asserted that 'half our football team are our most distinguished scholars'. Football, in his view, made boys 'feel proud of their college, and it is this principle which will, doubtless, hereafter make them feel proud of being citizens of the most progressive city of the United Kingdom, and subjects of the greatest empire on earth'.[15]

Schools elsewhere in Ireland were slow to emulate their Ulster counterparts in inaugurating competitions, though this was not for the want of teams, particularly around Dublin. R. M. Peter listed thirty rugby-playing schools in his *Irish Football Annual* of 1880, almost all of which were Protestant and half of which were in Leinster. But hardly any of these were affiliated to the IRFU. In 1876, just three schools – Rathmines School, Arlington School and Walker's Military Academy – were members of the IRFU.[16] In order to encourage affiliation and the growth of the game more generally, the Union committee proposed the establishment of a schools competition as early as 1876. But nothing came of this proposal in the short term, and schools that played football tended to confine most of their activities to internal matches between scratch teams.

The Rev. Charles Benson's Rathmines School was one of the pioneering rugby schools in Dublin, though Benson himself did not care for the game, considering it too rough.[17] He preferred cricket, but it was better to have a rough game to fill the winter months than to have no game at all. Rathmines affiliated to the Irish Football Union in 1875, and from around then a regular set of external fixtures took place, mainly against other Protestant schools.

The school's intake of 1877 and 1878 produced three future international players: Joseph Chambers, Robert Warren and Daniel Rambaut. All three were selected for Ireland's first victory over England in 1887. Warren – later Crown Solicitor for County Wicklow and one of the great talents of the day – was selected at half-back for Ireland within a year and a half of finishing school. Rambaut, a brilliant athlete who defeated Dan Bulger in the 1887 national hurdling championships, starred in the victory over England, converting both of Ireland's tries.

By the time rugby was established in Ireland as a game dominated by a Protestant elite, the social, political and economic dominance of that class was already in decline. The Intermediate Education Act 1878, which introduced a system of payment by results, led to a trebling in the number of Catholics attending secondary school between 1871 and 1911. University education was also reformed. The founding of the Royal University of Ireland and, later, the National University of Ireland led to a notable increase in the number of Catholics enrolling on degree courses.

The children of the most well-to-do Catholics now had a clear route to university education, the professions and careers in the civil service. Between 1861 and 1911, the proportion of Catholic lawyers, doctors, civil servants, teachers and engineers increased considerably, though Protestants remained over-represented in all of these professions.[18] In that context a feverishly competitive atmosphere developed both within and between secondary schools, and places at the best Catholic institutions were highly coveted.[19] Clongowes Wood, a long-established Jesuit boarding school in County Kildare, was the most prestigious, but other schools soon caught up. The boarding schools at Blackrock and Castleknock, and the Jesuit day school Belvedere, became highly influential as the nurseries of a new ruling class.

One activity clearly united the growing Catholic elite with the longer-established Protestant middle class: rugby. In Leinster, between the mid-1880s and the opening decade of the twentieth century, internal scratch matches gradually gave way to a calendar filled with external fixtures. Catholic and Protestant schools freely arranged matches with each other, and the Leinster Schools Cup was inaugurated in January 1887 by a subcommittee of the Leinster Branch of the IRFU. Once schools rugby became public-facing and the subject of press coverage, its importance stretched well beyond the physical and moral benefits that it provided boys. Cup fixtures were occasions when the school colours were on display in a strikingly visceral way; stories of cup glory allowed a lasting emotional connection to be forged between boys and their school. The Schools Cup became highly ritualistic, a rite of passage that bound generations of old boys together.

Fr Martin Ebenrecht, a priest at Blackrock College, kept a detailed journal of events at the school throughout the 1880s and 1890s. Ebenrecht knew next to nothing about rugby, but his journal is a useful record of the growth of the game. In the inaugural season of the Schools Cup, he noted that Blackrock was 'the only Catholic college to enter the cup'.[20] Blackrock won the cup in 1887 and retained it in 1888. In the opening round of the 1889 competition, Blackrock were giving Wesley College such a hiding in the first half that the latter did not reappear after halftime. In the semi-final, they faced Galway Grammar School, who, in the absence of a similar competition in Connacht, tended to enter either the Ulster or the Leinster Schools Cup. Blackrock duly trounced their opponents, but were later disqualified for fielding an over-age player. Ebenrecht devoted six pages of his diary to the controversy, including several newspaper clippings.[21]

Blackrock cup victories soon became viewed as the natural order of things: the school won fourteen of the first twenty Senior Cups. From 1890, all boys were expected to attend Schools Cup matches. The cup was now more than just a competition – it was a ritual, the hordes of schoolboys descending on Lansdowne Road like pilgrims visiting a sacred site.

Other schools were desperate to emulate Blackrock's achievements. School teams in this era were often a motley assemblage of past and present pupils, but a key to the success of the Leinster Senior Cup was that it was confined to enrolled pupils under a certain age. The Senior Cup team was usually 'elected' at the beginning of the season. The composition of the team was the subject of much debate in school magazines, where portraits of players adorned the pages. It is scarcely surprising that these young men embarked on their post-school lives brimming with confidence and self-assurance.

The growth of the Senior Cup was decisive in drawing more Catholic schools into the game. At Belvedere College, games had been discontinued altogether in the late 1880s and were not revived until 1898, when the school chose soccer as its preferred code. But before long, according to *The Belvederian*, 'a determined agitation led to the dethronement of Association and the triumph of the handling code'.[22] The school entered the Senior Cup for the first time in 1904 and finally won it in 1923.[23]

St Mary's College, a Catholic day school in Rathmines, first entered the Schools Cup in 1898 but made no impact in the competition until well into the twentieth century. For the school historian, Fr William Maher, St Mary's had a patchy rugby record because it was a day school, dependent on 'weedy, city-types', as opposed to schools like Blackrock with their 'beefier boarders'.[24]

More successful was Castleknock College, which, like Belvedere, initially devoted its energies to soccer. In January 1898, the college adopted rugby at the request of students. 'For some time past,' a contributor to the school magazine explained, 'great interest has been centred in the Rugby code. This was attributable principally to the intense interest taken in the great Rugby internationals, especially this year, when Ireland led off with such a brilliant victory over England.'[25] The school continued to play soccer, however, and only dedicated itself exclusively to rugby from 1910 onwards, owing to the boys' eagerness to enter the Senior Cup.[26] Castleknock entered the Senior Cup in 1912–13 and won it at the first attempt, defeating Blackrock. A procession of a dozen brakes took the cup and the players home. When they arrived back at the college, a bonfire was lit on the hilltop, and stayed ablaze until the following morning. 'Never was such a scene of joy beheld at Castleknock', one boy recalled. The team had been coached by a Protestant, George Hamlet, himself a Wesley College man and ex-Ireland international.[27]

In Munster, organized schools competitions were slightly slower to get off the ground. Cork and Limerick each had their own schools cups, and a province-wide competition was not inaugurated by the Munster Branch until 1909. From the outset, three schools dominated it: Rockwell College in Cashel, County Tipperary, and Presentation Brothers College

(Pres) and Christian Brothers College (Christians) in Cork city. The two Cork schools had been founded specifically to provide elite education to wealthy Catholics. When Christians opened its doors in August 1888, the Lord Mayor of Cork described the new school as 'a want which had been frequently spoken of among the intellectual middle classes of our city'. There was now 'no reason why any Cork merchant should send his children out of Cork to be educated'.[28] Rugby rivalry between Christians and its slightly older neighbour, Pres, soon took root and survives to the present day. One of the first generation of boys to attend Christians would later recall, 'It almost looked as if our brand new college was the reincarnation of the soul of some ancient college, long dead, that bore enmity to "Pres" from eternity.'[29] The ritualistic combinations of songs, colours and banners that characterized the Leinster Schools Cup soon became the fashion in Munster as well.

The reason why Catholic schools opted for rugby over soccer or Gaelic games was a matter of timing. At the period when these schools were choosing their preferred sports, rugby was on a sounder organizational footing than the others. By the time the GAA was founded in 1884, Blackrock College, for example, was already a rugby-playing school. By the late 1880s, the GAA looked to be in terminal decline, whereas schools rugby was blossoming. The prestige of the Leinster Schools Senior Cup cemented rugby's status as the preferred sport among elite institutions. It was only in the second decade of the twentieth century that the GAA made earnest efforts to embed their games in schools. By then it was too late to supplant rugby in elite Catholic schools: the game was simply too ingrained in the everyday life of those institutions. And both soccer and Gaelic games lacked the social status of rugby – an important factor in the elite Catholic schools.

Another key factor in the growth of Irish rugby was the softening of sectarian divisions in the club game. In Dublin, clubs such as Lansdowne and Bective Rangers, both of which had strong Protestant origins, soon developed a multi-faith membership.

Belvedere College's school magazine noted which clubs past pupils had joined. Of the Belvedere XV in 1899–1900, ten joined Bective Rangers after school, 'and were instrumental in the subsequent revival of that club'.[30] In 1910, six of Lansdowne's cup team were ex-Belvedere boys, while there was a similar number on the Bective team.[31] Bective Rangers was founded by ex-pupils of Bective College, a Protestant school based at Rutland Square in Dublin; but by the turn of the twentieth century it became the preferred destination, along with Lansdowne, of Catholic rugby players eager to compete at senior level. The club's first eight Ireland internationals, starting with James Waites in 1886, were Protestant, but the next nine were Catholic. This was not some kind of Catholic takeover; club membership remained cross-faith. When the Clongowes-educated Magee brothers, Louis and Joseph, made their Ireland debuts in 1895, they lined up beside two of their Bective teammates, Ben Tuke and John O'Conor, both of whom were Protestant.

Founded in 1892, Cork Constitution (Con) was a Protestant and unionist club in provenance, but by the turn of the twentieth century it had a number of prominent Catholic members, and leaned heavily on Pres and Christians to fill its playing ranks. One of its most prominent administrators at the turn of the century was Edward Fitzgerald, a Catholic publican from Blackrock. He was educated at Pres and sat, simultaneously, on the committees of Con and Blackrock Hurling Club.[32] Meanwhile, Pres and Christians started to attract Protestant pupils. Harry Jack, a Methodist, and Ivan Popham, a Church of Ireland member, both learned their football as schoolboys at Christians before joining Con and eventually gaining selection for Ireland.

Religious boundaries were maintained in clubs created by and for the past pupils of particular schools. Old Wesley, for example, initially restricted membership to those who had attended Wesley College, a Methodist boarding school then based in Dublin city centre. The same was true of the clubs eventually set up by Blackrock, St Mary's and Terenure colleges. Even when a school attachment wasn't necessary, religious identity was sometimes to the fore. In 1922, a member of Old Belvedere RFC expressed the hope that boys arriving in Dublin from Clongowes would join in order 'to carry out the object for which the club was founded, i.e., to have a Jesuit club'.[33] Wanderers, with their longstanding connections to Trinity, seem to have maintained an overwhelmingly Protestant membership, though Catholics were never entirely excluded.

The multi-faith membership of some clubs speaks to rugby's capacity to unite people from different backgrounds in Ireland. A man who had attended Rathmines School might have taken part in school functions where the Queen was toasted and the British national anthem sung.[34] He might have joined the school's auxiliary to the Dublin University Church Missionary Association. In 1883, Dr Benson proudly reported that 'Rathmines School had already furnished three men to carry the Gospel to the heathen – a higher honour . . . than the much prized Indian Civil Service.'[35] 'Though they were proud of being Irishmen,' one Rathmines old boy would later state, 'they were still prouder of being part of the great British Empire.'[36] For the man who attended Blackrock College, Belvedere or Castleknock, by contrast, the equivalent school function might have observed a toast to the health of the Pope, and he might have joined a Catholic sodality.[37] Without rugby, these groups might never have interacted socially.

While there may have been diversity within Irish rugby, especially along the lines of religion, these men had an overarching feature in common: middle-class social and professional ambition. Snobbery cut across sectarian lines. In school magazines, those of both Catholic and Protestant institutions, the only details of past pupils recorded more carefully than their rugby careers were their professional accomplishments. Of the Belvedere College rugby team of 1901, for example, the school magazine recorded that 'The majority of the fifteen . . . reside in Dublin. Eight are engaged in commercial pursuits, while among the others we have two barristers, one doctor, one engineer, one solicitor, one architect, and one journalist accounts for the fifteen.' Though none were 'sufficiently long enough engaged in the world of work to have yet made a name for themselves', the author reassured readers that 'this, we trust, is just a matter of time'.[38]

Of the cohort of men who played for Ireland before the First World War for whom we have reliable information, almost a third entered the medical profession in some capacity. Others entered law, engineering, the (Protestant) clergy, the civil service, the colonial service, financial services and the military. The remainder included a light sprinkling of farmers and gentry, some businessmen – including textile magnates from Ulster – and those, mainly clerks, occupying the lower rungs of the middle-class ladder. A pub owner from Cork,

Billy Riordan, was also capped, though this seems to have escaped the notice of the *Church of Ireland Gazette*. Manual workers of any type are almost entirely absent from the sample, though Paddy Healy (a butcher) and Tom Halpin (a plumber) managed to earn international honours. Both men were from Limerick, a city where rugby took an idiosyncratic trajectory – as we will see in the next chapter. Myley Abraham, a Catholic clerk from Clontarf, was the son of a coachman and a domestic servant. He was the only Dubliner from a working-class background to play for Ireland before 1914.

There was a wider context to all of this. By the late 1890s, and for the century that followed, Ireland was viewed by the rugby world as one of the sternest defenders of that great symbol of class distinction in sport: amateurism. Amateurism was much more than a mere description of the relationship between payment and play: it was a complete moral framework. Fair play, privileging participation above winning, and gentlemanly conduct were key components of this ideology. Apart from the mortal offence of accepting money or payment in kind for playing, strict adherents of the amateur code frowned on careful preparation and training, excessive competitiveness, and gamesmanship.

Amateurism was as much a device for keeping working-class players out as it was a set of genuine values. This was particularly pertinent in England, where, in the industrial towns of Lancashire and Yorkshire, the game attracted working-class players and supporters from the late 1870s onwards. Intense rivalries between towns, consummated on the field of play through cup competitions, led to money and other payments in kind exchanging hands as clubs scrambled to attract the best players. A transfer market of sorts developed. In 1879, for example, Teddy Bartram left Harrogate for Wakefield Trinity, where he had his rail fares paid, was lent money and was eventually given the invented role of assistant secretary, earning him a generous stipend.[39] Matters came to a climax in the early 1890s when northern clubs attempted to legalize so-called 'broken-time' payments to compensate working-class players for wages lost while playing rugby. The Rugby Football Union, dominated by upper-middle-class ex-public schoolboys affiliated with London clubs, voted against this initiative. Twenty-two northern clubs immediately withdrew from the RFU and, after a meeting at the George Hotel in Huddersfield, announced the founding of the Northern Football Union. Thus, the new professional sport of rugby league was born.

This birth of professional rugby, through the League code, only intensified the quasi-religious status given to strict observation of the amateur ethos. In Ireland, there was a consensus among officials and press commentators that amateurism needed to be defended. As early as 1887, at a time of deep paranoia in English rugby about veiled professionalism in the northern counties, Jacques McCarthy offered a crass assessment of a visiting Hull team:

> the men who are over here look like artisans or mechanics of some sort. Now, these men don't play for nothing, and the question is – where do they get the money? . . . I have been in Yorkshire often enough; seen all the clubs, and if I was in the witness-box to-morrow I could not swear that I saw a single amateur.[40]

When the Hull delegation arrived for a post-match dinner in Dublin, McCarthy claimed that they were 'dirty, with their mouths open and ate as if they never got a bit', that they drank excessively, and that the IRFU should 'discourage importing such gentlemen to this country'.[41] Professionalism, or the suspicion of it, was thus conflated with the working classes and a whole range of undesirable behaviours. 'If men cannot afford to play football or indulge in other luxuries,' McCarthy had stated a year earlier, 'they must do without them.'[42]

At a general meeting of the IRFU in 1903, the Union's treasurer, H. C. Sheppard, went on an extraordinary verbal solo run. He told the meeting that temporary stands would no longer be erected at grounds and that admission prices would be raised to 'keep out the roughs'. 'Rugby', as distinct from soccer, he continued, 'was still followed by respectable crowds, and they did not want roughs into their ground to break up everything.' He specifically blamed Welsh fans for damage to the ground, before aggravating the insult further, telling delegates that

> They would notice by the balance sheet that over £50 had been paid for a dinner to the Scotchmen and only about £30 for a dinner to the Welshmen. The reason for this was that champagne was given to Scotchmen, and beer – and plenty of it – to the Welshmen. Whiskey and porter was always good enough for Welshmen, for they were used to drinking. The Scotchmen, however, were gentlemen, and could appreciate a dinner when it was given to them.[43]

Sheppard probably assumed he would get away with this calumny of the Welsh, but the *Irish Independent* published the speech. The Welsh press were furious. There were talks not only of that season's Ireland v. Wales fixture being abandoned, but of a permanent rupture between the Irish and Welsh unions. The Ireland international Mossie Landers of

Cork Constitution, a bookie's clerk and the son of a publican, expressed his disapproval of Sheppard's comments. Various Irish clubs also made plain their displeasure. Bective Rangers, for example, issued a statement to the press condemning Sheppard and sent it to the Welsh Rugby Union. The *Irish Independent* closely reported Welsh reaction and, in an editorial, criticized the tendency among Irish rugby men to look down on those they viewed as their social inferiors.[44] The same editorial criticized other newspapers for not reporting the speech.

Rugby's Welsh heartlands were located in the dense coal-mining areas of the south, where the game acquired a mass working-class following and player base. This bred a suspicion among the other rugby-playing nations that Wales were less than faithful to amateurism. There was also something in the brio and innovation that Wales brought to their style of play that annoyed the other unions, who preferred a more stolid, 'manly' version of the game. A few years earlier, Wales had raised a testimonial for their great international centre Arthur Gould, the money being used to buy his house in Newport.[45] Scotland and Ireland viewed the testimonial as a breach of amateurism, and in protest they refused to play against Wales in 1897. The Ireland match resumed the following year, but the Scots froze out the Welsh for another season.

Ireland and Scotland saw themselves as close allies in the battle to defend amateurism. When Ireland won the Triple Crown in 1899, according to McCarthy, 'the victory of Ireland was the victory of amateurism which we established and in which we were assisted by the other amateur nations composed of our brother Celts and amateurs of Scotland'.[46] The Scots, in turn, were thrilled with Ireland's success. 'It is hopeful for the prospects of Rugby amateurism when we find such staunch supporters as the Irishmen are at the top of the tree', the *Scottish Referee* observed.[47]

When both Ireland and Scotland defeated England in 1899, it was amid a sharp downturn in the latter's fortunes on the rugby field. Ireland's and Scotland's success, in McCarthy's view, was 'simply because they stuck to amateurism'. This, in rugby terms, was the doctrine of salvation by faith alone: steadfast belief in amateurism was essential for victory. McCarthy's view was entirely wrong. It was England's dogged adherence to amateurism that had brought them low in the first place. It had caused them to haemorrhage players to rugby league. In the five seasons prior to 1895, players from clubs that later defected to rugby league accounted for around 40 per cent of those selected for the international team. When England won the Triple Crown in 1892, ten of the fifteen players selected for the final match were from such clubs.[48] The starkest evidence of England's decline was in their results against Ireland. In nineteen meetings between the teams prior to 1896, Ireland won twice. In the eleven fixtures that followed, Ireland won nine.

Irish officials, no doubt, took pride in sticking to their principles. But it is easy to have principles when circumstances mean that they will never be tested. Professionalism was no threat to Irish rugby whatsoever. The essential precondition for professional football of any kind – a large industrial working-class population with disposable income – simply did not exist in Ireland outside the Belfast region. The likelihood of players defecting to rugby league – something that afflicted Welsh rugby from time to time – was very remote indeed in Irish rugby. For middle-class professionals living in serene suburbs and enjoying the status that rugby union brought with it, a move to the mining or textile towns of the industrial north of England for a short, precarious, and poorly rewarded career in rugby league cannot have been tempting. It would have wasted their fathers' expensive investment in their education. There was simply no incentive for Irish footballers to swap Dublin for Dewsbury or Belfast for Batley.

'All the Irish clubs', the *Church of Ireland Gazette* declared in 1908, play rugby 'in a fair and chivalrous manner ... Ireland and Scotland are sworn brothers, and work together to keep the game pure. No hint of "professionalism" is ever made against the players of either country.'[49] This was a comforting illusion. Ireland's stout defence of amateurism in the 'war' against professionalism was imaginary, like children playing at soldiers believing they are engaged in a real battle. But as we will discover in the coming chapters, Irish rugby had its own conflicts to contend with. Jacques McCarthy's view that Irish rugby was entirely composed of 'gentleman amateur schoolboys' did not reflect the complexity of Irish sport.[50]

4. The 'foreign' game?

'Limerick is literally swarming with clubs', the newspaper *Sport* joyfully reported in 1886 before announcing the founding of a new club, Kincora FC. The club secretary claimed the club had a membership of seventy-nine and 'some of the best halves and quarters in Munster'.[1] Quite how the fledgling club achieved such rude health so early in its history is unclear, though it seems plausible that the secretary, Walter Brazier, got carried away at the prospect of coverage in the national press and overstated the club's progress. It was certainly the case, however, that Kincora soon became one of the finest junior clubs in Limerick ('junior' in this context being the adult rank below 'senior'). Brazier, a Catholic clerk who later worked for the city council, and William Lamb Stokes, a Protestant merchant, organized a junior rugby tournament in Limerick in 1887.[2] The tournament had one strikingly unusual feature: the fixtures took place on Sundays.

Kincora FC had taken the precaution in 1886 of writing to the IRFU asking if this was allowed. The Union, in turn, passed a motion 'That there is nothing in the rules of the Irish Football Union which prevents clubs from playing one day more than another.'[3] Most IRFU officials were Protestants who, irrespective of denomination, would have been encouraged to observe the Sabbath; and Sunday sports, as we will see, were bitterly opposed by many Protestants. The Catholic Church was much more relaxed about these matters. Jacques McCarthy, a Catholic, was responsible for the motion that permitted Sunday rugby – though its seconder, J. R. Blood, was Protestant.

'To deal with the Sunday clubs in Limerick would be to write a history', *Sport* claimed in 1887; '– they are simply innumerable. Every youth from five summers upwards has his club and his colours'.[4] It is difficult to specify exactly the number of clubs that emerged, though McCarthy's claim that there were 'more than two dozen' seems excessive.[5] Around half that number seems more plausible. None of them was affiliated to the IRFU, meaning that a precise record of their comings and goings does not exist. Many of these clubs had a precarious existence, their vitality often dependent on the efforts of one or two eager officials. The loss of key men to emigration or other commitments could lead to a club's demise, or force mergers. Kincora, having attained senior status in 1888, suffered a chastening defeat to Queen's College Cork in their first competitive outing at that level. Rather than return to the junior ranks, Kincora amalgamated with Limerick Football Club in 1889, taking the name of the latter.[6]

The meteoric rise and fall of Kincora notwithstanding, a culture of junior rugby, with fixtures mostly played on Sunday, survived and prospered in Limerick and, in the form of Young Munster and Shannon, gave the city some of its greatest clubs. Each junior club tended to be associated with a particular locality in the city, and intense rivalries soon emerged. One fixture in the 1887 Sunday tournament attracted over a thousand spectators to the field at the rear of the Tait's clothing factory.[7] The tournament was held again in 1888. From 1895, a new competition, the Transfield Cup, became the focal point of junior rugby.

Junior rugby took the game in Limerick down a divergent path from the rest of Ireland, and reflected the demographics of the game in the city. The fact that they played on Sundays means it is likely that most of the players involved were Catholic. It also suggests that these players worked on Saturdays, the day when rugby matches typically took place in Ireland. Though this does not necessarily imply that they were from working-class backgrounds, it probably means that they occupied a lower rung of the socioeconomic ladder than the footballers that we met in chapters 2 and 3.

Some clubs even dabbled in nationalist politics. In November 1887, the Kincora club held a general meeting at the town hall in Limerick. Two resolutions were passed. Members agreed that the club would take part in a demonstration honouring the Manchester Martyrs, and the meeting condemned the government's treatment of political prisoners, specifically the imprisoned National League MP, William O'Brien.[8] When the Manchester Martyrs commemoration took place the following week, there were serious disturbances in Limerick. The police, intending to seize two flags from the Kincora contingent, approached the clubhouse only to find that members had barricaded themselves inside. The Kincora men chided the police, lustily singing 'God Save Ireland' from the windows.[9]

The surroundings in which Limerick's Sunday clubs played offered a striking contrast to those enjoyed by more elite clubs. In 1886, for example, Kincora played a fixture on a Sunday against Thomondgate in the field adjoining the Limerick workhouse – a far cry from sedate weekday afternoons in College Park or Clyde Road in Dublin.[10] The footballers of Ulster, where the Sabbath was observed with particular severity, would almost certainly have disapproved.

With its inter-parish rivalries and Sunday fixtures, junior rugby in Limerick had conquered terrain coveted by the

GAA before the latter had an opportunity to lay down roots in the city.

The Gaelic Athletic Association was founded in 1884 to take control of Irish athletics, to revive the ancient pastime of hurling, and to draw up rules for a new code, Gaelic football. As the sporting branch of the broader cultural revival, the GAA saw as their mission the rescue of Irishmen from the 'denationalizing' effects of 'foreign' games. The Association's founder, Michael Cusack, had himself been immersed in the Dublin rugby scene from the mid-1870s to the early 1880s. Cusack, who was relentlessly pugnacious – the type of character who would pick a fight with his own shadow – was also an astute observer of the world around him. The social and cultural elitism of rugby that we observed in Chapter 2 would have been obvious to him. When Ireland was defeated by England in a rugby international in 1886, Cusack was typically scathing in his *United Ireland* column: 'For the twelfth time representatives of the foreign faction in Ireland met their English friends to play England's game . . . Imported games have been a source of humiliation to us.'[11]

The nationalist critique of rugby was not confined to issues of culture and identity; it also had a clear class dimension. 'Thanks to the unfailing and constant patronage of our colleges,' a correspondent in the *United Irishman* claimed in 1900, 'Rugby football occupies the leisure moments of our young men whose destiny is one of the learned professions or the Indian Civil Service.' Gaelic games, the writer sarcastically claimed, are 'altogether unfitted for and beneath the scions of country grocers and police pensioners'.[12] The great irony here, of course, is that fringe nationalist publications were offering an almost identical critique of elite Catholics as the one that we observed in the staunchly unionist *Church of Ireland Gazette* at the beginning Chapter 3. *Young Ireland* in 1919, for example, informed readers that

> At Blackrock Rugby is played . . . it is the parents who pay and hence call the tune which they demand is one which will ennoble . . . The provincial shopkeeper who profiteers in porter is most anxious that his children should be reared in an atmosphere where even the smell of cork should never penetrate. The local solicitor, who exists on drunks, disorderlies, licence transfers and odd pickings from local councils . . . ambitions the Indian Civil Service for Ignatius Arthur.[13]

The lampooning of the schools rugby player clearly did not begin with Ross O'Carroll-Kelly – it is a genre with a rich heritage.

Intemperate voices like Cusack's were not necessarily a faithful barometer of the wider GAA membership's mood. The mentality that later crystallized into a series of rules prohibiting members from playing rugby took some time to develop. The idea that one sport was more patriotic than another was not as intuitive to the footballers of the 1880s as Cusack's loud voice made it sound. Moreover, Gaelic football was not an especially attractive code for football clubs – its rules were quite vague and in its early years it remained, as the historian Paul Rouse has put it, 'a game very much in the making'.[14] In the short term, then, there were no compelling cultural or sporting reasons for young men to choose Gaelic over rugby.

Rugby's appeal in Limerick was built around the intense inter-parish rivalries that developed in Sunday junior rugby tournaments. The organizational stability of Sunday rugby was guaranteed by the fact that Garryowen FC, Limerick's greatest club, acted as an administrative body for the junior teams. Garryowen had been founded in 1884 and quickly became one of the city's most important sporting institutions. Among their founding members were Mike Joyce and Tom Prendergast, Catholic nationalist politicians later elected to the city council on a mandate to improve wages and conditions for the working classes. Joyce was later a Home Rule MP. The club's founding president was a Protestant, William Lamb Stokes. With their striking light-blue jerseys bearing a five-pointed star embroidered on the breast, Garryowen FC quickly became a remarkably popular Limerick institution, especially when provincial cup contests started in 1886.

A durable system of mutual dependence developed between Garryowen and the Sunday junior clubs. Garryowen effectively served as the governing body for the junior clubs' competitions, while enjoying an advantage in recruiting players for their own senior team.

Once the GAA established a toehold in the city, it was not unusual for men to become involved in both rugby and Gaelic games. Joyce and Prendergast were founding members of the St Michael's Temperance Society GAA club, where Joyce was captain of the hurling team, while Prendergast refereed the first ever hurling match held under GAA rules in Limerick. In September 1886, however, the GAA introduced their first ban on members playing 'foreign' games. Prendergast immediately resigned from the Association. St Michael's passed a motion 'That the members of this club deeply regret the loss of Mr T Prendergast, and hope that the rule which caused him to leave will be soon rescinded.' The same week Prendergast was elected vice-captain of Garryowen.[15]

It seems clear that St Michael's believed the ban would never be enforced. The club made no secret of the fact that members played rugby. A couple of months later, the club arranged a hurling fixture with South Liberties, a team based a few miles outside the city. When the opposing sides lined out in the middle of the field before the match, however, the Liberties captain refused to allow his team to play until St Michael's replaced the known rugby players on their team. A *Munster News* reporter described the behaviour of Liberties as 'disgraceful'. 'In St Michael's Club,' the reporter continued, 'as in many other clubs under the Gaelic Association, are many members who have a preference to Rugby football to that of Gaelic.' The stance adopted by South Liberties was especially frustrating given that St Michael's had 'identified themselves so strongly with the revival of Gaelic sports'.[16]

St Michael's continued to honour the ban in the breach. When the club won the county Gaelic football final in 1887, they were forced to replay the match because their opponents, Commercials, objected to the rugby players on the St Michael's team. The latter lost the replay by a disputed goal and Commercials went on to win the All-Ireland title. An incandescent St Michael's man, Joseph O'Reilly, wrote to the *Munster News*:

> The Commercials objected to our having men who played Rugby football still, they themselves, took a prominent Rugby player to Dublin to play for them . . . many clubs in this district cannot do otherwise but resign from the Gaelic Athletic Association until a change is made in reference to the Rugby footballers, many of whom have done far more to forward the Gaelic Association than the County Boards of Limerick.[17]

Limerick GAA soon fell into disarray. The County Board, heavily infiltrated by the IRB, split in 1887. In December, Joyce had been nominated for president in opposition to the IRB incumbent. Described by his proposer as 'a true-hearted Irishman and Gael' and 'one of the prime movers of the Gaelic clubs', Joyce eventually withdrew his nomination and the 'constitutional' faction, opposed to the IRB, withdrew to form their own rival County Board.[18] The resultant decline in the number of affiliated clubs, accelerated by the Parnell Split from 1891, allowed rugby to consolidate its position as the favoured sport of the masses in Limerick city.

All of the factors that led to the popularization of rugby in Limerick also existed in Cork. Here, as in Limerick, rugby had established itself before Gaelic became a serious option, a lively Sunday rugby culture developed, and the GAA went through periods of organizational chaos.

One club, Lee FC, tried to have it both ways. They started playing 'under the Rugby rules' in 1883.[19] But the club's president, J. F. Murphy, was elected a vice-president of the new GAA the following year,[20] and the club attended a GAA convention in October 1885 as the Lee Athletic and Cricket Club.[21] The club wanted to be attached to the GAA but not to Gaelic football, so Murphy and others devised a code of football called 'National Rules', and an associated Munster National Football League was founded. The new rules were brought before the GAA convention in October 1885, where they were deemed 'entirely foreign to the objects of the association'.[22] Cusack had already taken to his column in *United Ireland* to attack the National Rules as 'rugby undisguised', a code 'specially cooked to suit the requirements of young men who have to stand behind drapers' counters with Mr Murphy'.[23]

Cusack might have been right in thinking that National Rules was a close replica of rugby. Sketchy surviving accounts of matches played under the Munster National Football League rules describe a game very similar to rugby, with forward drives, and touchdowns leading to kicks at goal.[24] The following February, Murphy was unceremoniously removed as vice-president of the GAA.

GAA officials, members of the Munster National Football League and various other local athletes called a meeting in Cork hoping to resolve the dispute. William Daly of Lee FC claimed in defence of Murphy that Maurice Davin, then the GAA's president, had given his club assurances that they could play football under any rules they wished without jeopardizing their status as GAA athletes.[25] John McKay, a senior GAA official and local journalist, argued that the GAA never intended to facilitate the formation of separate associations. He also conceded that he and GAA colleagues were willing to discuss revisions to the Gaelic rules.[26] The meeting passed a vote of confidence in Murphy, and Cusack was booed as he left the meeting.

The matter was discussed at the GAA convention in April. Daly, the Lee FC representative, justified the club's membership of the Munster National Football Association by claiming not only that there were several Gaelic clubs in the South playing under rugby rules, but that the GAA did not debar them from doing so.[27] This line of argument was unsuccessful, and the meeting decided to disaffiliate Lee FC from the GAA.

The row originated in practical and sporting considerations, not ideological ones. Many of Cork city's footballers were shop assistants: 'if they went to work in the morning with a black eye, they would be sent playing football for the other six days of the week'.[28] Daly and Murphy, it seems, had no problem with Gaelic football – they simply could not convince club members to play it. On the surface, it may seem odd that rugby – a game whose dangers were often remarked on – was considered safer than Gaelic football. But Gaelic was a vastly different sport in 1885 from what it became even a few years later. In 1885, its rules were vague and such practices as wrestling off the ball were permitted. It is plausible, therefore, that there was some merit in the idea that rugby was less hazardous than Gaelic in 1885.[29]

The new football association petered out quickly, and in December 1886, Lee FC formally adopted Gaelic rules.[30] By then the club's great antagonist had departed the scene. Cusack's colleagues had grown tired of his confrontational style and his mismanagement of GAA affairs, and he was voted out of office in July 1886.

This was far from the end of code-hopping in Irish football. Another club that had joined the Munster National Football Association were Nil Desperandum FC. Founded in the mid-1880s as a rugby club, Nils then joined the Munster National Football League for the duration of their brief existence, before returning to rugby – and then switching to Gaelic, winning the Cork county title in 1889 and 1890, before again returning to rugby. In 1890, Nils played both rugby and Gaelic fixtures, were counted among a list of GAA clubs in Cork city, and were said by some to be on the brink of joining the IRFU. By 1891, they seemed to decisively opt for Gaelic football, and they went on to win the All-Ireland title representing Cork in 1895.[31]

The Cork County Board of the GAA, the *Irish Independent* reported in 1893, were 'up in arms against the abuse practised by members of Gaelic clubs playing Rugby and Gaelic alternately . . . doing the "double shuffle"'.[32] In November

1892, Tom Irwin, William Riordan and Michael Downey, all of Nil Desperandum, were expelled from the GAA for playing rugby.[33] All three were soon reinstated despite continuing to play rugby.[34] Irwin won an All-Ireland senior hurling medal in March 1893 with Redmonds.[35] And by October 1893, all three were selected for a Cork city Gaelic football representative team.[36]

Where objections arose, they were motivated by cynical opportunism rather than any kind of idealistic commitment to the ban. In 1895, Redmonds were beaten by Blackrock in the Cork senior hurling final and subsequently demanded a replay on the grounds that the winning team had fielded three rugby players. When the objection was heard by the Cork County Board, it was none other than the code-hopping Tom Irwin, himself a Redmonds man, who tabled the motion in favour of a replay. Irwin also confessed that he had known since the beginning of the championship that the rugby players were also hurling for Blackrock. In that light, the Redmonds' objection looked unprincipled and County Board members voted it down.[37]

Irwin, a serial offender, was again expelled from the GAA by the County Board in 1896 for playing rugby. By then the GAA's Central Council had dispensed with the ban, having recognized the injurious effect that it was having on Gaelic games. The Cork Board had therefore acted outside the rules of the Association. Irwin appealed and won, with the Central Council informing Cork officials that 'any member is perfectly at liberty to play any game he wants'.[38] (The ban on 'foreign' games, though, was soon reinstated.)

Although elements within the GAA tried to erect a wall between their games and those of English origin, a significant number of footballers simply would not have their sporting preferences dictated to them. In 1888, at a meeting of Queenstown GAA, the subject of members who played rugby was raised. The club, it seems, had been inactive for some time, tempting the young men in the town to play rugby. The chair asked any rugby players present to leave, prompting three delegates to do so, stating that they would not play under Gaelic rules. When another delegate asked who the 'leaders of the Rugby movement in Queenstown' were, 'Bailiffs', came the hissed reply from some of those present.[39] Two weeks later the Cove National Football Club was founded in the town, a new Sunday rugby team.[40]

Cove Nationals became part of a thriving Sunday rugby culture in Cork city and Queenstown between the mid-1880s and the mid-1890s. One curious feature of this activity was that it existed almost entirely parallel to rugby played by clubs affiliated to the IRFU, which tended to play on weekdays and Saturdays. In Queenstown, Midleton and Bandon, there were Saturday-playing and Sunday-playing clubs whose paths never crossed. It is likely that the majority of the players on the Sunday-playing clubs were Catholics who simply preferred rugby to Gaelic. In time, Sunday rugby in Cork died out, with many of its players, we can speculate, drifting to Gaelic games. In 1888, one journalist queried why the Sunday rugby clubs of Limerick and Cork could not find their way to make fixtures with each other.[41] Had that happened, or indeed had any of the established IRFU-affiliated clubs embraced Sunday football in Cork and nurtured it – as happened in Limerick – it might have developed the organizational momentum required to survive. Evidently, the Sabbath-observing Protestants who dominated Cork rugby were reluctant to involve themselves in such an enterprise.

Between 1896, when the GAA lifted the ban, and the

opening years of the twentieth century, when attitudes hardened again and it was reintroduced, there was a brief window
when footballers could play whichever code they wished
with impunity. Ned McCarthy, who won a Cork county
championship while playing for Lees in 1896, was selected
to play rugby for Ireland against Wales in 1898, having 'not
played ten matches under the code in his life'. He had joined
Cork Constitution, a club that was, according to Jacques
McCarthy, 'most liberal in its embrace of membership'.[42]
Ned McCarthy was Constitution's first international player – an
ironic turn of events, given that the club's parent organization, the *Cork Constitution* newspaper, despised the GAA.
Tom Aherne was selected to play for Cork in the All-Ireland
football final in 1899 and for Ireland in a rugby international
against England the same week. For reasons that have not
been recorded, he appeared at Lansdowne Road, but not at
Croke Park the following day.[43] Winning his sole international
cap, which came during Ireland's Triple Crown season, Aherne
lined up beside the Ryan brothers, Mick and Jack. Later that
year, they played for Arravale Rovers, a Gaelic football team in
Tipperary.[44] Dr Bill O'Sullivan played in an All-Ireland Gaelic
football final for Kerry before gaining a cap for Ireland in
rugby in 1895. When attempts were made to revive a rugby
club in Killarney in 1898, Dr O'Sullivan told a meeting that
'Most of the men in the Rugby Club, and he himself, would
be prepared to play for the Gaelic Club any time they were
wanted . . . he thought that the Gaelic Club should look upon
the starting of the Rugby Club with favour'.[45] At one stage in
1899, an English reporter claimed to have been told 'by the
most competent judges in Ireland that a new recruiting field
had been opened up, and that men who had hitherto played
the Gaelic game were about to relinquish it for Rugby'.[46] This

was especially the case in Munster, where code-mixing seems to have been most common.

The window of opportunity soon closed. The GAA's infiltration by the Fenians in the late 1880s had almost poisoned the Association to death. Its slow recovery in the 1890s was due in part to its renewed focus on sport over politics. From 1898 onwards, however, the GAA slowly re-embraced a more assertive nationalism, involving itself in the 1798 Rebellion centenary activities, and taking a strongly pro-Boer stance. From 1901, the GAA reinstated the ban on 'foreign' games, and this time the instrument carried a sharper ideological edge.[47] At that year's GAA convention, Thomas F. O'Sullivan, a hardliner from Kerry, condemned 'the anglicisation of our people'. Rugby supporters were 'contemptible shoneens' (a highly derogatory term used to describe Catholics perceived to be loyal to Britain). Rugby took place on fields '"decorated" with the Union Jack', and involved social functions 'marred by the toast of the English King – the man who swore that they, Catholics, were idolators'. O'Sullivan asserted that rugby supporters were 'enemies of their country and should not be tolerated'.[48]

Despite all of this, many footballers retained a taste for both codes. After Kerry defeated Louth in the 1909 All-Ireland football final, for example, the losing county contested the result, claiming that Johnny Skinner – who had given a match-winning display – had played rugby for Cork County and that M. J. Quinlan had played for Blackrock College.[49] Though Skinner had certainly played rugby, the appeal failed.[50]

'How tolerant this sensitive board of the GAA appear to be' was the sarcastic response of the *Cork Constitution* to news of Tom Irwin's expulsion from the Association in 1892.[51]

It must have been galling for Cork GAA members to take lectures on tolerance from the *Constitution*. The GAA's rules might have been illiberal and exclusionary. But bigotry flowed both ways. The unionist press was openly hostile to the GAA, viewing it as a subversive organization that governed uncivilized games. The GAA, according to this view, encouraged riotous Sabbath-breaking and intemperance. It was Fenianism by sporting means.

Quite apart from any connection between the GAA and the physical-force tradition of Irish nationalism, one suspects that the staging of fixtures on Sundays would have been enough to make the unionist press disapprove of Gaelic games. 'Gaelic football is a game detrimental to the interests of the locality in which it is encouraged', the *Skibbereen Eagle* argued in 1889. The paper deplored

> the utter want of discipline on the Sabbath day by those intoxicated fanatics, who glory in what they call their national game . . . If an amusement of that kind is necessary, why not have 'Rugby' football, a game universally practised in Ireland, England and Scotland, and one that can be indulged in without the slightest danger to the players.[52]

Underlying such views, also frequently aired in the *Cork Constitution*, were ancient assumptions about the barbaric tendencies of the 'native' Irish. The GAA were a disloyal organization promoting brutish games. Rugby, by contrast, was civilized and scientific, a game for gentlemen. 'The game of Gaelic football, as it is now played, is a stumbling block, a stone of offence', the *Church of Ireland Gazette* claimed in 1907; and it 'were far better not to play at all than to play at a game where the rules and the referee are as little regarded as good manners'.[53] Rugby, the same publication noted soon afterwards, provided invaluable training in self-restraint and discipline. 'No game suits so well the Anglo-Irish temperament, as it gives abundant scope for the more aggressive qualities, and also calls for much endurance and patience.'[54]

In 1892, the Rev. Frank Marshall commissioned Jacques McCarthy to write a chapter about Ireland for a book called *Football: The Rugby Union Game.* McCarthy brazenly played to the prejudices of his English readership in a passage that was frequently quoted in the British newspapers:

> Football in Ireland may be said to consist of three parts – Rugbeian, Associationist, and Gaelic. The rule of play in these organisations has been defined as follows: – In Rugby you kick the ball; in Association you kick the man if you cannot kick the ball; and in Gaelic, you kick the ball if you cannot kick the man.[55]

As we shall see in Chapter 6, as the IRFU gradually took more control of the club game in the interwar era, officials – who had been players in the 1890s – developed a marked distaste for Sunday rugby. The rugby authorities might not have codified their exclusionary practices, but an unwritten rule can be just as powerful as any formal resolution.

As in any culture war, the conflict between those who viewed rugby followers as degenerate shoneens and those who viewed the Gaels as feral Sabbath-breakers was dominated by cranks. In between the extremes was a vast number of people who enjoyed playing and watching their games while giving barely a thought to politics or culture. It seems clear, for example, that from the 1890s onwards mainstream nationalists in considerable numbers became rugby supporters. Rugby, and particularly the international team, received favourable coverage in the nationalist press. This was partly the result of the one great advantage rugby enjoyed over Gaelic games: the opportunity to defeat England at its own game in international contests. From the mid-1880s, the rugby team took its first tentative steps towards becoming a national institution of sorts.

Ireland's first victory over England came in 1887. In Cork, where the battle between rugby and Gaelic was intense, there were spontaneous victory parades in the city and in Midleton. One of the chief organizers of the procession in the city was W. J. M. 'Jumbo' Barry. A world record holder in the hammer throw, Barry was a founding member of the GAA in Cork and was elected vice-president of the County Board in 1885, though he seems to have had a tepid relationship with the Association thereafter.[56] The parade also included Nil Desperandum, the club that so freely moved between rugby and Gaelic. In Midleton, a procession was led by the local brass band carrying a blazing tar barrel. The local Catholic priest addressed the crowd and likened Ireland's success to a recent by-election victory for the Irish Parliamentary Party.[57]

Ireland's first sustained period of success in international rugby came in the 1890s. Between 1894 and 1908, Ireland won ten out of fifteen matches against England. Ireland also won the Triple Crown in 1894 and 1899. After the defeat of England in 1899, the avowedly nationalist *Dublin Evening Telegraph* featured the match in its editorial, paying tribute to 'Irish muscle and Irish mettle'. The victory was 'a triumph for the representatives of a small section of a small nation over the best talent available amongst a population of more than thirty millions'.[58] Even *United Ireland*, a newspaper that had thrown plenty of stones at rugby in the past, had Ireland's victory in the 1899 Triple Crown as its main editorial item. 'Ireland, by that dash that has never failed the Celtic race either on the athletic or battlefield, came through victorious.'[59]

Part of the reason for this was the composition of the Irish team. The 1887 team that beat England for the first time was a union of Catholic, Protestant and Dissenter. Not many organizations in Ireland could unite those three factions in aid of a common purpose. The XV was backboned by Church of Ireland men. But there was also a smattering of Presbyterians, including John Dick, a Lisburn man then studying at medicine in Cork. The celebratory procession in the city led by the erstwhile GAA man Jumbo Barry gathered outside Dick's residence on York Street, where the victorious Ireland player was given a 'tremendous cheer'.[60] There were also two Catholics on the team: Ned Walshe, a Blackrock College man, and Jack Macaulay, who worked in a mill in Limerick. According to Irish rugby folklore, Macaulay, who was employed by an austere Presbyterian who disapproved of rugby, brought forward his wedding in order to secure leave of absence to play against Scotland two weeks after the victory over England.[61]

T. F. O'Sullivan's assertion, made in 1901, that the Ireland rugby team were nothing more than 'Trinity College mudslingers and other degenerate Irishmen', jarred badly with the composition of the 1899 Triple Crown winners.[62] The stars of the team were the Ryan brothers, Mick and Jack, committed nationalists who possessed the 'racy of the soil' quality so cherished by the GAA. In 1899, a memorial committee for the Ryans was initiated and an illuminated address was presented to them by the 'supporters of Rugby and Gaelic athleticism in Tipperary'.[63] The sons of a prosperous farmer from Racecourse, Cashel, the Ryan boys were educated at nearby Rockwell College, where Mick developed a close friendship with Éamon de Valera. Before the brothers became famous rugby players, Mick was a GAA half-mile champion as well as a noted hammer-thrower and hurdler, while Jack, though less heralded, was twice a medallist at GAA athletics championships. The Ryans were also accomplished hurlers and Gaelic footballers, with Mick winning a national title for raising and striking a hurling ball in 1892 – the equivalent, then, of the modern Poc Fada (long puck) competition.[64] They were joined, as we have seen, by Tom Aherne, who forwent an All-Ireland football medal to play against England that season. This was not lost on GAA writers, one of whom noted that 'The two Ryans and Tom Aherne, whose athletic careers began in the Gaelic Association, did their own part in turning the tables on them [England] last Saturday'.[65] Another attempted to claim that the success was entirely the work of Mick and Jack Ryan: 'The two Gaelic men won for Ireland.'[66]

Limerick's Sunday rugby tradition offered a clear pathway for men outside the rugby establishment to achieve international honours. The O'Connors, Jack and Joe, capped for Ireland in 1895 and 1909 respectively, were pig buyers who started their rugby careers playing on Sundays for Shannon. They caught the eye of the Garryowen selectors, who chose them for their Munster Senior Cup team. This opened up a route to selection for Munster and eventually Ireland. A neighbour of the O'Connors on Athlunkard Street, Paddy Healy, also gained international honours via Sunday rugby at Shannon and selection for Garryowen. A butcher whose feats of strength in handling animals are written into Limerick folklore, he won ten caps for Ireland between 1901 and 1904. He was also an accomplished boxer and oarsman, and is probably the only former Ireland rugby international who has a road named after him in his native city. Only the foolhardiest of Gaels would have called Healy a 'shoneen' to his face. Tom Halpin, a plumber from St Lelia Street, gained thirteen caps between 1909 and 1913, having started playing on Sundays with Shannon.[67]

In terms of accent, habits, tastes and, indeed, religion, these Limerick men were vastly different from most of those men that they shared a dressing room with on international duty. George Hamlet, one of Ireland's greatest forwards of the early twentieth century, was later a vocal critic of Sunday rugby, in keeping with his Methodist background. One can only wonder if he knew that three of his Ireland teammates, Healy, Halpin and Joe O'Connor, were the products of the Sabbath-breaking he so bitterly decried.

5. Patriotic games

Jasper Brett earned his first cap for Ireland in March 1914. He didn't know it at the time, but he was the last man to achieve this honour before Europe descended into war. A nineteen-year-old winger from Monkstown in Dublin, Brett had every reason to believe that a long career in the green jersey lay ahead. But the war put international rugby into hiatus for six years.

What turned out to be Brett's only cap came against Wales in Belfast, at the conclusion of the championship. The game was a grim pre-echo of the conditions that soldiers would soon face on the Western Front: played in torrential rain, it was the rugby equivalent of trench warfare. The young debutant, by all accounts, gave a plucky display. Six months later and with war declared, Brett, then a trainee solicitor in his father's practice, did what many rugby men saw as their patriotic duty and joined a volunteer corps set up by the IRFU. Part of this corps eventually became D Company of the 7th Royal Dublin Fusiliers, later to see action at Gallipoli. (Such companies, with their strong social and personal bonds, were known as 'Pals' units.) From the outbreak of the First World War in August 1914 to the cessation of hostilities in the Civil War in May 1923, Ireland was embroiled in near continuous conflict involving the mobilization of many thousands of young men. For Irish rugby the impacts were many and complex, with players' loyalties being dragged in several directions. We can surmise with some confidence that Brett, a young

Protestant educated at Armagh Royal School, was firmly on the side of King and Country.

Having served at Suvla Bay and elsewhere in the Balkans, Jasper Brett was severely traumatized by his war experiences and was medically discharged due to shellshock. Having attempted suicide by throwing himself overboard on the journey back to England, Brett spent a few months in a hospital for mentally ill officers in Surrey before returning to Dublin in January 1917. A couple of weeks later he lay in the path of an oncoming train on the Kingstown line between Dalkey and Killiney. His father, William Brett, gave deeply moving evidence to a subsequent inquest, claiming that his son had been tormented by witnessing the loss of so many friends in the doomed campaign in Turkey. In his suicide note Brett had wished 'all to think of him as he once was'.[1] William Brett himself later developed 'mania' and died at Bloomfield psychiatric hospital just a few days before the fourth anniversary of his son's death.[2]

Jasper Brett's name is listed alongside seventy-nine others on the Monkstown Football Club Roll of Honour. Dozens of these men were killed in the war, including several of Brett's contemporaries, some of whom served alongside him at Suvla Bay. His teammate on the first XV in 1914, Edward Millar, was killed 'whilst exhorting men from another regiment to "stand firm"' on 9 August 1915.[3] Two other Monkstown clubmates and members of the Pals, Cecil Keller and Charles Dowse, aged seventeen and nineteen respectively, were killed in a foolhardy assault a week later. Dowse's brother, Cecil, was Brett's teammate on the Monkstown, Leinster and Ireland teams. He survived the war, having been awarded the Military Cross for his service in France. Less fortunate were two other members of the Monkstown first XV of 1914, John Lane and William

Kee, both of whom were killed in France. News of the carnage at Gallipoli was too much for another Monkstown man,
Ewen Cameron. He had not been deployed to Gallipoli as
his regiment was above strength. Back in Dublin, and with
word of the bleak succession of casualties filtering through,
Cameron developed severe depression. Apparently desperate to get to the front and beside himself with worry that he
might be considered a shirker, he shot himself dead on a train
in Dublin in late August 1915.[4]

Reports of Jasper Brett's inquest offered a sombre contrast
to the sort of oafish enthusiasm that greeted the outbreak
of war in 1914. 'Our sturdy young "forwards" and clever
young "backs"', the *Irish Times* asserted in September 1914,
'are just the right men for that supreme game – in which
is at stake our national existence – that we are now playing
against Germany.'[5] It was as though the newspaper anticipated schoolboy tales of derring-do to emerge from the front,
not the brutal reality of mechanized warfare. But this kind
of commentary was in keeping with the fashion of the time.
The themes of death and glory were widespread in public
school literature in Britain, and in the eyes of some observers
the war was an opportunity for rugby to fulfil its historical
mission.[6] When St Andrew's College, a Protestant school then
located in Dublin city centre, did the seemingly impossible
and defeated Blackrock College in the Leinster Schools Cup
final in 1906, a celebratory verse was suffused with martial
language.

> Stern the battle was and long,
> Hard the foemen died,
> Many a dauntless rush they made,
> Many a ruse they tried.

Mark where Sandy led his men
To conquer or to die,
Think how Wilson broke away
And scored the winning try.[7]

During the course of a speech at the same school in 1915, Mr Justice Dunbar Barton of the Chancery Division observed how 'marvellous' it was to see 'what a narrow space divided the football field from the battle field. Many glorious deeds would have been done before this campaign was over by those who had learned the lessons of courage and how to obey and command upon the football field at St Andrew's College.'[8] At Portora Royal School the same year, the Church of Ireland Primate and former Wanderers rugby player, John Baptist Crozier, told an audience that one of the 'great objects of education' was teaching boys to work in union. This 'was what had made the men they were of the soldiers and sailors who had been educated at public schools. They had learned to cooperate with others. And what had taught them that? More than anything else, he ventured to say as an old Rugby captain, it was Rugby football.'[9] With their education in manliness, patriotism and moral purity, rugby men were ideally placed to answer the Empire's call.[10]

In Ireland, of course, the militarization of society was already well underway before 1914. The Home Rule crisis of 1912 had led to the formation of two paramilitary groups: the Ulster Volunteer Force (UVF) and the Irish Volunteers. The UVF, committed to resisting Home Rule, would be the first of many military outfits to profit from the rugby man's sense of mission. In what can credibly be considered the most brazen political intervention by any club in the entire history of Irish rugby, NIFC ceased playing activities in favour of military drilling with the UVF in January 1914. This was not some self-effacing group of patriotic men quietly going about their duty: the club was determined to make as public a show as possible of its decision. A letter to Ulster Unionist Party leader and UVF founder Edward Carson, widely published in the Belfast press, announced that 'The North of Ireland Football Club is the leading Rugby Football Club in Ulster . . . Its members are all of the public school and university class, some of the leading Belfast merchants and professional men.' The letter went on to inform Carson that the club had 'enthusiastically decided' to cancel all fixtures from January 'so that members might be able to give up their entire time on Saturdays to drilling and military training'. Among those now forgoing football were, according to reports, fifteen Irish internationals, including five former Ireland captains.[11]

Edmund Vesey Ross, a clergyman in the Church of Ireland and member of NIFC, composed a poem that figured the politics of Ireland and Union in rugby terms:

> With Union fervour, till their strain, heart-whole,
> Out of the scrimmage, bear the fight along
>   Over the Redmond-Asquith traitor line,
> And Smith to Carson pass, and, going strong,
>   He, 'tween the goal-posts, gain a try divine,
> And Bonar Law convert to such a win
> That to Home Rule no more the ball will spin.[12]

The example of NIFC, according to the *Belfast Telegraph*, must 'bring home . . . the concentration of bitterness with which the people of Ulster take the threat to place on their necks the yoke of nationalism'.[13] This was striking hypocrisy. The very newspapers that scorned the GAA for mixing sport and politics were now praising NIFC for doing so. This must have been discomfiting for at least one NIFC man, Charles Le Fevre. A linen agent by profession, Le Fevre had been a member of the Ireland selection committee and refereed international fixtures. Le Fevre differed from the great majority of Ulster rugby men in two key respects: he was Catholic and nationalist. Before enlisting in the Royal Inniskilling Fusiliers, he had been an officer in A Company of the 2nd Belfast Battalion of the Irish National Volunteers.

Not all Ulster clubs immediately followed NIFC's example. At a meeting of Malone FC, chaired by former Irish international Alf Tedford, a motion to cancel all fixtures was narrowly defeated. A number of senior players resolved, nonetheless, to swap rugby for drilling with the UVF.[14] Under the headline 'Rugby or Rifles?', the nationalist *Strabane Chronicle* caustically dismissed the 'absurd movement to convert Rugby football organisations into an annexe of the Carsonite movement'. Malone FC deserved credit for delivering a 'nasty snub' to the 'football politicians'.[15] This was premature. By the end of the month, Malone had ceased activity on the field due to pressure from players.[16] Queen's University and Knock FC soon followed.[17] A parade of inspection of the UVF's East Belfast Regiment in late January put paid to the weekend's fixture list.[18]

We know of several Irish internationals who joined the UVF. Fred Gardiner, whose father William played for Ireland before him, earned twenty-two caps – a considerable number by the standards of the time – between 1900 and 1909. He was an 'ardent member' of the UVF and a member of the Ulster Unionist Council.[19] Robert Stevenson, another old Irish international, commanded a battalion of the South Tyrone UVF and served throughout the First World War, even though he was in his late forties.[20] A significant proportion of rugby men later enlisted in the 36th (Ulster) Division and fought in France. One Malone man, Captain William Edwards, survived a head wound and being gassed in France, only to be killed in Palestine in 1917 while serving with the Royal Irish Fusiliers. Edwards, a pre-war officer in the East Belfast Regiment of the UVF, had been twice capped for Ireland on the eve of the war.

A much greater mobilization of Irish rugby players would follow later in 1914, of course, with the outbreak of war. The IRFU followed the example of the British unions and cancelled fixtures for the remainder of the season. From then until the end of the war, rugby was confined to military teams and schools competitions. In any case, clubs could scarcely have fielded teams even if the usual fixture calendar had remained in place. More than half of the men who played for Wanderers and Clontarf in the 1913–14 season joined the war effort, while Dublin University lost more than three quarters of their pre-war playing strength.[21] Of the St Andrew's College Senior Cup team of 1912 – most of whom we must assume were now playing for clubs – fourteen joined the colours.[22] The Castleknock College senior XV of 1911 were less enthusiastic – five joined up.[23]

In August, the IRFU, mindful of the raw materials it potentially had at its disposal, had decided to establish a volunteer corps. The moving spirit behind the initiative was the Union's president, Frank Browning. Having advertised his intentions as early as 6 August, Browning soon gained the support of several Dublin rugby clubs, which, in turn, issued press circulars encouraging members to join up. By early September, the Irish Rugby Football Union Volunteer Corps had a membership of 250 and was regularly drilling at Lansdowne Road.

The corps soon separated into two groups: those younger men of military age who would volunteer for active service, and those – generally older with professional commitments – who would remain in Dublin as a home defence unit.[24]

The first group, dubbed 'the toffs in the toughs', became D Company of the 7th Battalion of the Royal Dublin Fusiliers.[25] Recruitment to D Company was boosted in early September when the commander of the Battalion, Lieut. Col. Geoffrey Downing – himself a former rugby player – addressed the IRFU Volunteer Corps at Lansdowne Road. Eighty-nine men immediately enlisted.[26] This, according to Downing, 'was a bad day for the Germans'.[27]

In late September, 120 rugby volunteers departed Dublin for the Curragh amid considerable patriotic pomp, marching through the city to Kingsbridge, led by the Royal Irish Constabulary band. One writer in the *Evening Herald* hoped that 'the Rugby Corps will get inside the enemy's goal-posts and score a point or two for Ireland in this "international"'.[28] Such analogies seem tastelessly hollow and whimsical in retrospect. D Company remained in Ireland until the summer of 1915, before departing initially for England, and then to the Dardanelles to fight German-backed Turkish forces in the hopeless Gallipoli campaign. By the time they arrived at Suvla Bay in August 1915, the rugby Pals numbered more than 200 men. When they departed in September, D Company's strength was reduced to seventy-nine. A number of the rugby Pals were lost on 16 August, when the company embarked on what was little better than a suicide mission, attempting to dislodge a well-entrenched Turkish position on Kireçtepe Sirt.

The great majority of Dublin rugby players who served in the war joined regiments other than the Royal Dublin Fusiliers. Young medics, for example, tended to join the Royal

Army Medical Corps, and engineering students gravitated towards the Royal Engineers. Some rugby men simply joined their local regiment. In March 1915, Sir Frederick Moore, the Trinity College botanist and future president of the IRFU, claimed that 'over 1,000 Rugby footballers were now doing their duty in the Dublin Fusiliers, the Munster Fusiliers and the Connaught Rangers'.[29]

In all, nine Irish internationals died as a result of the war, seven killed on active service. For some clubs, the death toll was almost unimaginably high. Twenty-four members of Clontarf Football Club died. The equivalent figure for Wanderers was twenty-nine. Dublin University FC lost forty-six members.[30]

Commentators who had energetically encouraged men to join the conflict now comforted themselves by pointing out the great sacrifice made by the game. The *Irish Times*, falsely reporting the death of Ireland international Dickie Lloyd in 1915 – he had been wounded, not killed, was capped again after the war and lived until 1950 – told readers that rugby men had been

> charged with the duty of maintaining the high traditions of the game, both on the playing field and off it . . . They did not fail when the moment of trial came. They showed to the very utmost of their ability that Rugby football trains men to discharge their obligations in the sterner business of life . . . If ever a sport justified its existence when the country required manliness and courage, it is Rugby football.[31]

Irish rugby also became embroiled in the tumultuous events at home, notably the 1916 Easter Rising. The rebel commander, Éamon de Valera, was a devoted rugby fan – and, before his entry into nationalist politics, a player. A useful three-quarter, de Valera played senior rugby for Rockwell alongside his great friends the Ryans in the early 1900s. Moving to Dublin, he lined out for Blackrock College, where he was a teacher. In a friendly match against Wanderers in 1906, he played against Poole Hickman, one of the rugby Pals commanders killed at Gallipoli on 16 August 1915.[32] Although most who shared de Valera's cultural politics gravitated to the GAA, Dev never abandoned his attachment to rugby. Speaking at the annual dinner of the southern branch of the Blackrock College Past Pupils Union in 1957, de Valera admitted that he had not attended a rugby match since 1913 'because I do not want it raised as a political matter'. He told his audience, however, that 'for Irishmen there is no football game like rugby'; and he would later state, 'if all our young men played rugby not only would we beat England and Wales but France and the whole lot of them put together'.[33]

The most significant rugby-related event of Easter week involved rebels under de Valera's command and the remnants of the IRFU Volunteer Corps that stayed at home. By then, the enthusiasm that had brought these men together in the giddy days of August 1914 had faded. Attendance at parades fell away, and by December 1915 around a third of the corps' men had allowed their membership to lapse.[34] A group of those who remained made the fateful decision to go to Ticknock, in the Dublin hills, on Easter Monday to take part in a route march. Returning to the city, the men were fired on from a rebel position close to the junction of Northumberland and Haddington Roads. IRFU president Frank Browning, whose idea it had been to set up the volunteer corps, was fatally injured. Reggie Clery, a 22-year-old Catholic who had attended Belvedere College and played for the Senior Cup team in 1910, also fell. It was a lamentable end for the IRFU Volunteer Corps, whose final act was to pass on the proceeds of a collection among the surviving Pals then serving in the Balkans to Browning's widow. It formally disbanded in October.[35]

Browning and Clery were not the only rugby men to die on Easter week. Lieut. Alan Ramsay of the Royal Irish Regiment survived wounds in France, only to be killed in action back home in Dublin, also on 24 April 1916. Ramsay, the Protestant son of a nurseryman, fell at South Dublin Union. He had been on the Wanderers first XV just two years previously.

The most famous of all rugby-playing republicans, aside from de Valera perhaps, was Kevin Barry. Executed for his role in an IRA ambush in 1920, the eighteen-year-old Barry instantly became a republican martyr. The most widely reproduced image of Barry is a striking photograph first published in the Belvedere College magazine in 1919. Child-like and innocent in appearance, with slicked-back hair and slightly plaintive eyes, Barry wears the black-and-white hooped jersey of the college rugby team. Alongside his more athletically imposing, square-jawed and earnest-looking teammates on the Senior Cup team, he cut an almost feeble figure.[36] He was on the senior second XV in 1918, but was selected for the Senior Cup team in 1919, when, as usual, Belvedere were beaten by Blackrock College. Barry, by then the honorary secretary of the college football club (and a member of the IRA), was now playing at hooker and had 'improved very much during the season'.[37]

The week of Barry's execution, the college cancelled all matches 'as a mark of respect to our "boy hero" . . . who died for his country on November 1st in Mountjoy Prison. Little we thought when we saw him play for the 2nd XV last year that he would be called upon to give the supreme test of devotion to his country – to die.'[38]

Barry was not the only Belvederian rugby player in the republican ranks. In November 1920, the captain of Old Belvedere, Michael O'Brien, was arrested by Crown forces and interned at Ballykinlar Camp in County Down. O'Brien later recalled his time at Ballykinlar, telling readers of *The Belvederian* of how among his camp comrades 'charity and self-sacrifice ruled in our little Commonwealth so knit by one universal devotion – the Cause of Caithlin na Houlihan [sic]'.[39] On his release, he was immediately reappointed captain of the Old Belvedere first XV. Belvedere and other private Catholic schools were hardly seedbeds of republicanism, but there were hints of radicalism in some of the school magazine's articles. A set of feature articles entitled 'Under the Terror' included Michael O'Brien's account of his time at Ballykinlar, and Fergus Murphy's stint at Wormwood Scrubs.

Dr Patrick O'Sullivan played rugby at Blackrock before returning home to Cork and joining the IRA, eventually reaching the rank of commanding officer of the 8th Battalion, Cork No. 1 Brigade.[40] He had successfully applied for reinstatement to the GAA after playing his last rugby match in March 1915, a victory over the High School in the Leinster Schools Senior Cup final.[41] Mortimer O'Connell, a Senior Cup winner with Blackrock in 1911, joined the Volunteers in 1914 and fought during Easter week 1916. After internment, he linked up with the IRA in Kerry, where he served during the War of Independence. He remained a committed member of Blackrock College RFC after hostilities ceased. Tom Cullen, a Dublin IRA commander and a close confidant of Michael Collins, was a Clongowes and Bective Rangers man whose son, his namesake, played for Ireland.[42]

In Limerick, rugby-playing republicans appear to have been far more common than elsewhere. After the Volunteer split in 1914, the 250 men in Limerick who opted not to follow Redmond's call to serve in the Great War were organized into four companies, three of which, James Gubbins claimed in his statement to the Bureau of Military History, had rugby players as captains. More than half of A Company, the same witness added, were rugby men. Limerick, then, had its own rugby Pals of sorts, only they were not willing to throw their lot in with the British war effort.

Limerick rugby men were active in the subsequent independence struggle. Among many examples was Jack Quilligan, a Shannon and Garryowen club man, who was a member of the IRA and was held hostage by the British during the War of Independence.[43] Quilligan played at interprovincial level for Munster on the eve of the First World War and was later an Ireland selector.[44] John Gubbins, a carpenter, who played for Young Munster and Garryowen and coached Young Munster, was an active republican during the War of Independence. The *Limerick Leader* claimed that 'when his country was engaged in the life and death struggle . . . with England's minions, John Gubbins took a man's part in defence of his motherland'.[45] The irony here, of course, is that a noisy strand of opinion within Irish nationalism viewed rugby players, by definition, as 'England's minions'.

Jim McInerney, pre-war captain of Limerick rugby club Lansdowne (which had no association with the Dublin club of the same name), had a period of imprisonment at Dundalk and internment at Ballykinlar, where he was appointed camp quartermaster.[46] In the immediate aftermath of the Civil War, Limerick's rugby clubs decided to suspend fixtures for the duration of republican hunger strikes in autumn 1923. We cannot confidently impute direct political allegiances to this decision; the clubs were worried, perhaps, of the repercussions of not doing as the local GAA clubs had done. In Cork, when rugby continued despite pressure from republicans, the goalposts at the Mardyke grounds were promptly felled by persons unknown.[47]

Amid all of this turmoil, the rugby authorities stiffened their upper lips and carried on. At international level, it was quite an achievement that Ireland fielded a team at all during the 1920–23 period. These international campaigns were played out in extraordinary circumstances. While the IRFU were preparing to host Wales in the 1923 championship, for example, the Civil War was in its most squalid phase, and the match was bookended by horrific events. The week before the Wales match, the notorious Ballyseedy massacre took place in County Kerry. The week after, the Free State Army executed eleven anti-Treaty republicans by firing squad. The army's senior legal officer, who had ultimate responsibility for the executions, was Cahir Davitt, an establishment figure in Irish rugby and later president of the IRFU.

By then the IRFU had also turned their focus to commemoration. As early as February 1919, the Union set up a subcommittee to arrange a memorial for players who had died during the Great War. In 1925, the Union agreed to erect a memorial at a cost of £306, a great deal of money for a tight-fisted organization to part with.[48] For years afterwards, the IRFU observed an annual tradition of laying a wreath at the cenotaph at Islandbridge. The war memorial at Lansdowne Road was understated and tactful, avoiding any mention of King and Country. In Ravenhill, perhaps unsurprisingly, the memorial was a more ostentatious affair, comprising a large rectangular arch and an eye-catching clock.

Irish public memory offered martyrdom to some, while consigning the memory of others to an obscure corner of the national narrative. Jasper Brett and Kevin Barry both sacrificed their lives for their country. All politically minded rugby men in Ireland who became involved in military conflict in the years from 1914 onwards – be they unionists, of the Southern or Ulster variety, nationalists heeding Redmond's call to the trenches in the cause of Home Rule, or republicans seeking to sever the link with Britain – had one thing in common: they were attempting to vindicate their vision of Ireland. From 1921 onwards, Irish rugby men were separated not only by the abstract borders of culture, creed and class, but by the physical border that divided the island, and the IRFU's jurisdiction, into two states.

6. 'The rugby game has no boundaries'

By the time he took the presidency of the IRFU in 1926, George Hamlet was a legendary figure in Irish rugby. Born into a farming family in Balbriggan, County Dublin, Hamlet was a railway cashier by profession and served in the First World War. At Wesley College, he and another future Ireland international, Billy Hinton, had spearheaded the school to their first and, to date, only Senior Cup title in 1898. In a ten-season international career, beginning in 1902, Hamlet won thirty caps – captaining the team in nine – and was regarded by observers as one of the finest forwards in the game. When he took to his feet to give a speech at a Wesley College old boys' dinner in March 1927, he was not only the most senior official in Irish rugby, but he remained the country's most capped player.

Given his profile, the speech he gave was remarkably indiscreet. Hamlet spoke of his anxieties about the future of Irish rugby. His fears were not about the game's survival; conversely, he was worried that it might become too popular. He told his audience that the game's increased appeal carried the risk of drawing a crowd 'who might not be educated in the true spirit of the game'. This strange intervention came amid a debate about playing rugby on Sundays, something that was still disapproved of by the IRFU. Hamlet fretted that if Sunday rugby was permitted, the scenes at Lansdowne Road would soon resemble 'Jones's Road of a Gaelic Sunday afternoon' – something that was seen as highly undesirable on social and cultural grounds. If the worst were to happen, he continued, then it was 'almost certain that Sunday in Ireland will be like the French Sunday, and that we will have most of our finals and cup ties played on Sunday'.[1]

The rugby correspondent at *Sport*, 'Judex', described Hamlet's speech as 'squalid, and narrow-minded', and wrote that the 'slur cast on the Gaelic playing community in no way represents the great body of opinion amongst Rugby men'. Hamlet, by this logic, had not just insulted Jack Ryan and Billy Riordan, the two erstwhile GAA men who had played alongside him for Ireland. He had also effectively cast a slur on Paddy Healy, Joe O'Connor and Tom Halpin, three Limerick men who began their careers playing on the rough-and-tumble Sunday rugby circuit in their native city and went on to represent their country.[2]

Hamlet probably assumed that his speech – made, as it was, at a fairly obscure event and in familiar company – would never be publicly reported. It is almost certain that he did not anticipate his thoughts being discussed at the inaugural meeting of the Drogheda branch of the Catholic Truth Society a few weeks later. Hamlet, one speaker at the meeting stated, was a 'representative of the Protestant brawn'. 'In the 26 Counties at least,' the speaker continued, 'these people have lost the political ascendancy they enjoyed up to a few years ago . . . We, Catholics of Ireland, must in our own land, where we are the large majority, take the social as well as the political leadership.'[3] As a Southern Protestant, George Hamlet hailed from a people heading towards the margins, a small and shrinking minority in the Free State, cut adrift from their Northern co-religionists by partition. Southern Protestants now found themselves stranded in a state where the Catholic Church had a pervasive influence on public policy. In this context, the question of what day of the week rugby was played on took on an outsize significance.

Independence, partition and the increased popularity and profile of the game meant that a stark question now faced the rugby public and the sport's leadership: whose game was it?

For the time being, power in Irish rugby remained vested in old establishment types. Of ten Southerners elected to the IRFU presidency in the first decade and a half after independence, seven were Protestants, and four of them had strong links with Trinity College Dublin. Ex-presidents were automatically given positions on the IRFU Council, and therefore had the power, as a bloc, to dictate the pace of any reforms.

On the field, however, the new elite was gradually replacing the old one. After independence, the number of Southern Catholics gaining international selection increased sharply. Between January 1923 and the close of the 1932 season, two thirds of the Southerners who earned their first cap for Ireland were Catholic. When Eugene Davy – a founder of Davy Stockbrokers – first captained Ireland in 1929, he became only the second Catholic to receive the honour in more than fifty seasons of international rugby.

If George Hamlet's speech at Wesley College betrayed sectarian feeling, open sectarianism was relatively rare in Irish rugby. In March 1924, a furious row erupted between Cork Constitution and their local rivals Dolphin after the Dolphin captain directed an insult at a Constitution player, Frank Wilkie, during a match. In a terse letter to Dolphin, the Constitution secretary wrote, 'the words used were "you bastard protestant"'. Wilkie, as the Dolphin man's ugly remark suggested, was the product of mixed marriage. When Constitution members gathered to discuss the incident, there were 'many old players who said in their experience of rugby football they never heard any reflection on any player's religion', and noted the 'good feeling between Catholics and Protestants wherever the game is played'.[4] Having received a letter of complaint from Constitution, Dolphin caused even greater offence by tersely advising their rivals to take the matter up with the offender directly.[5]

An altogether more benign example of religious cleavage appears in the Blackrock College community journal the following year. When the school was unexpectedly defeated by Belvedere in a cup tie that year, an entry to the journal observed: 'The fact that the selectors of the interprovincial team, *the majority of them Protestants* [emphasis added], selected 8 players of our team goes to prove that the high hope we entertained for a win were fully justified.'[6] The various college diarists at Blackrock were so accustomed to victory that any defeat, in their vivid imaginations, was invariably someone else's fault: incompetent referees, nefarious opponents and so on. But on this occasion, defeat was incomprehensible because even the Protestants thought they had the best team.

In 1927, the IRFU secretary, Rupert Jeffares, boasted that the IRFU now had 190 affiliated clubs, the 'highest in the United Kingdom'.[7] Jeffares' remark showed a shaky grasp of the constitutional position of the Irish Free State, but the statistic was remarkable. In Connacht, clubs cropped up in locations previously untouched by rugby: Ballina, Castlebar, Castlerea, Gort, Portumna, Salthill and Westport. In Munster, there was barely a population settlement of any significance without a club. But their existence was precarious. In order to field teams consistently, many of these clubs, particularly in the remoter areas of Connacht and Munster, needed to attract players whose work commitments meant that they could only play on Sundays. If they fell below a certain membership threshold, as many often did, they would lose their affiliation to the IRFU.[8] Arranging fixtures for Sundays, the only day when almost all workers had a day off, was critical to the survival of these clubs.

From the mid-1920s, the IRFU started receiving letters from provincial clubs regarding Sunday play. The Union's replies were generally high-handed. When a cup competition was inaugurated by County Longford RFC for clubs in the midlands and west of Ireland in 1926, the IRFU committee informed J. J. Callanan, the organizer, that the Union would 'not sanction the playing of rugby football competitions under the jurisdiction of the Irish Rugby Football Union on a Sunday'.[9]

For close to fifty years, there had been a culture of Sunday rugby hiding in plain sight in Limerick, where a saltier variant of the game was played and where concerns about violence on the field and among the crowd were legitimate. Indeed, the IRFU had warned the Munster Branch about discipline in Limerick rugby on more than one occasion.[10] Yet no measures were ever taken by the officials to suppress Sunday rugby in Limerick, and men who had encouraged the practice had held high office in the IRFU. Matters changed, however, as the IRFU began to take a more active role in managing the grassroots clubs and competitions. Aspects of the game came under the pedantic gaze of Rupert Jeffares. The greater the number of clubs, the higher the risk of some trivial infraction of the amateur code. Clubs were obliged to submit annual accounts to the Union on pain of losing their affiliation. The IRFU were capable of heroic achievements in pettifogging, as when, for example, Garryowen were scolded for paying

a player's medical expenses in 1946. It was no justification
that the player was injured on the field and that he could not
afford the bill: these expenses were 'the personal responsibility of the individual member', according to Jeffares.[11] If one
was not of sufficient financial means to bear the physical risk
of playing rugby, then one ought not to play it.

Regarding Sunday rugby, matters came to a head in 1929
when the Connacht Branch grew restless with the IRFU's rigid
attitude. In March, the Union wrote to all branches informing
them that permission would not be granted for competitive
or gate money fixtures on Sundays.[12] Looking for allies, the
Connacht Branch approached their Munster counterparts
with a view to sending a joint delegation to meet the IRFU.
Munster, reluctant at first, eventually agreed, and in September
the meeting went ahead. Two of the four members of the
delegation, Connacht's Henry Anderson and Munster's Peter
Galbraith, were Protestants.[13] The IRFU refused to relent,
claiming, as though to confirm George Hamlet's fears, that
reports which had 'reached them of the behaviour of players
and spectators at certain matches which have taken place on
a Sunday have confirmed and strengthened their views that
such play is undesirable'.[14] Most of the clubs affected were
playing in the junior ranks, and though the Union recognized
'the importance of junior football nevertheless do not regard
it as paramount'.[15] The 'tone' of the game was everything; if
a few clubs in the remote provinces went to the wall, so be it.

The Connacht Branch ignored all of this and decided to
schedule their provincial league and cup competitions on
Sundays anyway, while the Munster Branch, around half
of whose officers and committeemen were Protestant, held
a meeting where delegates agreed that 'all present were in
favour of Sunday football'.[16] Eventually, in December, the

Munster Branch formally decided to ignore the IRFU's ruling and to permit Sunday fixtures.[17]

Suspecting that their edict was being defied, the IRFU went looking for evidence of Sunday matches. They instructed the Munster Branch to reprimand the Fethard and Clonmel clubs for playing a Cantwell Cup fixture on a Sunday. When it turned out that the Cantwell Cup was a Gaelic football competition, the Munster Branch gently mocked the IRFU, advising the parent body 'not to take so much notice of newspaper reports'.[18] The Connacht and Munster branches received further letters demanding to know why newspapers were carrying details of Sunday fixtures in both provinces.

Ireland had a star-studded team in the late 1920s. Agonizingly narrow defeats to Wales and England (twice) denied Ireland the Grand Slam in 1926, 1927 and 1928. Led by the full-back Ernie Crawford, the teams were backboned by what was arguably the first generation of truly great players from the elite Catholic schools: Denis Cussen and Morgan Crowe from Blackrock; Eugene Davy from Belvedere; and four Castleknock College men, Mike Dunne, Charlie Hanrahan, Jimmy Farrell and Jack Arigho. These players – featured on cigarette cards, spoken of in reverent tones in the press – were as close as one could get to sporting celebrities at the time.

What was concerning the IRFU in 1929, however, was the fact that several of these players had taken to playing Sunday exhibition matches at provincial clubs around the country. The players' motive seems to have been purely to promote the game. In January 1929, for example, the Naas club hosted an exhibition match featuring Irish internationals Jimmy Farrell, Mark Deering and Claude Carroll, all of whom were guests of honour at a whist drive and dance that followed.[19] In November, the same club hosted a fifteen led by Mike Dunne, then an emerging talent with three caps to his name. This fixture earned those involved a severe reprimand from the IRFU.

The Union were especially peeved the same month to learn that Ernie Crawford, the man who had captained Ireland for four seasons, had taken part in an exhibition match in Waterford. Crawford was a Belfast Methodist; doing anything on a Sunday other than attending to religious devotion was nominally at odds with his background. In reality, he was a long-time and unapologetic advocate of Sunday rugby and had been involved in several similar fixtures. He spoke publicly of the necessity to remove restrictions on the practice, especially if the game was going to remain healthy in Connacht and Munster. 'I may be called the leader of the Bolshies', Crawford told an audience after a match in Galway. 'I am not a Bolshie; but rugby appeals very strongly to me.'[20] In the case of the fixture at Waterford, Crawford wrote to the Union, claiming that there was no truth in 'the suggestion that the match was arranged to thwart the Irish Rugby Football Union in their prohibition of competitive Sunday matches', before airily stating that he did not take any notice of whether a gate was taken or not. The Union replied, warning him not to repeat the offence.[21]

A significant element within the Leinster Branch (encouraged by UCD rugby club) were worried about the effects of the prohibition on Sunday rugby on the game in the south and west of the country and secured a meeting with the IRFU on the issue.[22] Had this problem remained confined to obscure clubs in Munster and Connacht, the IRFU might well have maintained a hard line. But with high-profile players flagrantly ignoring the policy and reformist noises growing louder in Leinster, the IRFU had no option but to relent. At a special meeting in January 1930, the Union committee adopted a new policy. All matches from then on were to be played on week-days and Saturdays 'except by the special permission of the Branch or Branches to which the competing clubs belong'. In practice, this amounted to blanket authorization of Sunday rugby; branches tended to treat applications for 'special per-mission' as a formality. The new policy was put forward by Sam Lee, a Northern Protestant. One of Ireland's greatest ever players and a Triple Crown winner in 1894, Lee was, above all else perhaps, an IRFU insider seeking a pragmatic solution.

Amid all of this, Sunday rugby had its greatest vindication on the field in April 1928, when Limerick's Young Munster defeated Lansdowne in the final of the Bateman Cup (effect-ively an All-Ireland club competition). The match, of course, took place on a Saturday, but the winning team's players all first encountered the game at junior level on Sundays. Competitions like the Transfield Cup and the City Junior Cup provided men with a rough-and-ready education in rugby, and 'the boys from the Yellow Road', as Young Munster were affectionately known, would not have been intimidated trav-elling to Dublin.

A senior club only since 1923, Young Munster had already caused something of a sensation by defeating Cork Constitution in the Munster Senior Cup final. The club's heartland was the working-class terraces and laneways off Parnell Street and Hyde Road, in the shadow of Limerick railway station. Indeed, several of the club's players worked on the railways, while a significant proportion were from labour-ing backgrounds.[23] In the Bateman Cup final, they faced a star-studded Lansdowne side, which included five current and two future internationals and was expected to make short work of their little-known Limerick opponents. A 6-3 victory for Young Munster was one of the greatest shocks ever witnessed at Lansdowne Road. The Limerick club's light, nimble pack dictated the game, playing a fast, dribbling style (then more associated with Scotland and now obsolete), while Eugene Davy, Lansdowne's magician at out-half, was well contained. Young Munster's victory, according to the Dublin newspaper *Sport*, was 'all the more creditable when one considers that the majority of their players are drawn from a class which has neither the time nor the opportunities for extensive practice'.[24]

Young Munster's victory brought very modest rewards in terms of international recognition. Just two players – Ter Casey (once in 1930 and again in 1932) and Danaher Sheehan (once in 1932) – were selected for Ireland. Casey was an outstanding front-row forward in the classic Limerick style: wiry, tough as nails, skilful in the loose. *Sport*'s correspondents were bewildered at the consistent refusal of the Irish selectors to pick him. 'For the last two years,' one commented in 1930, 'his claims have been urged in terms which seldom have erred on the side of moderation.'[25] His omission, in the view of the Limerick press, was straightforward class prejudice – Casey was a labourer.

Limerick clubs generally set aside their fierce rivalries when one of their own was playing against outsiders. In that spirit, Young Munster's victory was greeted as a triumph for the city, not just the club. On their return home, the winning team were treated to a procession through the streets of Limerick, led by the Lord Mayor. By producing a champion team moulded in the hothouse conditions of Sunday tournaments, Limerick rugby thumbed its nose at the establishment.

*

The battle over Sunday matches was far from the biggest challenge facing the rugby establishment in this period. The IRFU had to manage a game that now spanned two mutually hostile states.

The IRFU's response to partition was quite simple: they behaved as though it had not happened. This was understandable. Rugby in Ireland had trundled along as an all-island sport for almost half a century. In 1926, Cavan RFC, in light of the club's location on the Free State side of the border, wrote to the IRFU seeking affiliation to the Leinster Branch. This was refused. The 'Rugby game has no boundaries and recognises no border', the IRFU told Cavan officials, and as 'the position of the Co Cavan RFC remains geographically the same as before the Treaty' they could affiliate either to the Ulster Branch or to no branch at all.[26]

The IRFU attempted to observe neutrality in political matters, but this was tricky. Sitting around the Union's committee table were men divided by a political and cultural border, who recognized two different, often antagonistic sets of rituals and symbols, and who owed allegiance, or respect, to two different sets of public figures. But sometimes the ambition to maintain neutrality collided with tradition. There was a deep-rooted convention in rugby, for example, of honouring public figures, especially when they died. For most countries, this was a routine feature of national sporting culture. This was not the case in Irish rugby.

In 1936, for example, the IRFU cancelled all fixtures on 25 January, as a mark of respect to King George V, who had just died. The IRFU could argue that, as a Dominion, the Free State had retained the British monarch as head of state, and a gesture of respect in those circumstances was standard procedure. But the cancellation of matches, taken together with the continued toast to the King offered at IRFU functions, provided rugby's critics with ammunition, and annoyed figures within the game. Members of the Munster Branch bristled at what they saw as kowtowing to a foreign monarch. 'The principal toast at Union dinners and functions should be Eire and not the king', a Munster Branch committee meeting agreed in 1933. Jack Quilligan, the Old IRA man, enthusiastically supported the motion.[27] It was rumoured that international full-back Dermot Morris had skipped the post-match dinner following his debut at Belfast in 1931 in order to avoid the toast to the King.[28]

The practice of honouring public figures applied regardless of political affiliations. In 1927, the IRFU passed a vote of sympathy to the widow of Free State minister Kevin O'Higgins after his assassination in Dublin by republicans.[29] In the course of one IRFU meeting in 1940, the Union's committee extended both their condolences to the widow of the former Ulster Unionist leader James Craig, and their congratulations to the newly appointed Catholic Archbishop of Dublin, John Charles McQuaid. It is difficult to imagine two historical figures as divided politically and culturally as these.[30] McQuaid, officials noted, was a 'warm supporter' of the game.

As we have seen in the Prologue, international sport put these sorts of political and constitutional questions very much in the spotlight. Anthems and other symbols were fraught with significance and ambiguity long before the first rendition of 'Ireland's Call'.

In 1925, delegates at the annual council meeting decided that the Ireland rugby team should have its own flag: a politically neutral one, bearing the coats of arms of the four provinces. The republican newspaper *An Phoblacht* described the flag as 'a patchwork design that means little to anybody'.[31] This, of course, was entirely the intention. In 1932, following an international match against South Africa, University College Galway RFC objected to the absence of the Irish tricolour at Lansdowne Road, accusing the IRFU of 'anti national bias'. The matter was taken up by the press, and soon dozens of clubs across the Free State joined in. Shannon RFC in Limerick, for example, described the IRFU's flag policy as 'a studied insult to every man of Irish birth'.[32] The IRFU were unmoved, and had the support of the four provincial branches.

The controversy was given a steady supply of oxygen by newspapers, particularly the *Irish Press*. Effectively a mouthpiece for Fianna Fáil, the *Irish Press* gave lavish coverage to rugby, sharing its founder Éamon de Valera's love of the game. But it was determined to steer Irish rugby away from its Anglophile roots. The controversy soon escalated to the highest level of government. In early February, the Connacht Branch of the IRFU – going over the heads of their parent body – sought and were granted an audience with President Cosgrave. Little was resolved in the meeting; Cosgrave told the Connacht delegates that the government 'could not intervene'.[33] But just three days later the Minister for External Affairs, Paddy McGilligan, while acknowledging that the IRFU were not 'exclusively an Irish Free State institution', made plain his view that the tricolour should be flown at Lansdowne Road on the occasion of international fixtures. The IRFU immediately agreed to do so from then on.[34]

There were other occasional instances of sporting partisanship within electoral politics. In 1929, for example, Galway County Council voted to disqualify rugby-playing schools from receiving county secondary-school scholarships, one councillor claiming that 'Masonic and imperial forces were at work against the national life of the people'.[35] The Fianna Fáil government also exempted the GAA from entertainment tax in 1932, a measure not extended to rugby.[36]

In general, however, Irish governments were reluctant to interfere with the business of sports organizations and were acutely aware of the sensitive position of Irish rugby. Here, they were able to call on the views of an insider. Sarsfield Hogan, a member of the IRFU's executive committee, was a senior civil servant in the Department of Finance. He informed the Department of Foreign Affairs in 1952 that the IRFU

> have to keep constantly in mind the susceptibilities of the Six County representatives on the Committee. It would not be fair to say that these representatives call any particular tune. It is rather the concern of the 26 counties representatives to avoid any issue which would disrupt the unity of Ireland in this sport, which determines the policy about flags, etc. What they feel they have to avoid is anything which would make it possible for Belfast diehards to assert that Six County members of the Irish Rugby XV are being used for political purposes.[37]

By then the constitutional landscape had shifted considerably from the post-independence years. Ireland was now a republic with no connection to the British Crown. This had implications for the relationship between sport and national symbolism.

After the passage of the 1937 constitution, the King was effectively replaced as head of state by the holder of the newly created office of President of Ireland. The first President, Douglas Hyde, became embroiled in a sport-related controversy early in his term when, as a consequence of his attendance at an international soccer match in 1938, the GAA took the crass decision to strip him of his position as patron of the Association. Hyde met with de Valera soon afterwards, and they promptly resolved that the President should attend international rugby and soccer matches.

Two years later, when it became known that Hyde planned to attend a rugby match to be held in aid of the Red Cross, J. J. Walsh, a minister in the first Free State government (and later a fascist sympathizer), phoned the President's office claiming that 'a large body of opinion' was perturbed at his potential attendance at a 'foreign' game. Walsh was politely informed by an official that 'the President was President of the whole State and not of a particular section which disapproved of all forms of sport except those to which they were attached'. Objections to the President's attendance at games were 'unreasonable and unpatriotic', the official added.[38]

An official in the President's office summed up the position in 1938:

> There is a possibility that the President's attendance at Rugby Football Matches will create an outcry among Gaelic enthusiasts . . . but in my opinion the President as Head of State cannot take sides in a matter of this nature. To indicate by his absence disapproval of a particular type of sport which is popular throughout the country would be the cause of widespread discontent.[39]

New constitutional arrangements did not alter some traditions. After independence, Southern Irish players continued to take part in British Isles (later British and Irish Lions) tours. In advance of the 1950 tour of Australia, in which the visitors were captained by a Dubliner, Karl Mullen, the *Sydney Telegraph* pointed out that the team's name was 'a title which placates the turbulent Welsh, the rugged Scots, the unpredictable Northern Irish and the touchy representatives of Eire'.[40]

'Touchy' was a description that clearly applied to Ireland's Chargé d'Affaires in Canberra, Brendan O'Riordan, who took a close interest in the tour. Though the twenty-six Southern counties had become a republic the previous year, Australia had not yet granted Ireland full diplomatic recognition. This aggravated O'Riordan, who was determined, it seems, to keep Ireland as symbolically separate from Britain as possible. When an Australian rugby official requested the loan of an Irish flag, O'Riordan refused, not wishing to see an Irish tricolour displayed in a 'British Empire solidarity display'. He complained that 'by its very name the team does not purport to represent the Republic of Ireland'.[41] He also refused to meet the players, deeming it inappropriate to offer any recognition to the team. When another request for a flag arrived at the Irish Legation, this time from a British diplomat, J. M. Hunter, O'Riordan again refused to assist. From his perspective, Hunter had airily overlooked any difficulties the Irish might have had with the tricolour's inclusion in an imperial flag display. Hunter, O'Riordan wrote, 'with typical British obtuseness' thought that the only potential difficulty was 'that players from Belfast might object to the Irish flag'.[42] O'Riordan had also tersely informed Hunter that Ireland was 'not part of the British Isles'. The British Isles team, in O'Riordan's view, was being used 'as an instrument for boosting the "Empire Spirit"'.[43] Though the Department of Foreign Affairs supported O'Riordan's decisions, it did not reply to most of his correspondence, and the whole affair looked a lot like the pet obsession of a bored official.

The issue that almost caused a rupture in Irish rugby was anthems. Republicans had adopted 'The Soldier's Song' – the original English-language version of 'Amhrán na bhFiann' – as their anthem during the revolutionary period, and it was usually sung at public occasions in the early post-independence years. The Free State government was wary of the song's partisan lyrics, and briefly groped around for an alternative before quietly adopting it as the national anthem in 1926.[44] From then on, the government gradually came to expect that the anthem would be played at public events. This inevitably led to controversy. 'God Save the King' remained the only anthem played at Trinity College Dublin, and was generally played at functions where ex-unionists predominated; in the hymn book of the Church of Ireland, it remained the national anthem. It was sung with gusto by Dublin Protestants to greet the British team competing at the Dublin Horse Show, when international competitions were first staged there in 1926.[45] It was also played solemnly on Armistice Day – an occasion marked every year by the IRFU.

Along with Trinity and the Church of Ireland, the IRFU belonged to a class of institutions that had been broadly loyal to Britain prior to independence, and now needed to adapt to a new political and cultural environment. 'The Soldier's Song' was played at Lansdowne Road for the first time at an international rugby match in January 1928 to mark the arrival of the Governor-General, James McNeill. The Governor-General would later describe how he was now 'determined . . . there can be no further ignoring of the fact that the Free State has a separate identity'.[46] Some observers were aghast. A correspondent to the *Belfast News Letter* wrote to express disgust that the 'rebel ditty' had been played at Lansdowne Road. 'Is it not a scandal that any Government within the Empire should so insult his Majesty as to authorise a defiant anti-British song being described as a National Anthem?'[47]

The disconnect between Ireland's constitutional status and the structure of Irish rugby seemed to cause the French rugby authorities great confusion. Either that or they were simply careless. In 1923, at the post-match banquet in Paris, the band, 'not knowing an appropriate Irish anthem, played "God Save the King"'.[48] When Ireland played in France two years later, 'The problem of what National Anthem should be played for Ireland was altogether too much for the authorities, and the Marseillaise was played when the teams came on the ground.'[49] Then, in 1927, 'God Save the King' was played before kick-off. This eventually became a matter of diplomatic concern. In 1930, the Irish ambassador to France, Count Gerald O'Kelly de Gallagh, wrote to the Department of Foreign Affairs in Dublin seeking advice on the protocols pertaining to anthems and flags at international rugby matches, having been invited to an international between Ireland and France, due to take place in January 1931. In reply, Seán Murphy, the Assistant Secretary at Foreign Affairs, warned O'Kelly that 'Irish Rugby football has never been partitioned, and the team which will go to France will represent all Ireland as in pre-Treaty times.' The minister, Paddy McGilligan, was 'very anxious to avoid any appearance of trouble in this matter'. Murphy advised O'Kelly that an Irish air such as 'St Patrick's Day', rather than an anthem, should greet the Irish XV onto the field, and that at the post-match banquet 'Amhrán na bhFiann' should be played. If the president of the French rugby union, C. F. Rutherford – described by Murphy as a 'complacent Englishman' – insisted that 'God Save the King' should be played, then O'Kelly was to request that either both anthems or none should be played.[50] Murphy noted that there were more players from the Free State on the Irish team than ever before.

In the event, no anthems were played, either at the match or the subsequent banquet. Some French press sources, according to O'Kelly, claimed that Ireland had yet to compose an anthem, others that the anthem was not well known enough to warrant inclusion in the musical programme. The Irish XV, in some newspapers, were tactlessly described as 'Les Anglais' and 'Les Britanniques'. O'Kelly concluded that

> we ought to make every effort to secure the recognition of the Irish Flag and the Irish Anthem as the suitable symbols at an Irish–French match in France . . . So long as we countenance the Union Jack and concur in the suppression of 'Amhrán na bhFiann' we have only ourselves to blame if the man in the street looks upon us as 'les Britanniques' . . .[51]

As it turned out, this was a problem for the future. The French were expelled from the championship at the end of the 1931 campaign – the other four nations were dissatisfied with the less than scrupulous observation of amateurism in France – and would not reappear in the tournament until 1947.

France's difficulties stemmed in part from the fact that international rugby's pre-match protocols throughout the entire pre-World Cup era were vague, and could vary from season to season. In general, throughout the first several decades of international rugby, teams would be played onto the field to the sound of a politically neutral air (in Ireland's case, 'St Patrick's Day' was often the choice). France, as a republic, was usually greeted by 'La Marseillaise'. These were often, though not always, followed by 'God Save the King' at UK venues (including in Dublin pre-1922). When playing in Belfast, post-partition, Ireland still took to the field to a neutral air, while 'God Save the King' was played at the end of the match, apart from when the Governor-General attended; then a line from the song was played to mark his arrival.[52]

From 1949, the four 'home' unions agreed that only the national anthem of the host state would be played prior to championship fixtures. It seems likely that this agreement stemmed from friction between the IRFU and the President of Ireland, Seán T. O'Kelly, the year before. In 1947, the IRFU departed from procedure and both 'Amhrán na bhFiann' and 'God Save the King' were played at Lansdowne Road on England's first trip to Dublin in nine years.[53] On Ireland's return to Twickenham the following season, 'Amhrán na bhFiann' was omitted from the pre-match programme.

Shortly before the Ireland–Scotland match at Lansdowne Road two weeks later, O'Kelly instructed an official in his office to meet with the IRFU secretary, Rupert Jeffares. The official informed Jeffares that the President would not be attending the upcoming match, and that he was not authorized to reveal the reason for the decision. It was hardly coincidental, however, that the official then questioned Jeffares about the English band's failure to play the Irish national anthem at Twickenham. Jeffares was told that this was 'contrary to international practice'. This was wrong: 'God Save the King' was not routinely played at Lansdowne Road in the pre-war era.[54] When asked whether any Irish players objected to the anthem's absence, Jeffares 'said no. Everyone on the team seemed to take it for granted, as it had been done before.'

Jeffares added that the IRFU were 'in a difficult position as there were members from the north on the team'. When the IRFU tried to smooth matters by offering to play only the Irish anthem before the Scotland match, O'Kelly still refused to attend. Sarsfield Hogan, the Department of Finance and IRFU committeeman, was under the impression that the President's absence was 'due to the fact that at the recent match at Twickenham, the British anthem was played, and the Irish one was omitted'.[55] O'Kelly, however, offered no reason for his absence but authorized his office to issue a public statement (which made no mention of rugby) to the effect that he was sick in bed.

Whatever the precise circumstances that led to the adoption of these procedures, from then on 'Amhrán na bhFiann' was the only song played before matches at Lansdowne Road, while 'God Save the King' was played before home fixtures in England, Scotland and Wales, and in Belfast.

Four years later, Rupert Jeffares offered a confusing, pseudo-legal explanation of the protocols:

The practice for some years passed has been to play the ceremonial anthem customary in Dublin or Belfast, as the case may be, in the way and at the time which is in accordance alike with usage and respect for the State; and to play no other National anthem.[56]

The intention of the new policy was to disassociate the anthem from the *team*: it was to serve as a gesture of respect to the host *state*. This might seem like a hollow distinction, but the formula kept all sides relatively content. Decades later, in Jason Tuck's sociological study of rugby and Irish identity, one (anonymized) Ulster player pointed out that 'The Anthem is officially played because the game is played in Dublin, not because it's the team anthem.'[57]

The anthems protocol worked smoothly enough when it was followed, but caused problems when it was not. In 1953, before a match against France in Belfast, the band played both 'God Save the Queen' and 'La Marseillaise', giving the impression to some observers that the British anthem was being played in honour of the Irish team. 'Had the British anthem alone been played as that of country of venue,' a memo to the President of Ireland read, '. . . that would be understandable.'[58] The Connacht Branch passed a resolution condemning the IRFU, imploring them never to allow a repetition of such an 'insult to the Irish nation'.[59] The Branch briefed the press about the resolution before informing the IRFU. Jeffares composed a snippy reply, accusing the Connacht Branch of behaviour 'wholly out of accord with the spirit of mutual loyalty and consideration which ought to exist between the Union and its Branches'. Moreover, Connacht were 'grievously in error in believing that any music was played at Ravenhill, Belfast, on the occasion of the recent match between Ireland and France as "the anthem of the Ireland fifteen"'. The playing of any anthem, he said, was purely out of respect for the state where the match was being hosted. The playing of the French national anthem, Jeffares claimed, was due to an error on the part of the band in Belfast. 'My committee deplore and take grave exception to the suggestion that the Irish Rugby Football Union was, or could be, associated with any insult to the Irish nation', he concluded.[60]

The letters editors of the newspapers were kept busy for days dealing with correspondence on the issue. One letter to the *Irish Times* accused the IRFU of 'pandering to the sensitivities of the Orange Lodges, rather than those of the country – Ireland'. The letter concluded that 'The Rugby clique, who never tire of criticising the narrow-mindedness of the GAA clique, can be very narrow-minded themselves.'[61] The *Connacht Sentinel*, in a lengthy editorial, accused the IRFU of being 'a clique which stands for British rule for part of the Northern province of Ireland and which . . . would like to see the Twenty-six Counties again occupied by Britain'.[62] Several local authorities across Ireland passed resolutions condemning the IRFU, and Sinn Féin stated that had the players been 'Irishmen worthy of the name', they would have refused to play.[63]

When Clontarf second row Paddy Lawlor was dropped for the following match, against England, rumours circulated that he had lost his place because he had 'let it be known in no uncertain terms what he thought of the playing of the British national anthem and the absence of the Irish national anthem in an Irish city'.[64] There is no evidence that these rumours were true, but we know for a fact that when Ireland next played at Ravenhill – against Scotland in 1954 – the prospect of standing to attention to 'God Save the Queen' caused an outright revolt among several of the ten Southern players selected for the match. On the journey north from Dublin, a conversation had started among three players – later described as 'rabid nationalists' by one of their teammates – who were particularly unhappy. By the morning of the match, attitudes had hardened and the three had decided that they would not take to the field until after the anthems. Not alone that, they had convinced several others to join their protest. Eventually, all ten Southern players decided to act as one, and effectively boycott the British national anthem.

Though he was not one of the originators of the protest, the task of informing the IRFU fell to the captain, Jim McCarthy.

The players were then summoned to a hotel room for a meeting with officials, where Cahir Davitt, a long-time IRFU committeeman, pleaded with the players to abandon their protest for the sake of unity in Irish rugby. Davitt, as we have seen, had nationalist credentials that were beyond reproach. He warned the players that their planned action would jeopardize rugby's status as a non-partitioned sport and that the Taoiseach, de Valera, would not approve. He also made the reasonable observation that Northern players stood to attention to 'Amhrán na bhFiann' before matches at Lansdowne Road without complaint. Crucially, he assured the players that they would not be put in this position again.

The players complied and swore to keep the incident secret. All the while, the Northern players were oblivious to the drama playing out in the hotel room, thinking that the Southerners had gathered to say a prayer for the Pope, who was then ill.[65] The identities of the three players who initiated the proposed protest is not known, but it is telling, perhaps, that when Paddy Lawlor – who had regained his place in 1954 – died in 2015, his death notice stated that he had been the 'last remaining of the "Ravenhill Rebels"'.[66]

Ireland did not play again at Ravenhill for fifty-two years. The decision to host all Irish internationals at Lansdowne Road was not, however, made in deference to the feelings of Southern players. The addition of a new tier to the West Stand at Lansdowne Road in 1954 increased the ground's capacity by 5,000. The IRFU, burdened with an overdraft of over IR£200,000, could not afford the loss of revenue that international fixtures in Ravenhill would now entail.[67]

With the Union's finances looking much healthier by 1968, suggestions of a return of international rugby to Ravenhill circulated. IRFU president Eugene Davy conceded that 'In fairness to Ulster they have never pressed their claim.'[68] Not everyone in Northern Ireland was quite as phlegmatic as Davy implied, but it was at least clear that the abandonment of Ravenhill was not political. An editorial in the *Belfast News Letter* the previous year complained that the IRFU's attitude to venues was 'based on economics'.[69]

The debate over returning to Belfast was overtaken by events. The deteriorating security situation in Northern Ireland carried risks from an international rugby perspective: the logistics of large gatherings in Belfast, the willingness of fans to travel there, and the headaches associated with anthems and symbols must all have weighed heavily on the IRFU. From the perspective of 1954, however, we don't know why Cahir Davitt gave such confident assurances to the Southern players that they wouldn't have to stand to 'God Save the Queen' again. Most likely, he knew that the redevelopment of Lansdowne Road would deprive Belfast of international matches in the medium term, and that this arrangement would comfortably outlast the careers of the Ravenhill rebels.

Despite such dramas, rugby achieved a *modus vivendi* between North and South that was generally absent from other aspects of Irish life. Bertie Smyllie (under his pen name, 'Nichevo'), commenting after Ireland's first home international against England after the Second World War, in 1947, observed that

> The field of Rugby football is the only common ground on which Irishmen of all shades of opinion can meet in absolute harmony. They recognise no such thing as partition . . . [I was] particularly glad to watch the Ulster members of the team standing stiffly to attention during the playing

of the Soldier's Song . . . [O]n Saturday it was an Irish team that took the field at Lansdowne Road and the border seemed to me, at any rate, to be a rather ridiculous thing.[70]

Matters in this regard were helped no end by performances on the field. In the years after the war, Ireland had its greatest team of the amateur era. The 1948 team defeated all four Five Nations opponents, thus securing what later generations called the Grand Slam. Victory over the Welsh in Belfast to secure the title was a moment of genuine national celebration. The match had drawn a huge crowd to Ravenhill, with ten special trains carrying thousands of fans from Dublin to Belfast.

The final whistle was greeted with scenes of unrestrained joy, as the crowd invaded the field. John Daly, a Catholic from Cork who scored Ireland's winning try, was carried off the Ravenhill pitch and had the jersey ripped from his back. It was not the only unusual sight that afternoon. The *Manchester Guardian*'s correspondent, commenting on the symbolic significance of the victory, told readers, 'whisper it gently – even Belfast has seen an enormous Eire flag being waved during and after the match without falling upon the bearer or casting him into the nearest dungeon'.[71]

Ireland won the championship again in 1951, denied another clean sweep by a draw in Cardiff. Ireland's era of success was built on an outstanding forward pack, featuring a dynamic back row of Billy McKay, Jim McCarthy and Des O'Brien. The team's star turn was the young out-half, Jack Kyle. A mesmerizing talent who played an off-the-cuff, instinctive game, Kyle soon became recognized as one of the greatest players in the world, a reputation copper-fastened by superb displays on the 1950 British Lions tour. He was a powerfully symbolic figure. Though raised Presbyterian in Belfast, he was revered across the island and cared deeply about the all-island dimension of Irish rugby.[72] In this, he was probably influenced by his headmaster at Belfast Royal Academy, Alec Foster. A former Ireland international and British Lion, Foster was a Presbyterian of the radical tradition, a member of the Wolfe Tone Society and a supporter of civil rights.[73] Though Kyle largely kept his political views to himself, he was later an outspoken critic of Paisleyism. On the island of Ireland consensus was a rare commodity, but people of all backgrounds could agree that Kyle was a national hero.

We should not get carried away, however. Smyllie's claim of 'absolute harmony' in Irish rugby was too optimistic, as the debates over national symbols demonstrated. But rugby remained capable of producing profoundly symbolic moments. In 1949, Father Tom Gavin, an English-born Catholic priest, defied Archbishop McQuaid by lining out for Ireland. Though an admirer of the sport, McQuaid thought that international rugby was no place for a priest. But Gavin was known for his independence of mind and, besides, was under the authority of the Bishop of Birmingham, in whose diocese he then served.[74] Thus he defiantly took to the Lansdowne Road field for his debut against France in January. Among his teammates was a Presbyterian clergyman, Ernie Strathdee. This was an achievement in sporting ecumenism that other games struggled to match.

7. Political football

In January 1970, Brian McRoberts, a prospective Unionist parliamentary candidate for West Belfast, made public his intention to organize a protest at Lansdowne Road on the occasion of Ireland's forthcoming rugby match against South Africa. He was not intending to join the broader anti-apartheid protest also planned for the fixture. In fact, his was a counter-protest – against the GAA. 'We feel the discrimination of the GAA is worse than the apartheid in South Africa,' he stated with a straight face, 'because it does not allow players in other sports . . . to become a member.' He claimed to have had 20,000 leaflets printed, and was going to lead a group of twenty people carrying banners exclaiming 'Ban the GAA' and 'Stop apartheid in Irish sport'.[1] After consulting with Gardaí, however, McRoberts dropped his plan, having been told that there 'were strong feelings in Dublin' against the picket. It is not clear how sincerely McRoberts believed the ludicrous proposition that the rules of a sporting organization were worse than the systematic racial segregation and oppression of the majority of South Africa's population. The GAA, for their part, accused McRoberts of attempting to 'divert attention from the monstrous bigotry and discrimination in the Six Counties that is firmly set on the Orange lodges'.[2]

Viewed in isolation, McRoberts's campaign appears merely absurd. There was political calculation involved, however. He was hoping to gain election to the House of Commons and he wanted to play on the darker prejudices of some of his potential supporters. The Nationalist MP Austin Currie plausibly suggested that McRoberts never had any intention of going ahead with the protest and was merely 'playing a pathetic make-believe game in order to gain cheap publicity'.[3]

The weightier row over the ethics of hosting a team from South Africa had been brewing for a while. Five weeks before the Lansdowne Road fixture, the Stormont government had cancelled an Ulster v. South Africa match – not because of a revulsion at apartheid, but because an anti-apartheid protest organized by the civil rights group People's Democracy was due to take place at the ground beforehand. The likelihood of a loyalist counter-protest and violent clashes prompted government action. Indeed, as MPs debated the fixture's fate, additional security measures were in place at Stormont due to 'a mass lobby of anti-Apartheid students . . . to get the match banned'.[4]

The cancellation of the match drew considerable criticism from some Unionist politicians, who felt the government had caved in to a gang of malcontents. Unionist MP Harry West was left 'angry, embarrassed and humiliated' by the cancellation of the match, while his party colleague James Stronge – later killed by the IRA – claimed that 'there had been a total abdication . . . to the militant element of the civil rights association'.[5] One over-excited correspondent to the *Belfast Telegraph* described the cancellation of the match as 'a victory for anarchy'.[6] This was the context in which McRoberts decided to use the Dublin fixture as a means of political positioning.

Meanwhile, there were threats from the other side. The IRA, anticipating clashes between stewards, Gardaí and demonstrators at Lansdowne Road, vowed to hold IRFU officials directly responsible for any injuries sustained by anti-apartheid protestors, and threatened to 'take action' against

'Mr Fitzpatrick'. No IRFU official of that name existed, and newspapers assumed that the Union secretary, Robert Fitzgerald, was the target of the threat. 'The IRFU', an IRA statement read, 'have been notorious in the past for anti-Irish snob attitudes.'[7] The UVF, wrongly asserting that the anti-apartheid demonstrations were orchestrated by the IRA, promised that 'the Fenians would suffer the consequences' if the protests went ahead.[8]

Though the Dublin government took no steps to have the match cancelled, the Taoiseach, Jack Lynch, refused to attend. The most prominent rugby voice amid all of this was that of a Presbyterian, Alec Foster, one of Irish and Ulster rugby's most complex characters, whom we met at the end of the last chapter. Foster was a zealous anti-apartheid campaigner. The touring Springboks, he asserted, were 'ambassadors' of 'a political system which is abhorred by civilised people all over the world'.[9] He took a prominent position among the leaders of the anti-apartheid protests. The IRFU, however, were steadfastly of the view that the game should go on at all costs, that international fraternal bonds had to be maintained and that rugby, an innocent pastime, must remain aloof from politics. The Union, responding to a request from the Irish Anti-Apartheid Movement to cancel their invitation to the touring Springboks in 1965, asserted that 'The Irish Rugby Football Union within its jurisdiction permits playing of matches against any team, regardless of race, nationality or political affiliations, which conforms to the accepted principles and disciplines of amateur rugby football.'[10]

Irish rugby, then, was positioned awkwardly in the midst of colliding political currents. The Northern Ireland Troubles presented an unprecedented challenge to the thirty-two-county unity that the IRFU had preserved so eagerly since partition.

And the foundation of a durable anti-apartheid movement meant that maintaining sporting ties with South Africa made the IRFU the focus of bitter criticism and protest.

Rugby's ability to bridge divisions on the island of Ireland had long been overstated. The working classes were notably under-represented in Irish rugby, and Northern Catholics were almost completely absent. The latter was largely a function of the broader segregation of Northern Ireland society along sectarian lines. The game in Ulster, from its very beginnings, catered overwhelmingly to middle-class Protestants. There were some eye-catching exceptions. The Ross brothers, Dan, John and Joe, Catholics from County Down, were capped for Ireland in the 1880s. St Malachy's College, a Catholic grammar school in Belfast, and St Columb's College in Derry dabbled in rugby from time to time. City of Derry RFC, the natural home for St Columb's old boys, had a cross-community dimension. A short-lived Old Malachians Rugby Club was founded in the early 1930s, but quickly fell away. When rumours emerged that St Malachy's were considering taking up rugby again in 1963, a correspondent to the *Belfast Telegraph* claimed that it was a development that

> fascinated our non-Catholic friends . . . For too long, they [St Malachy's] have found themselves barred from that universally popular student game, while they have watched with some bewilderment the fruitful sporting contacts of our Northern Protestant colleges with all that is best represented by such colleges as Belvedere, Blackrock and Clongowes.[11]

Nothing came of the rumours, and in 1964 the president of the college, Fr Walter Larkin, felt compelled to explain his institution's preference for Gaelic over rugby. 'It has been suggested that as part of the ecumenical movement St Malachy's should play rugby. As far as the present pupils are concerned, they have ample opportunities to meet non-Catholics through chess, water polo, golf, athletics and debates.'[12] Then, in 1982, the church correspondent to the *Belfast Telegraph*, in the context of a discussion about ecumenism, sincerely asked readers, 'when, God help us, is St Malachy's going to discover Rugby football?' It would be 'nice', he claimed, if the Ulster rugby team were 'representative in every sense'.[13]

It was telling that the future of multi-faith rugby in Ulster was vested by commentators in the most prestigious Catholic school in the province. The school's failure to take up the game, one noted, was something for which 'it was occasionally taken to task'.[14] At least one former St Malachy's boy managed to gain selection for the Ireland rugby team. Paddy Agnew was already thirty-two when he won the first of his two caps for Ireland in 1974. Agnew, who grew up in the staunchly republican area of Andersonstown in Belfast, had taken up rugby in his mid-twenties with the fourth XV at CIYMS (Church of Ireland Young Men's Society – by its very essence a Protestant institution).[15] Such a path to international rugby was freakishly rare in Northern Ireland, the exception that proved the rule.

Soccer, of course, was different. Working-class Protestants and Catholics had a shared passion for the game. But here, sectarian divisions were stark. Derry City, for example, were forced to seek refuge in the Southern League of Ireland in 1985 after the security forces deemed their home ground, the Brandywell, too dangerous for visiting clubs, especially those with links to unionism.[16] The working-class housing estates of Belfast, Derry and other Northern towns – the recruiting grounds for paramilitary groups and soccer's heartlands – were not seedbeds of rugby.

Long before the security situation in Northern Ireland deteriorated in the late 1960s, rugby matches had occasionally seen protests by opponents of partition. On the occasion of the Ireland v. Wales international at Ravenhill in 1950, a UCD student, Joe Hughes, ran onto the pitch with the Irish tricolour before being roughly handled by the RUC. 'While a district Inspector and two constables grappled with him for possession of the flag,' the *Irish Press* gleefully noted, 'Joe gallantly defended it and triumphantly emerged from the scrum still holding the Tricolour and a great cheer went up from the crowd, Irish and Welsh.'[17] The nationalist *Derry Journal* congratulated the RUC for giving the 'Anti-Partition cause a tremendous filip' through their overreaction to Hughes's high jinks.[18] The unionist *Belfast Telegraph* did not see matters this way, chiding those fans who arrived from Dublin bearing 'the Eire colours' as 'politically rather than rugby minded'. The *Telegraph* also took issue with 'an ill-mannered youth' who shouted 'up the rebels' during the RUC band's rendition of 'God Save the King'.[19]

The following year, the Anti-Partition League staged a protest on the occasion of a fixture between Ireland and the Combined Services, a team made up of British armed forces personnel. In advance of the match, the group wrote to the IRFU, reminding them of Bloody Sunday, when Crown forces opened fire on players and supporters at Croke Park in 1920. 'On this occasion', the letter read, British forces 'succeeded in inflicting casualties . . . on the home team, who were unable to score'. 'The home team', it went on, 'turned the tables at Crossbarry [the scene of an IRA ambush in County Cork in 1921], and other venues.'[20] Sarsfield Hogan passed the letter to the Secretary of the Department of Justice, Tommy Coyne, noting that it was 'very close to incitement'.[21] A poorly written leaflet was distributed to supporters arriving at Lansdowne Road, telling them that by attending the match 'you are encouraging fraternisation with the forces of the enemy thus creating an unrealistic attitude towards the crime of Partition and discouraging workers for Irish unity at home and abroad'.[22] The government decided not to intervene, and the protest was a damp squib: it consisted of twenty people carrying placards bearing slogans such as 'Why play ball with the enemy' and, weirdly, 'this is not an anti-rugby picket'.[23] This was not an isolated protest; small pickets usually took place when Ireland hosted the Combined Services.

By the outbreak of the Troubles, international fixtures at Ravenhill and matches against the Combined Services were things of the past. But as the upward curve of violent deaths in Northern Ireland steepened from 1971, rugby teams grew reluctant to travel there. In November of that year, Shannon (Limerick), Highfield (Cork) and Fylde (Lancashire) all called off fixtures in Belfast.[24] This trend intensified in the aftermath of a second Bloody Sunday in January 1972, when fourteen unarmed civilians were shot dead by British paratroopers in Derry. Days after the massacre, the Leinster Branch requested all teams taking part in that weekend's fixtures to observe a minute's silence in honour of the victims. As a result of the demand, Malone and Instonians rugby clubs, both due to play in Dublin that weekend, refused to travel south.[25] A Malone official cited the old formula that 'rugby was above politics'.[26]

Amid the menacing atmosphere that immediately descended on the island after Bloody Sunday, the IRFU came under pressure to withdraw from the Five Nations, and various local authorities petitioned the Union to boycott the upcoming match against England at Twickenham as a protest against the British government. A more sinister intervention came from an unnamed 'extreme Republican organisation' which threatened to force the cancellation of the match. 'The rugby bosses should realise', a statement read, 'that the Irish nation will not tolerate any fraternisation with Englishmen during the present political tension.'[27] When the match went ahead, a *Belfast News Letter* editorial saw it as striking a 'blow for sanity amid the political hysteria . . . All sporting bodies – and especially one which draws its players from Ballymena to Cork – have a particular duty to press on with their fixtures.'[28]

With sports teams across many codes refusing to travel to Ireland and with the British Embassy a burnt-out shell in Dublin, Scotland and Wales pulled out of Five Nations fixtures at Lansdowne Road that season. These decisions, according to the Leinster Branch, were 'without regard to the realities of the situation in Dublin' – a city mostly un-affected by the Troubles.[29] After the Scots had resolved to stay at home, the IRFU president, Dom Dineen, and captain Tom Kiernan, both Southerners, described the move as something of an overreaction. The *Belfast News Letter*, while conceding that rugby was 'the last bastion of Irish unity', told readers that 'There always has been a certain naivete in Eire with regard to public opinion across the Channel.'[30]

Ireland won its matches in Paris and Twickenham that year, but the championship was not awarded owing to the unful-filled fixtures. France came to Lansdowne Road for a friendly in April, which eased the IRFU's financial pain somewhat; but this was a grave crisis for Irish rugby. Not only did it call into question the viability of the Irish team as an all-island entity, but it had the potential to cause the IRFU financial ruin. Home fixtures in the Five Nations were the Union's main source of income. And from the perspective of observers in 1972, there was no knowing how long it would be before Welsh, Scottish or English teams would be willing to fulfil fixtures in Dublin.

Irish rugby ploughed on, and something resembling a normal fixture schedule was maintained. Protestant schools in Northern Ireland and Catholic schools in the Republic continued their tradition of cross-border fixtures. In June, the Ulster Branch wrote to their Munster counterparts, thanking them for maintaining their full schedule that season.[31] Then, in January 1973, Irish rugby was given a welcome boost by the arrival in Dublin of the All Blacks, a match in which Ireland secured a 10-10 draw – the first time they'd ever avoided defeat to New Zealand, and the last time they did so until 2016. The All Blacks had also visited Belfast, where 20,000 spectators – then the biggest non-political gathering in Belfast for three years – witnessed their victory over Ulster.[32] The annual report of the Leinster Branch gratefully recorded that 'The decision of the All Blacks to play in Dublin and Belfast at the height of the campaign by "disaffected persons" to cancel fixtures in Ireland displayed all the characteristics which have made the New Zealanders such formidable opponents on the rugby field.'[33]

Then, in February, the English RFU decided to fulfil their Five Nations Championship fixture at Lansdowne Road. Observers pointed out that the English had shown a level of intestinal fortitude notably absent among Ireland's Celtic cousins the previous season. In the words of the *Sunday Independent*, the English visit to Dublin 'inflicted quite a kick in the pants to the Scottish and Welsh Unions'.[34] This was slightly unfair, perhaps, on the Scots and the Welsh. Their fears in 1972 were reasonable enough in the immediate aftermath of Bloody Sunday, and the atmosphere in Dublin was much less tense by the time England arrived the following year.

The England fixture led to an intense security operation: police both North and South put tight border checks in place, roads were closed in the vicinity of Lansdowne Road, and the visiting players – who, it was feared, might be targeted – were chaperoned by Gardaí. It was, according to one Garda officer, 'the biggest security operation ever mounted in the city'.[35] Before kick-off, John Pullin and his English side were greeted by a standing ovation. 'In our fifty thousands we stood, cheering and applauding, howling with ghoulish delight as the fifteen white-shirted Englishmen bounced onto the pitch', the *Irish Times* beamed.[36] Ireland won the match, but the result was treated as something of a footnote: the mere fact that the game went ahead dominated the press narrative. A *Belfast Telegraph* editorial told readers that 'in a real sense, the true winner was the game of rugby itself'.[37] At the after-match dinner, John Pullin took to his feet and told attendees that 'we might not be much good, but at least we turn up'. The English team set a welcome precedent at a time when the Troubles were only just getting started. Though future visiting teams were subjected to threats – some more serious than others – in the years that followed, the fixture list was uninterrupted from then on.

The bravery of the English players in 1973 might have rescued Irish rugby in the short term, but it was the Northern Irishmen who continued to play for Ireland throughout the Troubles that kept the show on the road. Travelling south for squad sessions and matches must have been a tense experience, especially around the border area, where, as noted in the Prologue, three Irish internationals were injured in an IRA bomb attack in 1987. This was amplified for players who were employed by the security forces. RUC men like Jimmy McCoy and John McDonald and British Army officer Brian McCall all had a tight, carefully planned security detail while on Ireland duty. Garda Special Branch officers would accompany the players during their stay in Dublin, escorting them to training and matches and patrolling the corridors of the team hotel.

In an interview in 2012, Jimmy McCoy, a tighthead prop who was first capped for Ulster as a teenager and who was part of the Triple Crown-winning Ireland team in 1985, told his former international teammate Donal Lenihan (the grandson of an Old IRA man from Kerry):

> I always thought my job was my career. I went into the RUC straight out of school. I had great pride in playing for Ireland and had no problem whatsoever standing for 'Amhrán na bhFiann'. People in the police were proud that I was playing for Ireland. They knew that we got on well with everyone in the Irish squad, that there was no political issues between the players. I never met anyone who gave me grief or said that you shouldn't be doing that. I loved playing for Ireland.[38]

Players' memoirs invariably record the amiable, often light-hearted relations between Northern and Southern players. Ken Goodall, a Derry man who played for Ireland in the 1960s, cheerfully remembered a Five Nations match against England where the team captain, Noel Murphy (a Catholic from Cork), went about the dressing room beforehand sprinkling holy water on the players. Ken Kennedy, a Northern Protestant and the team's hooker, ducked to avoid this impromptu ritual, claiming that 'if the drops fell on his head they would burn right through him'.[39] When they wore the green jersey,

Kennedy, Goodall, McCoy and other Northerners were simply proud Irishmen who delighted in beating England.

This blend of identities found its most extreme personification, perhaps, in the figure of Davy Tweed. A pugnacious second row from north Antrim, Tweed played at club level for Ballymena and was already thirty-five when he was first selected for Ireland in 1995. Though visibly emotional when making his Ireland debut, Tweed was a hardline unionist. He was a member of the Orange Order's Royal Black Institution, and his hulking frame was an imposing, intimidating presence as he faced down police attempting to reroute Orange marches in the 1990s and 2000s. In 1998, while sitting as a DUP member on Ballymena Council, Tweed launched a campaign to have special bins placed outside council buildings where unionists were invited to dump their copies of the Good Friday Agreement.[40] As the DUP drifted towards the mainstream, Tweed defected to Traditional Unionist Voice, a fringe anti-Agreement party. After his death in 2021, Tweed's family made serious allegations against him of sexual and physical violence; he was a very dark figure, indeed.

Tweed's political views, at least in their public expression, were not the norm among Ulster's Irish internationals. Much more common were figures like Trevor Ringland, a Belfast Protestant, who, along with his former Ireland teammate Hugo MacNeill, a Dublin Catholic, arranged the Peace International in 1996. Taking inspiration from Nelson Mandela's full-blooded embrace of rugby as a symbol of unity in South Africa, the match pitted Ireland against a top-class Barbarians XV at Lansdowne Road. Before kick-off the teams were introduced to children from both communities in Northern Ireland who had lost loved ones to paramilitary violence. It was a poignant, symbolic moment. But symbolism was as much as rugby could offer. The likelihood was modest indeed that events such as the Peace International could inspire the residents of the Falls Road and the Shankill to think better of each other, something readily acknowledged by Ringland at the time.[41]

The idea that 'the game must go on' served Irish rugby well during the Troubles. This was emphatically not the case when it came to relations with South Africa. Sport and politics in this context were so densely intertwined that any pretence that they could remain apart was the rugby equivalent of arguing that the Earth was flat.

When the National Party came to power in South Africa in 1948, it went about creating a system of apartheid, under which the races were strictly segregated and the non-white majority were denied basic civil rights. As these policies intensified, South Africa became an international pariah. It was expelled from the Commonwealth in 1961, and in 1966 the United Nations adopted a resolution identifying apartheid as a crime against humanity. A sporting boycott ran alongside these developments. South Africa was flung out of the Olympics in 1970 and did not return until 1992, while the national cricket team was excluded from international matches from 1970 to 1991.

Like all other features of life in South Africa, rugby was racially segregated. The South Africa Rugby Board (SARB) was a white-only organization, a policy which extended, until 1977, to the selection of the Springbok XV; non-white players had their own governing bodies and representative teams. Prior to 1968, touring New Zealand teams in South Africa were prevented from selecting Maoris. When the All Blacks visited in 1970, the four Maori players selected were declared 'honorary whites' by the SARB.[42] Despite this vile system, South Africa remained inside the international rugby fold. Indeed, until the 1980s, rugby unions in the northern and southern hemispheres brazenly faced down bitter domestic protests against hosting and visiting South Africa, valuing fraternal relations above all else. 'The IRFU knows no politics', Union president Robert Ganly would write in 1981; 'playing Rugby Football against other countries does not indicate acceptance of that country's political system. The IRFU have had continuous contact with the South African Rugby Board since its foundation . . . continuing contact and communication will achieve far more than ostracism and boycott.'[43]

Ireland had hosted South Africa in 1951 and 1960 and had toured there in 1961; these encounters did not cause controversy. When the Springboks toured Ireland in 1965, the Irish Anti-Apartheid Movement protested and distributed leaflets, but the whole affair was muted. Speaking in the Dáil, the Taoiseach, Seán Lemass, mildly scoffed at the suggestion of opposition TD Dr Noël Browne that the government should ban ministers from attending the fixture, telling deputies that he did 'not see how attendance at an international football match could imply any point of view regarding the policies of the Governments of the countries concerned'.[44] Five years later, though, the government in Dublin had no representative present when the South Africans pitched up at Lansdowne Road for their only fixture against Ireland in the 1970s.

A turning point for South Africa's status in international sport came when Prime Minister John Vorster refused entry to Basil D'Oliveira, a mixed-race England cricketer of South African birth, for a proposed tour in 1968.[45] From then on the sporting boycott of South Africa gathered momentum. In 1977, the United Nations adopted a Declaration on Apartheid in Sport (the Gleneagles Agreement) calling on member states to cut all sporting ties with South Africa. Ireland abstained but resolved to implement the agreement as far as possible. This resolve was soon tested.

In 1979, the South African Barbarians, a multiracial team, were to tour Britain and Ireland, with fixtures scheduled against Munster and Leinster. By then international attitudes towards South Africa had hardened, and the Irish government's position was clear. In January, the Minister for Foreign Affairs, Michael O'Kennedy, had addressed a conference organized by the Irish Anti-Apartheid Movement on European Economic Community relations with South Africa, claiming that 'our sympathies in Ireland naturally go to those who are now oppressed . . . Europe has a special duty to reject the claim of White South Africa that it defends "Western values"'.[46] The Irish Anti-Apartheid Movement (IAAM) was now an influential organization that governments could scarcely ignore. Led by the energetic South African academic Kader Asmal, the IAAM attracted support from across the political spectrum, including several sitting politicians. Conor Cruise O'Brien was chairman from 1969, while Garret FitzGerald chaired IAAM conferences while serving as Minister for Foreign Affairs in the mid-1970s. The movement also counted among its members major figures in Irish culture, academia and religion, and had close links with the trade union movement and other civil rights organizations.[47]

The 1979 tour first entered the government's purview in September, when the Department of Foreign Affairs issued a public statement condemning the proposed visit, stating that sporting contacts with South Africa raised questions about 'our fundamental attitude' to the 'degrading system' of apartheid.[48] Soon afterwards, officials prepared a briefing note for the Taoiseach, outlining the situation as it stood. Any pretence towards integration in South African rugby, the briefing claimed, was bogus. The banner of 'South African Barbarians' was a method of avoiding objections based on the nationality of the team while the inclusion of non-white players in the Barbarians selection was 'superficial'.[49] The Taoiseach was also told that the arrival of the tourists would lead to widespread protests, might damage Irish relations with other African countries, and could lead to Ireland's expulsion from the Olympics. Indeed, the president of the International Olympic Committee, Lord Killanin (an Irishman), had written to the government warning of 'considerable repercussions' if the tour proceeded. He also wrote to the IRFU pleading with them that the invitation 'really should be reconsidered'.[50]

In advance of a meeting with the government on 12 September, Jim Montgomery, president of the IRFU, told the *Belfast Telegraph* that the Union would do 'exactly' what they were told: 'If the people who run the country tell us we are not allowed to have the Barbarians here, we will not have them.'[51] To all appearances, Montgomery was making things very straightforward for the government; yet the reality turned out to be different. We do not know exactly what happened at the meeting, but it resolved nothing, and the IRFU did not withdraw their invitation to the touring South Africans. In correspondence with the government, the IRFU were keen to stress that the South Africans had received a joint invitation from the Irish, English, Welsh and Scottish rugby unions. The IRFU were apparently privileging their relations with the British unions and the SARB over their relations with the Irish government. (The British government, for its part, was opposed to the tour, but took no action to prevent it.)

The IRFU's determination to brazen it out prompted the government to issue a statement on 18 September telling the public that the tourists would be refused entry to Ireland. The statement praised the contribution of rugby to Irish life, and acknowledged the independence of sporting organizations, conceding that 'the government should only involve themselves in such questions in the most exceptional circumstances'. But in light of the international position on apartheid and the South African tendency to use sport for political leverage, the government decided to act because the IRFU had refused to withdraw the invitation.[52]

There was palpable tension between the government and the IRFU. The Union wrote to the Minister for Justice, Gerry Collins, on 25 September seeking more detail on the basis for the government's decision. The IRFU were left waiting three weeks for a reply and when it came, it was a verbal smack in the face. A brief letter tersely informed the Union that the minister had nothing to add to the public statement that had been issued almost a month earlier.[53] The government stance drew praise from several quarters, not least, perhaps, because the British government, while voicing opposition to the tour, was not willing to deny entry to the South Africans. The tourists thus arrived in London, greeted by furious protests.[54]

The following year, the IRFU started to consider the possibility of a tour of South Africa in 1981. As the plans were firmed up, the government became increasingly concerned. In December, the Minister for Foreign Affairs, Brian Lenihan, told Dáil Éireann of the government's opposition to the proposed tour. But he would not take the draconian action of withholding the players' passports – a move that probably would not survive a court challenge.[55] News in January that the tour was definitely going ahead was met with stern opposition.

As was the case in 1979, the consensus among press commentators, politicians, churches, trade unions, local authorities and so on was that the government should intervene to prevent the tour. At this stage rugby was the last major international sport holding out against the boycott of South Africa. France toured there in 1980, and England were to do so in 1984.

In January 1981, the *Belfast Telegraph* delivered a withering assessment of the IRFU's decision, accusing the Union of putting 'a seal of approval not only on the state of rugby in South Africa but on the state itself'. 'Since Ulstermen were involved', the paper continued, the British government would have to follow the example of their Dublin counterparts and condemn the tour.[56] The Rev. Ronnie Craig, a former Ireland international and then Moderator of the Presbyterian Church in Ireland, was also opposed to the tour. But reaction to the tour was not uniformly hostile. DUP deputy leader Peter Robinson saw no reason why 'sportsmen should not visit South Africa'. Referring to the hosting of sports events in communist states, Robinson argued that 'Sportsmen have been taking part in games in countries with a great deal more to complain about their political regime than South Africa.'[57]

Brian Lenihan met with the IRFU officials in January and in March, and made clear the government's position. The IAAM wrote to the Taoiseach, Charles Haughey, in March, telling him that they had reached 'the inescapable conclusion that only the head of our Government, with all the political and moral authority vested in him, can by his intervention dissuade the IRFU from this foolish and possibly tragic venture'.[58] Haughey also had to hand a sobering list of potential consequences of the tour going ahead. From an economic perspective, growing trade links with Nigeria, whose government 'don't accept that the government cannot stop the tour', and Libya, which had started withholding contracts from Irish firms, were threatened. Ireland had also been denounced by the United Nations and the Organisation of African Unity, and there was the prospect that the country would be frozen out of international sport.[59] An Ethiopian team had withdrawn from a cross-country race in Cork, and the government of Zimbabwe refused entry to Greystones RFC for a tour in May. Irish athletes had invitations to competitions withdrawn because of 'a threatened boycott by the powerful Ethiopian team'.[60]

Haughey summoned IRFU officials to Government Buildings on 1 May. The written record of the meeting suggests that he gave them a detailed rehearsal of the tour's potential consequences. He warned them that it 'would cause serious damage to vital national interests', and 'put it directly and without qualification . . . that the tour should be cancelled'.[61] Haughey had enough on his plate at the time. IRA prisoners had launched a hunger strike, and Bobby Sands was days from death. A general election was weeks away, and Haughey's republican flank was threatened by the fielding of H-Block protest candidates, hunger strikers among them. It is a measure of how seriously he viewed the potential fallout of the rugby tour that he made space in his diary to meet the IRFU in the midst of all this political turmoil.

The IRFU, despite the weight of pressure from all directions, remained unmoved: the tour would go ahead. This was nothing short of an extraordinary decision. The Union haughtily declared that 'we have a deep conviction that within our mandate of responsibility we have acted rightly as administrators of an amateur sport . . . and . . . object to being made an unwilling weapon of political protest which is not the business of an amateur sporting organisation'. While ministers had warned of the dire consequences of the tour going ahead, the IRFU asserted that 'the situation at this present critical time in Ireland is such that any deviation from our traditional position would not only be injurious to the Irish Rugby Football Union but to Ireland as a whole'. 'Our responsibility within our respective communities', they continued, 'is to ensure the continuation of a respected institution – the Irish Rugby Football Union – and to keep it constant to its principles.'[62] The IRFU also stressed their longstanding relations with the South African Rugby Board. The Union, ultimately, chose loyalty to their own 'respected institution' and to their blazers-in-arms in South Africa over the clear desires of the Irish government and the moral force of the anti-apartheid movement.

The government, accepting defeat, issued a statement stressing that 'the touring team should not use the name of Ireland or any emblem or signs that would suggest they are representative of Ireland'.[63] This was an empty gesture that the IRFU ignored. Aer Lingus staff refused to handle any flight related to the tour, so the party of players and officials had to skulk out of Ireland using decoy travel arrangements. Meanwhile the government dedicated vast quantities of energy to publicizing their opposition to the tour, while also monitoring the behaviour of the touring party, noting how members had 'praised South Africa's changes in the apartheid laws affecting sport', had been greeted by senior ministers, and how the tour manager, Paddy Madigan, had stated that 'as far as rugby is concerned, there is no apartheid in South Africa'.[64]

There were some consequences of the tour for the IRFU. Two officials, Robert Ganly and Ronnie Dawson, were placed on the UN's Register of Sports Contacts with South Africa, the so-called 'blacklist'. The government refused the Union's application for a grant to aid schools rugby and made it clear that they should not bother applying again.

There is no evidence that any Irish player or official condoned, let alone supported, apartheid. In his autobiography published in 2004, Willie John McBride, the highly decorated second row who had captained Ireland and the Lions, was utterly unrepentant in his view that it was right to maintain sporting links with South Africa. He captained the Lions to a series victory in South Africa in 1974, and while his career as an international player was over by 1981, he managed a World XV on a tour in South Africa in 1989. McBride took the slightly odd view in his autobiography that 'connections should be kept open through tours, so that South Africans could be gently persuaded to the viewpoint of the outside world as to the horrors and impracticalities of the apartheid system'.[65] He also described the anti-apartheid protestors who opposed the 1989 tour as a 'rent-a-mob' and 'despicable'.[66]

In 1981, there was no default option for players selected to tour South Africa: a choice had to be made. For some, the choice involved more than weighing sporting ambition against politics. Michael Gibson and John Robbie both worked for Guinness, a company for which Nigeria was a large export market. As the toxicity of the public discussion around the tour intensified, Guinness withdrew permission for Gibson and Robbie to take leave to join it. Gibson stayed at home; Robbie resigned his job and went on tour. Later settling in South Africa and becoming a talk radio host, Robbie became a vocal critic of apartheid. In 2020, he told the *Irish Times*: 'I used to think: did I actually know how bad apartheid was? Of course, I did. I should never have toured. Despite what I went on to achieve, I consider it a stain that will never leave me.'[67]

Gerry McLoughlin and Jerry Holland also resigned from their jobs to take part in the tour. For some, the choice was taken out of their hands: Paul McNaughton and Ciaran Fitzgerald were both state employees and were thus denied leave. Three players – Tony Ward, Moss Keane and Donal Spring – refused to travel on principle. Ward said that he had been disturbed by what he witnessed on the 1980 Lions tour. 'I have thought deeply about South Africa', he told journalists, 'and feel I do not want to return.'[68]

As for the players who did travel to South Africa: what were they thinking? In the amateur era, opportunities to earn caps were restricted. There were fewer fixtures and strict limits on substitutes. Scores of players earned fewer than five caps and the whole business of team selection had a pronounced 'flavour of the month' quality to it. Once a player was in the selectors' line of sight, he needed to take advantage of that fact. Representing one's country in a relatively exotic location must have been very tempting for the young men offered the opportunity to do so.

The government changed in June, but the rift with rugby persisted, such was the political consensus in Ireland on the issue of apartheid. When the IRFU invited the President to Lansdowne Road for an international against Australia in November, the advice from the Department of Foreign Affairs was that he should not attend, 'in the light of the recent IRFU tour to South Africa which went ahead despite repeated appeals from the Government'.[69]

Not content with having antagonized all and sundry in 1981, the IRFU agreed to take part in the SARB's centenary celebrations in the summer of 1989. South Africa had been frozen out of international rugby since 1984. IRFU president Ronnie Dawson and other officials travelled as Ireland's representatives. Willie John McBride, as noted, managed a World XV in a fixture with South Africa to mark the centenary, while Ireland hooker Steve Smith travelled as a player. McBride and Smith were from Northern Ireland, so their travel plans were none of the Irish government's business. Dawson, also a senior International Rugby Board official, was the focus of intense criticism, not only from civil society organizations and the Dublin government, but from rugby clubs and schools as well. He faced multiple calls to resign, including from Dick Spring, the former Ireland international who now led the Labour Party.[70]

In the midst of the controversy, the Irish rugby team was on tour in North America. A planned reception for the team with Senator Edward Kennedy was shelved in accordance with the wishes of the Irish Department of Foreign Affairs.[71] Facing the prospect of collapsing sponsorship deals and having embarrassed the Irish government yet again, the IRFU issued a rather mealy-mouthed statement offering vague expressions of contrition, but, crucially, resolved to finally cut ties with South Africa. The IRFU also noted in the statement that the centenary celebrations in South Africa had been 'approved by the International Rugby Football Board' – the sport's global governing body; and England, Wales and Scotland all participated. Once again, the rugby brotherhood had chosen to stick together, come what may.[72] It was as though the imbroglio of 1981 had never happened.

The end of apartheid led to the rehabilitation of the Springboks as a major force in international rugby. No sooner had one crisis passed, however, than a fresh one appeared on the horizon.

8. Amateurism: decline and fall

In August 1997, the *Irish Times* journalist Gerry Thornley called for the interprovincial championship to be scrapped. The Munster, Leinster, Connacht and Ulster teams, he suggested, ought to be replaced with new city-based franchises. These would be fed by local All-Ireland League (AIL) clubs in a system closely resembling the structure of professional club rugby in New Zealand.[1]

Thornley's was a radical suggestion – but it was a time when radical suggestions were needed. The arrival of professionalism in rugby union had abruptly upended the game's traditions. In order to meet the financial demands of running a professional sport, rugby authorities across the world were forced to create new teams and competitions, professionalize the game at administrative level, and adopt modern coaching and scientific innovations. Irish rugby, never enthusiastic about professionalism, had been caught on the hop. A large number of Ireland's elite players had decamped to English clubs, the performance of the provincial teams in the first two seasons of the Heineken Cup had been patchy, and most rugby fans were still far more interested in club rugby than in the provincial teams. The problem with the provinces, as Thornley saw it, was they had 'no real sense of identity'. 'Munster', he claimed, 'is not a tribe', and 'Who in their right mind says, "Oh, I'm from Leinster"?' Thornley, a deeply informed and astute observer of Irish rugby, was giving his readers an accurate portrayal of the provincial sides as they stood at the time. Within a decade, however, the utterly unpredictable had happened: the provincial teams had become hugely successful professional clubs feeding off a strong sense of identity.

It turned out that the old provincial structure actually provided a sound basis for a domestic professional game. Though none of the provincial teams, apart from Ulster, had been especially popular during the amateur era, the consolidation of Irish playing strength into four teams provided a sustainable way forward, especially when new European competitions were inaugurated. The fact that the teams had been around for a long time, and that they represented provinces, meant that they attracted fan loyalty more easily than, for example, the newly minted Welsh regional teams.

Ireland benefited from three further factors in the early years of professionalism. First among these was luck: the opening decade of the twenty-first century was one of those rare cycles (like the 1890s and late 1940s) when Ireland unearthed a golden generation of players, who made the provincial and international teams highly competitive. Second, a dramatic Irish economic boom coincided with the first decade and a half of professionalism in rugby. In an era of cheap air travel and high disposable incomes, European away fixtures, for example, attracted large numbers of travelling Irish fans. Rugby became fashionable as its success dovetailed with the country's new-found wealth and confidence. Finally, the elite education system, particularly in Leinster, effectively became an academy system, deeply intertwined with the provincial teams. The two decades after 1999 were the greatest era in the history of Irish rugby: the provinces won seven European Cups between them, the international team won four championships (including two Grand Slams) and an additional three

Triple Crowns, and Ireland had unprecedented numbers of players selected for the Lions. The nation that was arguably least prepared for professionalism ended up being perhaps its biggest success story. But the transition was protracted and painful.

Amateurism in rugby came under pressure for a long time before it was finally abandoned. One early source of this pressure was South Africa. From the late 1960s, the South Africans enthusiastically embraced commercial sponsorship. During the northern hemisphere summer, when there was no rugby activity in Britain, players would travel to South Africa, where they would be paid to play and coach. Most contentiously, rebel tours brought rich rewards to international players willing to defy public opinion at home and travel to South Africa. Then, in 1986, the New Zealand Cavaliers, an unofficial touring team, defied the International Rugby Board and the wishes of their own government and headed to South Africa, where they were paid with considerable sums of money to play a series of fixtures.

Another source of pressure was less about commerce than about standards. In countries where the amateur ethos was observed most fondly, training and fitness standards were low. The shortcomings of rugby in Britain and Ireland were badly exposed on the Lions tour of 1966, where the tourists' palpably unserious approach to preparation was completely at odds with the direction of modern sport. So disheartened was the brilliant Welsh full-back Terry Price that he immediately resolved to turn professional and throw his lot in with rugby league. Price described tour captain Mike Campbell-Lamerton as a 'grand bloke but far too nice', who, at team talks, sounded like 'a chairman telling shareholders the firm wasn't doing too well'.[2] Though the Lions defeated Australia twice, they were easily beaten in all four Tests in New Zealand, unable to match the physical conditioning of their opponents. The tour manager, Des O'Brien, described by one commentator as 'an unusually witty Irishman of nationalist tendencies', was utterly unrepentant. For him 'the dictatorship exercised by coaches' in New Zealand meant that the 'spirit of rugby football' was coming 'under the whip'.[3] Though the English and Welsh were then moving towards specialist coaching, the Irish and Scots – over whom amateurism maintained a theocratic hold – remained suspicious of it.

In the northern hemisphere, the 1960s belonged to France, the nation least loyal to amateurism. It had long been the practice among French clubs to offer players so-called 'social aid' in the form of jobs and housing. A keenly contested and prestigious national club league (something that did not exist in Britain or Ireland until much later) provided French players with a competitive edge.[4] Still, France remained light years behind New Zealand and South Africa. The brilliant French team of 1968 lost every Test match as tourists in New Zealand that summer and as hosts to South Africa that autumn.

After a routine drubbing in Paris in 1964, an exasperated former international, Mike Dunne, wrote to the *Irish Press* complaining that 'Rugby in Ireland has remained static for too long', and predicting that in the absence of reform, the game 'will not survive to any appreciable extent'. The blame, in Dunne's view, lay squarely with the aged and conservative officials who ran the IRFU, particularly in their failure to nurture the game outside cities. (Dunne's radical suggestion was that an intercounty competition modelled on the GAA championships should be inaugurated.)[5] Each province had a senior cup competition that was relatively prestigious, but

FOOT BALL AT RUGBY.—(SEE NEXT PAGE.)

Football as played at Rugby School, *c.*1840s. In the nineteenth century, thousands of Irish boys attended boarding schools in England, where organized sports first became popular. Irish boys who attended Rugby were central to the early growth of the school's code of football in Ireland.

Engraving depicting a football match in an edition of *Tom Brown's Schooldays* (1857), the novel that established the primordial form of rugby in the popular mind. Until the latter part of the nineteenth century, there was no clear distinction between the games we now know as rugby and soccer. Games were rough and all permitted both handling and kicking the ball. Precursors of the distinctly Irish code, Gaelic football, had few rules and permitted wrestling.

The Ireland rugby team that won the Triple Crown in 1899. Until the mid-1890s, Irish rugby was dominated by the Protestant elite. As the game grew in fee-paying Catholic schools, it became more religiously diverse. The 1899 side, composed of both Catholics and Protestants, was arguably the most representative Ireland rugby team ever to take the field. *(Evening Herald, 4 February 1899. Content provided by The British Library Board. All Rights Reserved. With thanks to The British Newspaper Archive, www.britishnewspaperarchive.co.uk)*

The newspaper *Sport* pushes the claims for international selection of Ter Casey, 1 March 1930. A front-row forward for Limerick club Young Munster, Casey received just two Ireland caps. His international prospects, some commentators believed, were hampered by his working-class background. *(Content provided by The British Library Board. All Rights Reserved. With thanks to The British Newspaper Archive, www.britishnewspaperarchive.co.uk)*

Cigarette cards depicting Ireland internationals Charlie Hanrahan, Eugene Davy, George Beamish and J. D. 'Jammie' Clinch, 1929. *(From a collection printed by W. D. & H. O. Wills cigarette company)*

Ireland's Bertie McConnell is embraced by fans as he and his teammates leave the field after Ireland defeated England at Twickenham, February 1948. Ireland went on to win their first Grand Slam that season. *(PA Images/Alamy)*

Anti-apartheid protestors hold a demonstration outside Lansdowne Road, while Ireland take on South Africa, January 1970. *(PA Images/Alamy)*

Armed British soldiers take in the action between Ulster and the All Blacks at Ravenhill in November 1972. Large gatherings of any type in Northern Ireland at this time warranted a strong security presence. *(Associated Press/Alamy)*

Ulster Unionist Party leader David Trimble *(right)* and SDLP leader Seamus Mallon, First and Deputy First Ministers of Northern Ireland respectively, wave to the crowd at Lansdowne Road before the start of the Heineken Cup final between Ulster and Colomiers, January 1999 – less than a year after the signing of the Belfast Agreement. *(PA Images/Alamy)*

Munster fans gather on O'Connell Street, Limerick, to watch the Heineken Cup final, May 2006. A decade earlier the province attracted relatively paltry crowds to fixtures in the same competition.

A demonstrator holds a placard outside Croke Park, protesting at the staging of a rugby match at GAA headquarters, February 2007. His disdain for 'foreign games' clearly did not extend to soccer; he wears a Glasgow Celtic shirt and tracksuit. (*PA Images/Alamy*)

Ireland players leave the field for the second time after floodlight failure during a Women's Six Nations fixture against France at Ashbourne RFC, County Meath, February 2015. Though Ireland had won the Grand Slam just two seasons earlier, there remained widespread concern among players and commentators that the women's game was under-resourced. *(David Maher/Sportsfile)*

Ulster's Luke Marshall is helped from the field after suffering concussion in a PRO12 fixture against Scarlets at Ravenhill, September 2016. From the mid-2010s, concern grew in global rugby about the long-term effects of repeated instances of concussion on players' long-term health. *(Oliver McVeigh/Sportsfile)*

C. J. Stander of Munster and Bundee Aki of Connacht following a Guinness PRO14 match at The Sportsground in Galway, December 2019. Both Aki, a New Zealander by birth, and South Africa-born Stander were selected for Ireland having qualified on residency grounds. Ireland's 'project player' system was criticized by commentators both in Ireland and abroad, but Aki's and Stander's genuine, unaffected embrace of Irish life made them heroes in their provinces and on the national stage. *(Seb Daly/Sportsfile)*

Raucous St Michael's College supporters look on as the school does battle with Blackrock College in the semi-final of the Leinster Schools Senior Cup, March 2023. Remarkable numbers of boys who played for these two schools progressed into the professional game. *(David Fitzgerald/Sportsfile)*

provincial league competitions drew small crowds and occasionally were not even completed.[6]

Eventually, the IRFU stopped swimming against the tide and facilitated the arrangement of coaching courses by the various branches. Ronnie Dawson was appointed Ireland coach in 1969 and a panel of twenty-five was named well in advance of the first international that season. The squad was allowed to assemble for training in November – a month before the first international. This, according to *Irish Times* journalist Edmund Van Esbeck, was 'a vindication of the policy advocated by the more progressive element in the game here'.[7] Dawson asserted, however, that 'all members of executives in all provinces have not enough conviction that coaching and teaching are both good and necessary'.[8] Noel Murphy, then still a player, thought the answer to Ireland's woes lay in the approach taken by New Zealand, 'who were years ahead of us because of the attention they have paid to coaching at all levels'.[9]

The pace of change remained glacial, however. Substitutes were permitted by the IRB for the first time in 1969, but only when the player being replaced was certified as injured by a medical professional. Prior to then, injured players either left the field without being replaced or limped through the remainder of a match. Tactical substitutions remained prohibited, as rugby was a gentlemanly pastime that should not be taken so seriously as to require in-depth strategizing. For traditionalists, substitutions and detailed preparation were seen as gateway drugs to professionalism. An IRB directive in 1969 forbade teams from assembling more than forty-eight hours before a match. Periodic get-togethers by national squads were not prohibited, 'provided the occasions do not interfere with the players' work or vocation and do not restrict their freedom as amateur players'.[10] A *Cork Examiner* rugby correspondent gave a rather quaint impression of these conventions:

> The traditional system is for the players to foregather the day before the match, have a run around that afternoon, of a concentrated or casual nature depending on the feeling of the captain and then set out, next day, to give battle for the prestige of their country – the very minimum of preparation.

And though this was 'true amateurism all right', the writer wondered how long it could last when the French and southern hemisphere nations were not observing such restrictions.[11]

Additionally, IRFU secretaries continued to ruthlessly chase down any suspected infraction, however innocuous, of the amateur code. In 1965, for example, the IRFU instructed the Munster Branch to admonish a Waterpark RFC player for accepting the 'Rugby Star of the Year' award from the Town Hotel in Waterford.[12] The IRFU official responsible either spent hours poring over the provincial press looking for non-events like this or benefited from a network of busybodies and snitches.

Perhaps the cruellest feature of amateurism – and one that underscored the quasi-religious devotion it attracted from its adherents – was the fact that turning professional was a sin that could not be expunged. For the few Irishmen who went to the north of England to play rugby league, this meant that they could have no formal association with rugby union, even long after they had retired and returned home. High-profile defectors like Paddy Reid, Robin Thompson and Ken Goodall could not even coach a rugby union club's under-fourteens, at least not openly. Some IRFU officials recognized how unjust this was and spoke out. Paddy Madigan, president of the

IRFU in 1987, campaigned for reform. Though he supported the ban on league converts returning to union as players, the blanket ban on those individuals from having any involvement in the game 'was contrary to basic human rights'.[13]

A clear sign that the whole ideology was in terminal decay came in the late 1980s, when the IRB adopted the slightly creepy system of 'reinstating' the amateur status of former code-hoppers, in some cases posthumously. In 1989, Reid, Goodall and Thompson were shown this act of clemency. The whole business was particularly cruel in the case of Reid. He had been one of the heroes of Ravenhill in 1948. Unemployed and about to get married, he had left Limerick soon afterwards to join Huddersfield Rugby League Club. Quickly transferring to Halifax, he was on the losing team in the 1949 Challenge Cup final, then the game's greatest competition. By the time of his reinstatement, Reid was in his mid-sixties and had been exiled from his beloved club, Garryowen, for forty years. Reid's family were a Garryowen dynasty, and the club was deeply inscribed in his DNA. Any position he had held at Garryowen in the decades after his return to Limerick had to be fulfilled furtively, under an assumed name. Forcing Reid to skulk behind the scenes like this was an act of schoolboyish vindictiveness on the part of the rugby authorities.[14]

A crucial staging post on the journey to professionalism was the Rugby World Cup. Driven by the efforts of Australian and New Zealand officials, the decision to inaugurate the tournament was taken by the IRB in 1985. When it had come to a ballot, Ireland and Scotland – raging against the dying of the light – voted against the development. Ronnie Dawson, the Irish representative on the organizing committee for the inaugural World Cup in 1987, assured readers of the *Irish Times* that the IRB had full control of the tournament and would protect it from the 'insidious increase in unbridled commercialism within the game' that had been seen in some countries.[15] But the genie was already halfway out of the bottle. The first two World Cup tournaments, held in 1987 and 1991, drew large television audiences and considerable revenue through commercial sponsorship. Players began to realize that their talent was a saleable asset.

With money now flowing into the game, the IRB introduced further reforms. From 1990, players were permitted to receive payment for 'non-rugby activities' such as media appearances and book contracts. But events had already overtaken this concession. In France, payments to players were now barely concealed. Then there was the curious case of Italy, where, from the mid-1980s onwards, major international rugby stars such as David Campese and Michael Lynagh started joining clubs in the domestic league. Tax reforms created incentives for companies to sponsor sports teams, and Italian clubs were suddenly awash with money.[16]

Amateurism, already stumbling precariously on a cliff edge, was given a final push by events in the southern hemisphere. By then, satellite television had begun to revolutionize sport. For owners of specialist sport channels, hungry to fill schedules, rugby union was low-hanging fruit. In the summer of 1995, New Zealand, Australia and the rehabilitated South Africa announced that they had signed a television deal with Rupert Murdoch's News Corp worth hundreds of millions of dollars for the broadcast of a new tri-nations international series and a provincial competition, the Super 12s. At the stroke of a pen, amateurism was dead. The official IRB announcement followed in August, when the northern hemisphere unions, faced with the prospect of a global split in rugby union, accepted their fate and sanctioned pay for play.

The IRFU was, to put it mildly, utterly unprepared for this development. In its conservatism and lack of self-confidence, Irish rugby was at one with the society around it. Results in the decade from the mid-1980s set baseline expectations of Irish rugby at an all-time low when professionalism arrived. There had been some isolated triumphs in the 1980s. In 1985, a draw against a woefully undisciplined French team in Dublin was all that had separated Ireland from the Grand Slam. From then, however, the direction of travel was steeply downhill. Ireland followed up the championship victory of 1985 with the Wooden Spoon in 1986. In the ten championship seasons between 1986 and 1995, Ireland won just nine matches.

The spring sunshine of Paris was a particularly harrowing stage for Irish rugby teams. Typically, in these matches, the home crowd would grow ever more raucous as their fleet-footed Gallic backs ran rings around the plodding Irish resistance. Only twice were Ireland beaten by fewer than twenty points in Paris in the decade to 1995, and on both occasions the margin was nineteen.[17] In 1992, the annual report of the Leinster Branch secretary noted that 'For the past one hundred years, we maintained the gap between our standards and those of the strongest nations at an acceptable level.' Now, however, Ireland had fallen far behind its rivals in terms of coaching, structures, commercial revenue and facilities. Crucially, stronger nations had interpreted 'their views of amateurism to their advantage'.[18] The report concluded that

the strict interpretation of our amateur laws will have to change. The views of those who administer the game will give way to the views of today's players who will rapidly become the administrators of tomorrow. Practically all sports have, over time, moved away from traditional views relating to amateurism.[19]

Early steps in the direction of commercialization were modest, almost quaint in retrospect. From the 1970s onwards, and in response to reforms introduced by the IRB, the IRFU permitted provincial branches to enter into sponsorship deals with private firms. In 1976, for example, Murphy's Brewery agreed to pay the Munster Branch IR£1,500 per annum for three years to sponsor the Senior Cup.[20] Any rewards for players, however, remained strictly prohibited. In 1973, for example, the IRFU reluctantly agreed to allow the inclusion of rugby in the Kerry Sport Stars awards, as long as the prize 'was of nominal value only'.[21]

There were few dissenting voices. John Horgan, writing in the *Irish Times* in 1983, pointed to the hypocrisy of amateurism, observing that only those in a particularly advantageous career situation could afford to accept an invitation to play for the Lions on their forthcoming tour to New Zealand. 'The class profile of the Irish rugby player', he observed, was 'overwhelmingly a business and professional one. This is so because the kind of demands that are made on rugby players tend to exclude from those levels all but those who can afford to play.'[22]

Horgan, however, was not a rugby journalist. Among the latter, the voice of the establishment was Edmund Van Esbeck, the *Irish Times* rugby correspondent. Though usually a cautious advocate of modernization, he was trenchantly opposed to professionalism. The Rugby World Cup, he wrote, 'holds many dangers', representing a slippery slope towards professionalism, and he urged Ireland and Scotland not to enter the tournament in 1987.[23] Van Esbeck's columns before and after the tournament read like a succession of mournful reflections on a glorious past, when the game was untainted by money. Any step, however small, in the direction of commercialization was greeted with melancholy. When the IRFU signed a kit supply deal with Adidas, for example, Van Esbeck told readers that

> We have been told that the Adidas motif or logo will not appear on the Ireland jersey, which will remain the old cherished shade of green, with the shamrock the only emblem emblazoned on it. May the day be far off, or indeed never, when we would see an Ireland side take the field with the stripes down the sleeves.

It was a matter of great regret to him that the Adidas logo was to appear on the team's shorts. He mourned the passing of Ireland's previous arrangement with O'Neill's, 'a dignified one', where there was 'no high-powered commercial exploitation'.[24] Warming to his theme in a later column marking the hundredth anniversary of Ireland's first victory over England, he described the Adidas deal as 'deplorable and absolutely unnecessary'. Referring to Ireland's hero of 1887, Dan Rambaut, Van Esbeck added that Ireland had 'come a long way' since he and 'his true amateur team mates fashioned that memorable win. I am not altogether sure we really have learned a terrible lot in the intervening century.'[25]

The French wore the Adidas stripes on their sleeves and reached the final of the first World Cup; Ireland endured a miserable tournament, during which coach Mick Doyle suffered a heart attack and the main talking point was the 'Rose of Tralee' fiasco. Reporting from the tournament, Van

Esbeck looked on in horror as referees were obliged to wait for a signal from 'TV advertisement men' to start games. The referee should always be 'the sole judge of fact and of law and of time', he quaintly concluded.[26] Rugby was drifting away from the one true church of amateurism, tempted into an idolatrous relationship with money.

When the 1991 World Cup came around, the Irish players, like their English, Scottish and Welsh counterparts, had grown restless. The IRB, by then, permitted players to earn money from commercial sources subject to a byzantine set of criteria, some of which were left to the judgement of individual unions. In theory, this meant that the IRFU could choose a far more restrictive approach than those taken by other countries. This almost led to an outright schism between the players and the IRFU before the World Cup, when the Union abruptly presented the players with a participation agreement essentially forcing them to sign away their image rights to the tournament organizers. The players were furious: the IRFU had known the contents of the agreement for months but had sat on it, hoping, it appeared, that if it was produced at the last moment, the players would not realize its full implications. They signed it but grew increasingly disgruntled as the tournament progressed, to the point where, in the absence of some gesture of recompense, they were willing to make 'the ultimate sacrifice', and refuse to take the field against Australia in the quarter-final.[27] The Union relented, and after the tournament the Irish squad secured sponsorship from Ballygowan, Daihatsu and Smithwick's. The sum, said to be in the region of IR£30,000, was to be shared among the players.

Even the IRFU looked progressive compared to the Scots. The Scottish Rugby Union, showing a characteristic yet mildly hilarious determination to remain anchored to the past, reported Ireland to the IRB for 'ex-gratia payments to players'. This was in connection with the sponsorship money raised after the tournament. The SRU's behaviour was demented: they also reported the Welsh Rugby Union for allowing clubs to wear advertising logos on their shirts.[28] As long ago as 1924, a British journalist had observed that the 'cult of amateurism in Scotland seems to have developed into a form of mental disease'.[29] Not much had changed in the seven decades that followed.

After the 1991 tournament, amateurism was on borrowed time. The addition of the World Cup and the AIL alongside the interprovincials introduced new time pressure on players, and the question of amateurism began to appear frequently on the IRFU committee's agenda. The Leinster Branch secretary's report in 1991 concluded that 'Amateurism is not a simple subject. Caution is probably the wisest move and while some extol the virtues of a more freer [sic] environment for the players, getting there in a slow and steady state is . . . the preferred journey.'[30] The prospect of such an evolution away from strict amateurism was abruptly scuppered by the events of 1995. Rugby had professionalism imposed on it and, from an Irish perspective, the timing was appalling. In 1995, Irish rugby was in a deep hole. Ireland won just five of their twenty-four Five Nations matches between 1990 and 1995, securing the Wooden Spoon in 1992.

Not only was Irish rugby amateur, but it was also deeply amateur*ish*. Irish players had a reputation for being fiery and impetuous, competitive until supplies of adrenaline inevitably gave way to fatigue, allowing opposition teams to pull well ahead down the home stretch. Supremacy was reasserted, however, in heroic post-match drinking sessions.[31] 'Win or lose,' one newspaper columnist observed in 1987, 'the Irish play with a refreshing elan and they remain one of the most popular sides in the world with an inexhaustible appetite for the off-field festivities and celebrations which characterise the game.'[32]

A profound change in culture was required. When, in 1994, the Ireland coach, Gerry Murphy, proposed the selection of an elite squad that would receive something approaching modern preparation in exchange for organizational and financial support, nothing happened, apart from Murphy receiving a dressing down from the IRFU for making the plans public.[33] Such was the plain lack of seriousness – not to mention money – invested by the IRFU in international success that George Hook, whose curmudgeonly manner would later make him a star analyst on RTÉ, was quite right in asserting that 'We're the good guys of international rugby; everybody's going to love us, but we're going to get our asses kicked.'[34]

A noxious cloud of recriminations enveloped Irish rugby, not least in the press. In the 1990s, the IRFU received a weekly kicking from the *Sunday Independent*, where Mick Doyle – something of a reincarnation of Jacques McCarthy – did not care who he insulted. Doyle, a qualified vet who attended UCD and Cambridge, had a public persona that oscillated oddly between boorishness and sophistication, fairly typical of someone who had spent a lot of time around rugby clubs, particularly those attached to universities. Though his rural Kerry background gave him an appealing earthiness, his sense of humour was quite juvenile. His first autobiography, *Doyler*, read in places like the diary of a feckless male undergraduate recalling his most debauched nights out.[35] Doyle struggled to navigate the territory between charming straight-talking and plain obnoxiousness. His background, however, allowed him to speak on rugby matters with authority: he had been an outstanding back-row forward for Ireland, had played for the Lions, and had coached an unfancied Ireland to the Triple Crown in 1985 playing in an exuberant style, with Doyle encouraging his charges to 'give it a lash'.[36]

In February 1995, the Ireland selection committee, smarting at accusations of bias, threatened to sue Doyle if he did not apologize for articles he had written in the *Sunday Independent* and statements he had made on RTÉ Sport. Doyle, with the support of both media organizations, was gleefully unapologetic.[37] Though RTÉ did eventually apologize, all the selectors achieved, if anything, was to draw further attention to Doyle's views. When, in September, the IRFU appointed another selection committee – a system totally unsuited to the now professional sport – Doyle fumed at the Union's 'taxidermist-like singular devotion' to outdated methods.[38]

Even when the arrival of professionalism looked certain, the IRFU remained implacably opposed to payment for play. A statement in May 1995 read, 'The IRFU firmly believes that the game is not a business but a recreational activity out of which over many years a way of life has derived.' They were willing to make mild concessions: players should be paid expenses and should also have the right to earn money from such activities as speaking, media appearances and writing books. (The Scottish Rugby Union had banned international players Ian McLauchlan and Gordon Brown for life in 1980 after both players published autobiographies.) In general, however, the IRFU position leaned heavily on nostalgia, wishing rugby to return to a mythical past, unspoilt by any grubby financial imperative. The Union, for example, wished to see reductions in the numbers of international fixtures, squad training sessions and preparation times. Excessive numbers of fixtures tended to 'lessen the mystique previously attached to top games'.[39] This kind of thinking would doubtless have caused belly laughs in the southern hemisphere, where the sport had been moving inexorably towards professionalism for a long time.

A sense of profound apprehension descended on Irish rugby after the formal announcement that the game would go professional in late summer 1995. So deeply ingrained was amateurism that divesting Irish rugby of it was like trying to remove the egg from a baked cake. There was no obvious way forward. For commentators, decline and irrelevance seemed a plausible outcome. In Mick Doyle's view, the IRFU would need to pay forty full-time professionals for the international team, and he said that if he were the team manager, he would not accept 'partial fitness or half-hearted performances, as is the current vogue'.[40] While southern hemisphere nations were agreeing lucrative full-time contracts with their best players, Syd Miller, the president of the IRFU, was keen for Irish internationals to hold on to their jobs. Irish rugby remained mired in complacency, with the IRFU comfortable to govern a sport that was socially exclusive.

Amateurism needed deference like an engine needed fuel. Yet deference was disappearing in Ireland. The country was beginning to look outward, becoming firmly intertwined with globalized capitalism, and was experiencing impressive economic growth. The grip that the Catholic Church once enjoyed over Irish society was rapidly loosening, while a liberal female politician was President. A young, self-confident population, soon buoyed by the abolition of university tuition fees, were able to satisfy their professional and personal ambitions without emigrating. When Irish rugby eventually found a workable formula for professionalism, these broader economic and social shifts contributed to its upturn in fortunes.

*

A number of key questions immediately arose. Who would be paid? At what level of the domestic game should players be paid? How much? In 1995, the Irish rugby pyramid at the senior grade had three levels: the international team, the provincial teams, and the network of clubs playing in the AIL. Although the middle layer, the provinces, would become the bedrock of the domestic professional game, it was far from obvious to officials in 1995 that this was the best way forward. Irish club officials voted unanimously against paying club and provincial players. They knew all too well, however, that under-the-counter payments, benefits in kind, and help securing employment were already a feature of Irish club rugby. The scores of non-Irish players (there were fifty-seven in late 1991) who began to appear on AIL team lists from the early 1990s had not travelled across the world to experience amateurism at its most pure. But Irish clubs did not have the means to sustain any kind of serious professional game. Club competitions attracted relatively small crowds, apart from in Limerick – and even there a crowd of 10,000 for a local derby would be considered newsworthy. And there was practically no television money in Irish club rugby. Sky Sports briefly flirted with the AIL, broadcasting a couple of matches; but this experiment soon petered out due to tiny audience numbers.[41]

That left the provinces. Here, again, the signs were not promising. Supporters had no great affinity with the provincial teams, and generally showed interest only when the provinces played against touring sides. The annual interprovincial championship was unpopular, leading to periodic calls for its abolition, not least because it was loss-making. In 1973, for example, a Munster official complained that the interprovincial matches were a 'drain on the resources of the Branch'.[42]

That season, just 500 spectators turned out to watch Munster take on Leinster in Cork. After the inauguration of the AIL in 1990, international players were told that they did not need to play in the interprovincial championship and Ireland selectors stopped attending its fixtures.[43] In 1990, Mick Doyle, outspoken as ever, referred to the series as 'an imposition stamped on the back of an already crowded schedule'.[44]

Little did he – or anyone at the time – suspect that professionalism would help bring about a dramatic rise in the fortunes of Irish rugby, and that the provinces would be at the very heart of it.

9. Four proud provinces

In November 1995, Munster strode onto the field at Thomond Park for their first ever European Cup match, against Swansea. They were greeted by a crowd of 6,000: considerably lower than the attendance at a big club match in Limerick at the time. And though Munster won, few of those present that afternoon would have foreseen the transformation in store for the province in the decade that followed. The build-up to the match had been soured by the stinginess of the Munster Branch. The players, still effectively amateurs, were not compensated for loss of earnings incurred during a training trip to Italy. Their families were not offered tickets for the Swansea match. And when the players checked into their hotel, they found that the Branch had ordered outgoing calls to be blocked, for fear expensive bills might otherwise accrue.[1]

Leinster managed to advance to a home semi-final against Cardiff, but they were defeated in front of just 7,000 supporters at Lansdowne Road. Only a few weeks before Leinster's elimination, Munster took on the Exiles (a quasi-fifth province) in what was essentially a play-off match to qualify for the following season's tournament; a crowd of '1,500 somnolent souls' witnessed a drab encounter.[2] The following March, 25,000 people attended the Leinster Schools Cup final between Blackrock College and Newbridge College, almost three times the combined crowd of the two key European Cup matches the previous winter.[3]

The IRFU, with some justification, were reluctant in the

short term to make fully professional teams out of the provinces. As it groped around for a workable system, the
inevitable occurred: Irish players in large numbers decamped
to England. If we measure the health of Irish rugby by
the performance of the international team, then 1996 and
1997 were among its most troubled years. In this period
Ireland were defeated convincingly by Samoa and Italy (twice)
and could only manage wins over the USA, Canada, and Wales
(who could be relied upon to provide Ireland with false dawns
in the 1990s). Thrown into the mix was a record thumping in
Paris in 1996 before Ireland, fielding nine England-based
players, conceded sixty-three points at home to the All Blacks
in November 1997. Rock bottom, however, had been a development tour to New Zealand the previous summer, recalled
in lurid terms by Brendan Fanning in his brilliant account of
the early years of professional rugby in Ireland.[4] Such was the
chaotic preparation, muddled playing philosophy and total
collapse of morale that the Irish team would have struggled
to contain a ragtag XV made up of local schoolboys. Keith
Wood, Ireland's first professional rugby star, set modest ambitions in 1997, hoping Ireland would get to a point 'over the
next three to five years' where they 'might actually beat France
once in a while'.[5]

The road to recovery began in the *annus horribilis* of 1997,
when the provinces turned professional. By 1998, each of the
four provinces had coaching directors and over thirty professional players per squad, most of them full-time. The terms
were modest enough for professional sport: full-time contracts were worth IR£25,000 each, plus win bonuses. Basic
pay, in other words, was around IR£10,000 above the average industrial wage.[6] The gradual repatriation of players from

England that followed quickly led to success when Ulster, out of the blue, won the 1999 European Cup.

In some ways, the provincial model suited Ulster best. The series of Home Rule crises that began in the previous century had given Ulster Protestants a strong sense of provincial identity. (The fact that three of Ulster's nine counties had ended up in the independent Irish state didn't matter: Donegal, Cavan and Monaghan were not rugby strongholds.) Ulster had dominated the interprovincial championship in the decade leading into professionalism, winning the title outright eight times and sharing it twice. Bolstered by the return from England of key players such as David Humphreys and Jonathan Bell, Ulster gave Irish rugby a badly needed confidence boost with their European Cup triumph.

Various factors added weight to the significance of the victory. The final took place less than a year after the Good Friday Agreement, and Lansdowne Road was the venue. Supporters from all over the island, including 30,000 from Northern Ireland, gathered to support Ulster, whose coach, Harry Williams, told reporters ahead of the match that his side 'wanted to be the first team to win it for Ireland'.[7] In advance of the match, an Ulster delegation visited Áras an Uachtaráin for an audience with President Mary McAleese, a Belfast Catholic whose family had been forced by loyalists to flee their home during the Troubles. Before kick-off, Seamus Mallon and David Trimble, the political leaders of mainstream nationalism and unionism respectively, took to the pitch to acknowledge the crowd, while Gerry Adams issued a statement congratulating the Ulster team. It was a timely reminder of the advantage rugby enjoyed over other sports as a unifying force on the island. The GAA's Rule 21, banning members of the Northern security forces from becoming members of the Association, was still in place, while memories were relatively fresh of the 1993 World Cup soccer clash between Northern Ireland and the Republic in Belfast, where the atmosphere had been thick with sectarian hatred. The DUP, sour-faced as ever, cautioned the public not to get carried away with Ulster's victory. Though they may have had a point, the occasion still had considerable symbolic weight.[8]

The meteoric rise of Munster was even more striking. Munster rugby, traditionally, had been factionalized between its power centres in Cork and Limerick cities. In Limerick especially, the loyalty fans felt towards their club far outweighed any sense of provincial belonging associated with the Munster team. In the 1997–98 season, Munster's aggregate crowd for Heineken Cup matches at home to Bourgoin and Harlequins was 13,000, while two club matches between Shannon and Young Munster that season attracted an aggregate of 15,000 spectators.[9] The AIL, since its inception in 1990–91, had been dominated by Limerick clubs. Teams from Munster won the league in each of its first nine seasons, with Limerick clubs winning it on seven occasions. In 1993, Young Munster repeated the trick of 1928, defeating St Mary's College in the league decider in front of a raucous crowd at Lansdowne Road.

The decisive try was scored by Ger Earls, a dynamic back-row forward whose failure to win international caps, many suspected, was due to his working-class background. In the future world of professionalism, where merit alone mattered, Earls's son Keith would win over a hundred caps. The case of Earls senior fed into a long-felt sense of grievance in Limerick towards the rugby establishment, especially in Dublin. This gave Limerick teams a psychological and competitive edge in the early years of the AIL. Visiting Dublin sides were greeted by hostile crowds and often played as though they longed for the bus back home. Young Munster's home ground, the Greenfields (nicknamed the 'Killing Fields'), was a particularly intimidating venue for Dublin teams.

The first generation of professional players in Munster all had extensive AIL experience and were accustomed to success at club level. This was especially true of Shannon, which provided Munster with John Hayes, Mick Galwey, Anthony Foley, Eddie Halvey and Alan Quinlan, players who would win over 200 Ireland caps between them. These players were the core of a ferociously competitive pack of forwards that helped Munster to reach the European Cup final in 2000, which they lost to Northampton by a point. From then on, the giddiness around Munster rugby grew dramatically. An estimated 35,000 Munster fans attended the 2000 European Cup final, a campaign during which Thomond Park was less than half full for a pool stage match against Pontypridd. Two years later, when Munster reached another final, fans queued through the night to secure tickets. Pool games now routinely sold out, and when Munster finally won the title in 2006, 70,000 Munster fans made the trip to Cardiff for the final.[10] Munster added another title in 2008, before their momentum was halted unexpectedly in 2009, when they were defeated by Leinster in front of over 80,000 supporters in the European Cup semi-final. The provinces, by now, were club-like entities rather than representative teams and the AIL retreated into relative obscurity.

There is a natural enough human tendency to try to observe patterns in order to make sense of novelty, upheaval and rapid change. In the case of Munster rugby, among supporters and commentators, this amounted to a collective act of hindsight bias. Success in the noughties was depicted as the inevitable consequence of Munster rugby's glorious tradition. This led to an entire genre of commentary and writing devoted to reimagining the history of Munster rugby. 'Munster is a state of mind or, if you like, a state of heart', the celebrated journalist Con Houlihan claimed in 2002. 'And rugby is the great unifying force. This was true a century ago and hasn't changed.'[11] When Munster reached the European Cup final in 2000, the *Irish Examiner* viewed the team's success as 'all the more intriguing when one considers the deep-rooted rivalries that have existed for many years between the clubs in the province'. By 2004, the same publication was much less equivocal, seeing provincial unity as a historical article of faith: 'Munster rugby has a proud tradition which has always incorporated Limerick and Cork.'[12]

Munster rugby, according to this way of thinking, was classless, egalitarian, honest and, above all else, 'ordinary'. A compelling storyline in this narrative was Munster's traditional rivalry with Leinster. Posh and flaky, Leinster were everything that Munster were not. And then there was Munster's citadel: Thomond Park. One journalist, getting a touch carried away in 2007, told *Irish Examiner* readers that

> Thomond Park has mystique, it has an aura all its own. It touches the Munster players in ways they cannot describe, it touches the fans likewise. It makes those players bigger, stronger, faster, it gives them power they never thought they had, but, conversely, it reduces the opposition, stifles them, handcuffs them, weakens them.[13]

But the Munster rugby 'tradition' was largely a figment of the public's and the commentariat's imagination. There was no historical sense of provincial unity. In fact, Limerick and

Cork officials had a noble tradition of bickering with each other. The widely held suspicion in Limerick for decades was that the selection of the Munster team was riddled with bias favouring Cork players. Then there was Munster's supposed egalitarianism or classlessness. As with most mythology, there was a grain of truth in this. Limerick rugby, as we have seen, had a working-class tradition. During Munster's glory years, players such as John Hayes, Alan Quinlan and Mick Galwey came from non-traditional rugby backgrounds in rural and semi-rural parts of the province. These were relatable individuals who gave the team a veneer of ordinariness. But Cork rugby was shot through with snobbery and had a similar class profile to the game in Dublin. Every one of the Cork-born players on the 2008 European Cup-winning team attended fee-paying schools.

The Munster–Leinster rivalry was also an invention of the professional era. Annual interprovincial championship matches between the provinces in the amateur era rarely caused more than the merest glimmer of excitement among the rugby public.

Finally, there was Munster's victory over the All Blacks at Thomond Park in 1978. The ink was barely dry on laudatory newspaper reports commemorating the victory when the annual call to scrap the interprovincial championship came. A commentator in the *Evening Press* three weeks after Munster's win referred to the interprovincials as 'a dull as dishwater series in which . . . nobody really cares who wins or loses'.[14] In Limerick on that day in 1978, the crowd was there to see the All Blacks, not Munster.

Munster's sudden surge in popularity was the product not of old, deep-rooted forces, but of new local and global trends. Just as professional rugby began to bed down in

Ireland, the economy took off. Young Irish graduates, now in well-paid jobs and living in cities or commuter belts, were precisely the market that professional rugby could take advantage of. As cities expanded and commuter belts developed, provincial teams provided a pleasing sense of rootedness. Non-traditional fans flocked to rugby. Gerry Thornley, trying to make sense of the newfangled Munster–Leinster rivalry in 2008, told readers of the *Irish Times* that 'A new breed of rugby fan has evolved in all the provinces . . . in the vast majority of cases, they rarely if ever see the sky above their local club ground.'[15] Indeed, the Munster Rugby Supporters Club, founded in 1999, specifically targeted as members new rugby fans who had no association with a club. Old, intimate ties of loyalty between members, supporters and clubs were no longer the bedrock of Irish rugby.

If Munster were Irish rugby's new money, then Leinster had all the appearances of a fading aristocracy. Long before professionalism became a reality, Leinster officials had started to think deeply about the future of the game. The Branch secretary's report for the 1989–90 season is an illuminating insight into the sense of despondency that had seized the game in Ireland.

It is clear that Leinster officials recognized that the clock could not be turned back on the commercialization of sport. In 1989, the Branch set up a 'high level committee' to consider the 'strategic directions' that were required to improve rugby in Leinster. Officials conceded that rugby had an image problem, in that it was indelibly associated with snobbery and exclusion. With the Republic of Ireland flourishing in international soccer, convincing young boys from working-class areas of Dublin to swap the spherical ball for an oval one was a difficult task. 'Much needs to be done', the report advised, 'to create a positive image in the communities to encourage parents to send their boys to play rugby.'[16] Specifically, measures were needed to 'market and support the development of rugby in North Dublin'.[17]

The Leinster Branch were adept at navel-gazing, and more reports followed. Tellingly, another aim was to 'establish a Leinster identity', a clear signal that no such thing existed at the time.[18] Strategies to achieve this included more fixtures for the provincial team, the creation of a development squad and the appointment of a long-term coach. The steering committee also recommended the appointment of a paid chief executive.[19] At the end of the 1994–95 season, the Leinster Branch recognized that the province would soon need to evolve into a club-like entity. Having observed the increased profile of provincial rugby in New Zealand and South Africa, the secretary's report for the season pointed out that Leinster needed to 'internationalise our profile as a matter of urgency' by playing against high-profile foreign clubs in order to 'advance both the Leinster team and the Leinster identity in the years to come'.[20]

Fashioning an identity around Leinster rugby (beyond whatever self-image the players had as a group) would have been a considerable challenge, if serious attempts had been made to do so. Put simply, in the popular imagination, Leinster rugby was shorthand for Dublin 4 rugby, as officials more or less admitted. The reality was a bit more complicated. Like Munster, Leinster had their own provincial tradition outside the cities: the Provincial Towns Cup, for example, was a long-standing and, for those involved, prestigious competition. There were also GAA overlaps of the kind often observed in Munster. Ned Byrne won an All-Ireland hurling medal with Kilkenny before switching to rugby, joining Blackrock and winning selection for Ireland in 1977. His cousin Willie Duggan, a fearsome back-row forward, was another ex-hurler who threw his lot in with rugby to great effect, winning forty-one caps for Ireland, again playing club rugby for Blackrock.

In the professional era, international players such as Shane Horgan, Seán O'Brien and Tadhg Furlong, none of whom had any connection to schools rugby, all graduated through the Leinster system. Leinster also made sincere attempts to attract those from non-rugby backgrounds into the game by appointing an extensive network of development officers throughout the province. Most eye-catching among these efforts was Liberty Saints, a club founded in Dublin's working-class north inner city in 2008, with a specific mission to provide a sporting outlet for children who might otherwise engage in anti-social behaviour.[21] There had even at times been some relief from the monotonous domination of the Leinster Schools Cup by fee-paying schools. De La Salle College in Churchtown, a state school, won the cup in 1983 and 1985.

Nevertheless, the heart of Leinster rugby was – and was seen to be – a few square miles south of the Liffey: hugging the coast from Lansdowne Road as far as Monkstown, then extending inland roughly as far as Terenure and Rathmines, with isolated north Dublin enclaves at Clontarf and Sutton. Its fictional avatar was Ross O'Carroll-Kelly, the schools rugby player in Paul Howard's satirical newspaper column, which spawned a successful series of novels and plays. An obnoxious, misogynistic snob, O'Carroll-Kelly became emblematic of both Leinster rugby and Celtic Tiger decadence in the popular imagination. Indeed, for a proportion of Howard's readership, their only experience of rugby was through the voice of O'Carroll-Kelly. But there was ample non-fictional commentary as well. An exasperated rugby-playing north-side Dubliner, recently relocated to Kerry, wrote to the *Irish Independent* in 2008 complaining that 'not until my move to the scarlet province have I witnessed amateur rugby unfettered by smallminded snobbery'. He accused the 'D4' rugby establishment of being 'blinkered' and 'class-paranoid', and asserted that Irish rugby would never succeed while it was dominated by 'Leinster-led "Lansdowne-Roadery"'.[22]

In practical terms, none of this mattered much. Leinster did not need an identity of the type nurtured in Munster. In any case, that kind of confected tribalism would have been an awkward fit for Leinster; it had a folksy quality to it that the Catholic elite had spent more than a century trying to distance themselves from. Leinster's route to success lay not in hiding their privilege, but in leaning further into it. Schools rugby, by far the most distinctive cultural feature of Leinster, held the key, and became a remarkable supply line of talent for professional rugby in Ireland.

Schools rugby in Leinster had long been something of a media obsession, particularly among the Dublin dailies. In advance of the Leinster Schools Cup each year, newspapers would carry in-depth, team-by-team profiles. In 2006, Gavin Cummiskey of the *Irish Times* admitted that the paper's sports section received more 'enquiries, complaints and compliments' about their Schools Cup coverage than any other event.[23] The six or so weeks from late January to St Patrick's Day was a rite of passage for generations of schoolboys. Highly ritualistic and carnivalesque, cup ties were one of the most powerful expressions of elite identity in Ireland. To the sober outsider, this might all seem a touch excessive. In

2004, *Irish Times* rugby writer John O'Sullivan pointed out that the size of the crowds at schools matches was 'wholly disproportionate' to the importance of the competition. But for those involved, it provided landmark moments in their lives. Young men who made a name for themselves on the schools rugby field were doing no harm to their life prospects.[24]

Such prestige led to suspicions of sharp practice. There developed among promising young players representing clubs rather than schools an unusual tendency to enrol in a rugby-playing school for just one year to repeat the Leaving Certificate exams. The schools would waive the fees and an informal transfer market of sorts developed. The Leinster Branch introduced new eligibility rules in 2014 to counteract this practice. In 2018, Cistercian College Roscrea threatened High Court action against the Leinster Schools Branch when nine of their players were deemed ineligible for the Schools Cup under the rules. The Leinster Branch caved.

The whole schools rugby scene was shrouded in brattish entitlement and a stout refusal to grow up. In 2020, Owen Doyle, writing in the *Irish Times*, described behaviour he had recently witnessed at a Schools Cup tie. Past pupils of the participant schools gathered together and engaged in chants of 'Your father works for my father'.[25] A couple of years earlier, rival groups of past pupils from Terenure College and St Michael's brawled with each other outside Kiely's pub in Donnybrook. Such common or garden hooliganism would scarcely have attracted any comment had it occurred just a few miles away at a soccer match in Dalymount Park, but elite misdemeanours have a certain voyeuristic appeal.

In 1998, Edmund Van Esbeck, still reeling from the arrival of the professional era, looked with hope to the upcoming schools cups, competitions that were 'about glory, honour, and pride in the cause – may I say, a noble cause'. Warming to his theme, he told readers that 'As sport builds character, so too does it reveal character.'[26] Schools rugby, in this view, was the last refuge of traditional rugby values. This view was probably illusory then; and it most certainly was so by the middle of the following decade. Elite schools developed systems of training and analysis that would have been the envy of many professional set-ups. Video analysis, dietary plans, and strength and conditioning programmes became the norm. In the case of St Michael's College, this was all overseen by a full-time director of rugby.[27]

The *Daily Telegraph* referred to Leinster schools rugby as a 'talent factory' in 2018.[28] The same year, Will Slattery of the *Irish Independent* described the rugby programme at St Michael's College, one typical of many schools. Here, a schoolboy rugby player's entire week was mapped out, with video analysis broken down into the finest points of the game, a database measuring individual players' strength and conditioning performance, and gym sessions beginning at 7 a.m. At the time, ten former St Michael's pupils were in the Leinster squad.[29] The entire rugby structure at the school had been the product of a 'strategic review' conducted ten years earlier. Remarkably, all of this effort and expense was directed towards a knock-out competition where defeat in the first round ended a school's season.

Backboned by former schools players, Leinster were extravagantly successful between 2009 and 2018, winning four European Cup titles. By the time this era of success came around, Leinster had astutely taken a lease on the RDS arena in Ballsbridge, a ground big enough to accommodate the team's growing fan base yet intimate enough to create an electric atmosphere. Irish rugby players also enjoyed a positive media image. Self-deprecating and friendly, Leinster players, in public at least, bore no resemblance to Ross O'Carroll-Kelly.[30]

The impact of the schools at the elite level was quite staggering. Fifty-one Leinster men (including those who made their debuts while playing for other clubs, but not including Irish-qualified overseas players) earned their first caps for Ireland in the twenty years from January 2000 to December 2019. Of these, forty-four (86 per cent) attended private rugby-playing schools. When we consider that less than 7 per cent of Irish children in 2023 attended private schools, it seems clear that more than a quarter of a century of professionalism had not done a great deal to lower the class ceiling in Irish rugby.[31]

Within the Irish rugby family, Connacht were treated like the gormless younger cousin that the elder relatives felt grudgingly obliged to humour. Among the provincial branches, Connacht were the last to join the IRFU, always had fewer clubs than the others, had meagre representation on the IRFU Council, had no representative on the Ireland selection committee for decades, and had to wait until 1937 before they had a member on the IRFU committee.[32] Connacht men rarely held high office in Irish rugby, and players from the province – apart from those who played in Dublin – had meagre prospects of international selection.

The Connacht Branch were, at times, something very like a one-man show. Henry Anderson, a Presbyterian dentist from Galway, became the province's first international player in 1903 (while playing in Dublin for Old Wesley), later held the presidency of the Connacht Branch for a quarter of a century, and was their first IRFU committeeman and their first IRFU president. In 1933, the IRFU wrote to Anderson seeking basic details regarding club numbers, grounds and officials in the province, the type of information that the Union already had a careful handle on when it came to the other three provinces.[33] This semi-negligent attitude towards Connacht persisted right down to the arrival of professionalism.

Connacht's prospects as a professional set-up were not promising. In 1999, they were designated a development team, with a budget capped at less than half those of the other provinces. The disruption caused to international rugby by foot and mouth disease in 2001, combined with the timing of the 2003 World Cup, led to significant forecasted financial losses for the IRFU. The Union's preferred solution – arrived at in December 2002 – was quite simple: the professional Connacht team would be scrapped. In some senses, this was deeply ironic. The IRFU, an organization that privileged amateur principles over market forces for so much of its history, were now attempting to cast aside one of the four traditional provincial teams in order to cut costs.

Connacht fought tenaciously to save their professional status, including a public meeting addressed by Joe Connolly, a legendary figure in Galway hurling. At the meeting, which drew a public response more enthusiastic than the average Connacht home match at the time, attendees resolved to march on Lansdowne Road in protest at the province's potential demise. The march attracted 2,000 people and Connacht's cause was publicly supported by a number of TDs and senators. The IRFU relented and Connacht were spared.[34]

The province remained a relatively infrequent contributor of homegrown players to the international team, but became a refuge for players struggling to make the grade elsewhere, particularly at Leinster and Munster. This, along with judicious use of the transfer market and effective promotion of the Sportsground as a home venue, helped Connacht to achieve a level of success that few would have anticipated in the early 2000s. Phil Coulter, in the end, was not pressed into a hasty rewrite of 'Ireland's Call'. The proud provinces remained a quartet.

10. The man's game?

Only the most attentive readers of the morning sport sections on 15 February 1993 would have noticed it. Amid the voluminous coverage of Young Munster's AIL-deciding victory over St Mary's College at Lansdowne Road that Saturday, the merest of footnotes was given to Ireland's first ever women's rugby international. The match, against Scotland, took place at Raeburn Place in Edinburgh, and resulted in a 10-0 win for the Scots. Commentators viewed the result as a creditable one for the visitors, considering the infancy of the women's game in Ireland.

The first Irish women's international team was coached by Alain Rolland, a men's international player (and future referee) who also coached Blackrock College RFC women's team. The inexperience of the team seems hardly credible in retrospect. The domestic women's club game in Ireland was barely three months in existence. The Irish full-back for that match against the Scots, Aoife Rogers, had played her first game of rugby the previous November. Ten of the Irish XV were based in England, where women's rugby was more firmly established. Of the five Ireland-based players selected, three were from Blackrock College RFC and two from Belfast club Cooke.

Women's rugby, in its early seasons, struggled to be taken seriously, and the Scotland match was not some profound moment of emancipation. Barely a week later, when the Irish men's team and their partners gathered at the Berkeley Court Hotel in Dublin for a post-match dinner after a Five

Nations meeting with France, the wives and girlfriends dined in a separate room, as tradition dictated. This was a more eloquent expression of gender relations in Irish rugby than the events at Raeburn Place. The ladies, on and off the field, were a frivolous appendage. Miriam Lord, in a sympathetic and supportive article in the *Irish Independent*, offered a typically satirical view of contemporary attitudes: 'Women rugby players? What would Mother Ireland think?'[1] Women's rugby was the subject of bawdiness and innuendo, rather than analysis and insight.

In common with other rugby-playing countries, the game in Ireland was historically oriented almost entirely towards men. Rugby, a tough, physical game, was a test of manhood that could not be rivalled by other codes. When Down Athletic gave up rugby in favour of soccer in 1885, one commentator asserted that the club's 'conduct to me appears very effeminate'.[2] But it was also a game for gentlemen: it promoted courage, leadership and self-sacrifice, qualities needed for future military leaders, businessmen and professionals – sectors that women were largely excluded from. Rugby, wrote 'Judex' in the Dublin newspaper *Sport* in 1926, was 'the greatest of all manly pastimes, calling for courage, self-control and kindliness'.[3] He described Ireland's victory over England as 'a gladiatorial battle, fast, fierce and fearless'. These were adjectives not commonly associated with women at the time. In places like Limerick, where local rivalries and civic pride were intense, the game was often violent. The pages of the Munster Branch's old minute books are filled with the record of disciplinary proceedings against players and clubs. The sport was clearly a male domain.

Throughout the nineteenth century and for much of the

twentieth, there existed a social and medical consensus that women were unsuited to sport, particularly field games such as rugby and soccer. Not only might it do them physical and emotional harm, but the exertion that such games demanded was inconsistent with commonly held ideas of femininity. Although these attitudes eased over time, rugby was possibly the last major international sport to offer meaningful playing opportunities to women.

Women did play a role in Irish rugby. Most clubs of any importance had a ladies committee by the early decades of the twentieth century. Here, women would reprise their domestic roles: washing kits, preparing food at the clubhouse and organizing events, fundraisers and so on. In 1979, Edmund Van Esbeck wrote an article in the *Irish Times* paying tribute to the contribution made by women to Irish rugby. 'No respectable rugby club is now without its ladies committee', he wrote.

> The wives and mothers have their part to play in the game. They have . . . to live with the concern for the welfare of husband and son, dispense the sympathy in the acute moment of disappointment that follows defeat or omission. They must learn to be philosophical about praise and criticism, and for the young wife or girlfriend, in particular, make sacrifices to the time their menfolk spend at the game.

'Go along to a schools cup tie', he continued, 'and see Mum in the stands. Her exhortations may not be learned in terms of the game and its complex laws, but her enthusiasm will be total, her anxieties profound.'[4] In rugby terms, then, women remained housewives and caregivers, all in the service of their male relatives. In turn, the complicated, brain-taxing elements of the game ought to be left to the men.

Mary Rose Doorly, writing in the *Sunday Press* in 1986, pointed out that although 'very few' women wanted to play the game,

> Rugby is a sport that would scarcely survive without women. Who would make the sandwiches at club functions? Who would urge the ten-year-olds on to great glory? Who would excavate the rancid jersey and shorts from the kit bag seven days later? And who would give rugby the veneer of decency apparently least evident in . . . the choice of lyrics in rugby songs?[5]

This gender division was a product of its time. It was only in 1973 that Irish legislators removed the marriage bar, a legal mechanism that forced women to leave public sector jobs once married. Women were under-represented in the professions and senior corporate roles, and in the great majority of cases were responsible for the unpaid domestic duties that kept households functioning. From 1968 to 1995, Ireland had a televised 'Housewife of the Year' competition.

Another conspicuous female figure in Irish rugby was the 'rugger hugger'. According to the stereotype, the rugger hugger was a privately educated young woman who, having attended one of a handful of elite schools in Dublin and Cork, made it her mission in life to woo a successful rugby player. In Dublin, this weird middle-class mating ritual, concentrated in certain pubs and nightclubs, had its own fashion trends, visual cues and vernacular. Writing in the *Sunday Independent* in 1995, Lise Hand recalled how her convent school 'had the misfortune to be within courting distance of the Shrine of the Oval Ball aka Blackrock College, and so the ultimate catch for trawling convent girls was a Rock Boy who exuded a heady whiff of muscle, status, prospects and wintergreen'.[6]

The phenomenon apparently extended into young adulthood. Katie Hannon, writing about the 'nocturnal wildlife' of the rugby season in 1993, told readers that the rugger hugger needed stamina because 'the males only notice that there are females present sometime after midnight', so 'a good tolerance for Ritz [a type of cider then marketed at women] and a high boredom threshold is considered vital'.[7] Carol Tobin, in a *Sunday Independent* article in 2007, claimed that some girls pretend to be interested in rugby

> and go to posh bars to watch the matches in the hope that some rich man goes, 'Wow, you like rugby; here are the keys to my seven-bedroom Georgian mansion in Ranelagh; here's your selection of no-credit-limit credit cards, and hey honey, don't forget the keys of your brand new SUV. In return, just stay blonde and thin and provide me with three kids, boys preferably.'[8]

In reality, for every young woman who coveted a rugby-playing partner, there were probably countless who were turned off by the preening self-importance of the SCT member. Likewise, it is difficult to lay too much blame at the feet of the young men involved; they were conditioned by their peers, their schools and their parents.

Coincidentally or not, the media preoccupation with the rugger hugger faded as women's participation in rugby increased and gained recognition in Ireland from the mid-2000s. Ireland had been one of the last major rugby-playing nations to embrace the women's game. Sporadic instances of women playing rugby date back to the 1880s, but nothing structured or sustained emerged until the 1960s. France were the European pioneers: a women's rugby association was founded in 1970, followed by a domestic championship the following year. The first international Test match, between France and the Netherlands, took place in 1982. That same decade the Women's Rugby Football Union was founded, initially with jurisdiction over the game in England, Scotland and Wales, though individual national unions would later follow.[9] There was little club rugby for girls anywhere, and many took up rugby for the first time at university. It was in the collegiate sport system that the game first became popular in the USA, whose national team won the first World Cup in 1991.

Early efforts to establish the women's game in Ireland encountered a wall of derision. In 1973, for example, women's teams from Trinity and UCD did battle at College Park. RTÉ's report of proceedings featured not in its regular sports coverage but in *Tangents*, a magazine-style show covering quirky current events across the country, and the match was treated like a novelty skit in some lowbrow variety show. The players were questioned about their femininity and whether the whole thing was an exercise in 'women's lib'. The noise from the mainly male crowd was a mixture of cheers and jeers, while the editing of action sequences and the soundtrack were designed for maximum ridicule.[10]

Occasional colours matches took place involving UCD, Trinity and Queen's. When UCD met Queen's in 1978, the usual belittling ensued. One male reporter claimed that the women involved 'lined out rather prettily, and tackled with innocence', but he was disappointed that the players did not swap shirts at the conclusion of the match.[11] Lame jokes about the swapping of shirts and who would play in the hooker position were common in male coverage of the women's game. The game was even on occasion the butt of practical jokes. In 1983, for example, a prankster, said to be a male member of the rugby club at Trinity, invited an American team to Dublin to play against the college's women's team. The touring Americans, the Rio Grande Surfers, duly arrived in Dublin only to find no opposition team to play against. The college recreation officer was forced to apologize to the tourists while telling the press that 'Needless to say, we don't have a rugby team for women.'[12]

Women playing rugby was often conflated with feminism. Reporting on a match between UCD and Old Belvedere in 1972, an *Irish Press* correspondent asserted that Germaine Greer, the Australian author who was then one of the world's most outspoken feminists, 'would have loved this . . . women charging around Anglesea Road playing rugby'.[13] In 1988, when Susan Mannion began a recruitment drive to launch a women's team at Queen's University Belfast, there were no women's clubs in Ireland. It was telling that Mannion felt compelled to tell an interviewer that she was 'not a feminist'.[14] Mannion's efforts clearly yielded modest results, as three years later, Jill Henderson, Ireland's first captain, was hosting introductory sessions in an attempt to establish the game in Belfast.[15]

For the most part, women's matches took place as novelty events during festivals and galas, often featuring during 'rag week' at various universities. Clubs were too few and far between for a regular programme of fixtures to take place. When, in 1985, Tallaght Ladies' Rugby Club was set up, members encountered an immediate problem: there were no teams to provide them with opposition. And though the local men's club was supportive, one of their committeemen warned the women that 'the game has to be taken seriously if it is not to become dangerous', before adding that 'If the women are just playing for a laugh then you could have a lot of injuries.'[16] When Sunday's Well from Cork put together a women's team in 1986 the only opposition available was a team from Tralee, eighty miles away.[17] The Tralee team was bolstered by members of the All-Ireland-winning Kerry Ladies' Gaelic football team.[18] In the absence of a governing body and meaningful competitions – the key ingredients for promoting and sustaining enthusiasm for the game among players – efforts to promote women's rugby remained piecemeal.

The women's game was clearly also stymied by patriarchal attitudes. As the *Evening Press* rugby reporter Karl Johnston asserted in 1990:

> though I strongly deny that I am in any way anti-feminist, I still find it hard to accept that rugby is a suitable game for women. Arguably it is the toughest body-contact sport of them all – fiercely aggressive, and the prospect of thirty women knocking each other about on the field does not appeal to me.[19]

In another column, he continued, 'having never seen women's rugby, maybe I shouldn't comment, but it's hardly the sort of sport I'd like my daughters to take up'.[20] This kind of commentary was at least partly the legacy of a long-held prurient obsession in Catholic Ireland with the behaviour of young women when they were not under the supervision or surveillance of their older relatives. The *Belfast Telegraph* summarized contemporary attitudes in 1994, telling readers that 'to many women's rugby is like ladies boxing – not the most eloquent pursuit for the "fairer" sex to be involved in'.[21]

Matters were improving, however, by the early 1990s. The formation of clubs at Blackrock College RFC and at Cooke gave the game secure anchors in Dublin and Belfast respectively. The women's game was given structure from 1991 with the founding of the Irish Women's Rugby Football Union, and a domestic competition was set up. The IWRFU became an affiliate of the IRFU in 2001 (having been affiliated to the English WRFU to that point) before an eventual merger in 2008. From 1992, there was a domestic competition sponsored by Smithwick's. This, according to the *Irish Press*, was 'what happens when women drink pints'.[22] The 1993 event attracted six teams.[23] Another landmark was Ireland's first ever home match, in 1994. In advance of the match, which took place at Ravenhill in Belfast against Scotland, one newspaper saw the fixture as an attempt by the women involved 'to remove the all-too-readily applied "joke label" from their beloved game'.[24] It was the first rugby international of any kind to take place in Ireland on a Sunday.

Far more crippling than the game's lack of moral support was its inability to meet basic expenses. Ireland entered the World Cup in 1994, but the IWRFU were still holding open trials for potential places in the squad just a few months before the tournament. Team selection was hampered by the fact that players had to cover their own travel expenses and take leave from work, and Ireland actually pulled out of the competition, before the players had a change of heart and decided to enter after all. Willie Anderson, the former Ireland international, ran the coaching sessions. Women's rugby in Ireland survived on minimal institutional support and was dependent on the efforts of a few dedicated individuals fearlessly risking ridicule to pursue their favoured sport. Among these was IWRFU president Mary O'Beirne, who reported in 1994 that her organization had reached 'crisis point' for the want of stable sponsorship arrangements and support from established clubs. Only at Blackrock College RFC were the women's team fully integrated with the club's structures.[25]

With a mixture of homegrown and England-based players, Ireland continued to send out makeshift teams for fixtures against nations with vastly greater experience. In 1997, Ireland captain Carole Ann Byrne, reflecting on the challenges of competing internationally without sponsorship, asserted that 'Basically we are living in a country where rugby is still a very chauvinist old school game.'[26] Fiona Steed, a tenacious back-row forward who drifted into rugby while studying in England and went on to earn sixty-two caps, pursued her international career at her own expense. One newspaper report in 2000 claimed that she had spent around IR£20,000 to play for Ireland.[27] Her reward in playing terms was frequent heavy defeats – Ireland only won three Six Nations matches between the tournament's first iteration in 1996 and its tenth staging in 2005. Joy Neville, later an international referee in the men's game, recalled the spartan set-up of the formative days of her international career in the early 2000s: 'At the outset we hadn't accommodation paid for. If you trained in Dublin you'd ring someone living up there and ask if you could kip on the ground.'[28] So while the men were fully professional and enjoying all the comforts associated with that status, the women's team enjoyed sleeping arrangements more in keeping with a crowded student house party.

Results on the field reflected Ireland's lack of resources. In the 1999 Women's Five Nations Championship, Ireland were heavily beaten in every match and were held scoreless in three of their four outings. The IWRFU decided to withdraw from the following season's championship to concentrate, according to women's rugby journalist Ali Donnelly, 'on strengthening their domestic game'.[29] Ireland returned to the tournament in 2002. Considerable progress was made in the interim. In 2001, the IRFU brought the IWRFU under their wing – a development seemingly unconnected to Ireland's withdrawal from the Five Nations – and resolved to give financial and technical support to the women's game. There was also, by now, an interprovincial championship for women and impressive growth in numbers playing the game. And although the volume of press coverage remained low, it must have come as some relief to the players that their sport was no longer treated like a daft counter-cultural fad.

By 2006, there were 1,000 women playing rugby in Ireland, including a great expansion at underage level.[30] In 2009, women's rugby had its own full-time development officer, and women's teams came to be more integrated with the men's set-ups within clubs. These developments fed a clear upturn in the competitiveness of the international team. From 2009 onwards, Ireland routinely finished in the top three of the Six Nations Championship, pulling clear of Scotland, Wales and Italy.

The team stepped into the limelight in 2013, winning the Grand Slam and denying England a seventh Six Nations Championship in a row. When Ireland secured the championship that year in the tournament's penultimate match, RTÉ devoted all of 152 seconds of coverage to the win in the men's Six Nations programme. The Grand Slam-clinching match against Italy a fortnight later was the first international women's match ever given live coverage by the state broadcaster.[31] A year later the team finished fourth at the 2014 World Cup, gaining notable wins over New Zealand – thus becoming the first adult international team from Ireland to do so – and the USA, before encountering an unstoppable England in the semi-finals. Another Six Nations title was secured in 2015, and with the World Cup due to be held in Ireland in 2017 it looked from the outside as though the women's XV were on a steady upward trajectory.

But the heroics of 2013–15 belied considerable structural problems within the game. For one, the pathways into rugby and up to the elite level remained haphazard: Ireland was dependent on players who stumbled into the game by accident. Nora Stapleton, from the Donegal village of Fahan – a location untouched by rugby until then – started playing tag rugby 'for a bit of craic' before taking up the fifteens game.[32] Dozens of international players first encountered the game by giving it a go in college when already in their twenties. Lynne Cantwell, Ireland's most capped player, enrolled at the University of Limerick intending to pursue athletics, before 'getting into rugby by accident'.[33] This was not a sustainable route to success in a game edging towards professionalism.

In the aftermath of a disappointing early elimination in their home World Cup in 2017, Irish players became frustrated that their ambitions were not shared by the IRFU. These fears surfaced again when Ireland failed to qualify for the 2021 World Cup. Sixty-two current and former internationals wrote to the government in protest at what they saw as the IRFU's 'historic failings' in fulfilling their responsibility to the women's game. Though the letter did not go into great detail about specific grievances, its tone clearly indicated a gaping breach of trust between the players and the IRFU. A tin-eared and defensive response from the IRFU, decrying 'the overall tenor of the document', led the government to seek a meeting with the Union. This was arguably the greatest display of player power in the entire history of Irish rugby, men's or women's.

The problems in the women's game were many: substand-
ard preparation opportunities, a near complete disconnect
between the IRFU and the club game, and officials with competing priorities. The women's game itself was dragged in
opposite directions: the women's fifteens and sevens had
overlapping schedules, depriving the Six Nations team of key
players. Fundamentally, there was no official for whom the
women's game was the sole area of responsibility. Instead,
the women's game was run by David Nucifora, the main focus
of whose role was the men's game, and Anthony Eddy, who
was also in charge of the sevens programme. Eddy made matters worse in the aftermath of Ireland's failure to qualify for
the 2021 World Cup by trying to direct the blame towards the
players: 'I know the girls, the coaching staff, the girls themselves are disappointed not to have qualified and disappointed
in their performances.'[34]

In the same month that Eddy made his comments, the
Connacht and Ulster teams were forced to change in squalid
conditions before an interprovincial fixture in Dublin. Though
Covid-19 regulations meant that teams technically classed as
non-elite could not access indoor changing facilities, for the
public it was truly shocking that the women involved were
forced to change in flimsy shelters, amid rats, wheelie bins,
abandoned shipping containers, and assorted other detritus.[35]

For some, this must have brought to mind various past
indignities. For Ireland's away fixture in France in 2012, the
IRFU booked the players on a flight to Paris. Then the squad
had to board a crowded train south to Pau, in the foothills of
the Pyrenees, where the match was to be played. The players
arrived twenty-three hours after leaving Dublin.[36] When
the Irish women played their first ever match at the Aviva
Stadium in 2014, it followed a men's Six Nations fixture the

same day. And though one could argue a positive case for giving the women's game such a billing, the occasion brought about another indignity: due to a post-match presentation after the men's match, the women's teams were not permitted to warm up on the main pitch.[37] In 2015, Ireland's match at home against France descended into farce when a series of floodlight failures caused a one-hour pause to proceedings at Ireland's usual home venue, Ashbourne RFC. By then the team had a Grand Slam and a fourth-place finish in the World Cup to their name, yet they were still being consigned to an obscure outpost in County Meath for their home fixtures.

Ireland was behind the curve as the women's game gradually embraced professionalism. Paid contracts were first offered in women's rugby for the seven-a-side game in the early 2010s. Sevens was a more glamorous circuit that had an Olympic title as its highest honour, and this made national sports councils happy to fund it. The Dutch were the first to offer their sevens players contracts. From 2014, the English were also paying their elite sevens players, with Ireland soon following. The English took matters a step further by giving temporary full-time contracts to members of their fifteens squad in advance of the 2017 World Cup. And they went yet further again in 2019, when they put in place a permanent system of full-time contracts for fifteens players. The RFU, recognizing that girls' and women's sports were entering an exciting new era of expanding playing numbers, and a growing media and commercial profile, made its aims clear: 'We are at a tipping point for women's rugby globally, and it is our ambition to be world No 1 and drive growth at every level.'[38] Wales followed in 2022, before expanding their professional ranks considerably in 2023.

In this context, the IRFU were more or less shamed into

offering professional contracts to Ireland's best women's players. In October 2022, thirty-seven contracts were offered to elite sevens and fifteens players, with a basic salary of up to €30,000. With some contracts worth as little as €15,000, it was clear that few of the players would be pursuing a full-time career in rugby. Eight players turned down contracts. Four of these were based in England and chose to stay there, while the four Ireland-based players chose to continue their day jobs outside of rugby, unwilling, perhaps, to commit to full-time training at the Union's high-performance centre in Dublin on such modest terms.[39] 'We fully understand', David Nucifora stated, 'that you have financial obligations that don't permit you to be able to take up those contracts.'[40]

In April 2023, the *Daily Telegraph* published the damning findings of an investigation – heavily disputed by the IRFU – into the treatment of the Ireland women's team. Among the report's claims were that a high-profile IRFU official wondered aloud, 'Who gives a fuck about women's rugby?' at a Union dinner in 2023. John Cronin, director of rugby at Railway Union RFC in Dublin, told the paper that '"An old boys culture tends to pervade the organisation that can be quite hostile to women's rugby".'[41] It was surely an indictment of the IRFU that a callow women's team were sent out to do battle in the 2023 Six Nations, a tournament where Ireland took the Wooden Spoon, scoring only twenty-five points in five matches. In the autumn of 2023, the road to recovery lay in the third – and bottom – division of the WXV, a new tournament inaugurated by World Rugby.

Women's rugby in Ireland profited greatly from the contribution of Gaelic football players. An early example of this was Sue Ramsbottom. One of the greatest Gaelic footballers of all time, Ramsbottom was first selected for Laois ladies as a young teenager. At the height of her GAA career in 1998, she was selected for the Ireland rugby team, having played for Connacht at interprovincial level. By then she had been playing rugby for just two years.[42] Niamh Briggs and Fiona Coghlan, arguably Ireland's two greatest captains, were also accomplished Gaelic players. Lindsay Peat, an All-Ireland winner with Dublin, was capped for Ireland in only her eighth ever rugby match.

Ireland's great teams of the early 2010s were built around women who had played Gaelic football and took up rugby relatively late, often after enrolling in college. Grand Slam winners in 2013 such as Claire Molloy, Larissa Muldoon, Niamh Briggs, Jenny Murphy, Mary Louise Reilly, Fiona Coghlan and Alison Miller all played Gaelic in their youth, some of them to intercounty level. This cross-code traffic went both ways. In 2000, the *Belfast Telegraph* carried a report of several members of the Cooke RFC first XV – all Protestants – who had taken up Gaelic football in the summer with their local club, Bredagh, in County Down.[43]

At schools level, the girls' game had a very different class profile from the boys' equivalent. Some state schools took up the game readily. When the Leinster Girls' Schools Rugby League was first played in 2005, St Brigid's from Callan – a town in County Kilkenny with no rugby tradition whatsoever – were the winners.[44] In 2023, none of the finalists in the Munster Junior and Senior Girls rugby cups were fee-paying schools. In Ulster, the schools game had a clear cross-community dimension. Mount Lourdes, a Catholic school in Belfast, won the Ulster Girls' Schools title in 2007. More recently, Erne Integrated College from Enniskillen have been one of the strongest teams in the tournament. Magh Éne College in

Bundoran happily accommodated both Gaelic football and rugby and have had girls selected for the Ulster underage teams.[45]

The Ireland women's rugby team notched up a win over New Zealand and a World Cup semi-final appearance before their male colleagues achieved either. By developing a cross-community and, to some degree, a cross-class game, the Irish women were pioneers in more ways than one. In that context, the sclerosis that set in after 2015 felt like a missed opportunity.

11. Putting his head where it hurts

Ken Nuzum had a remarkably long rugby career. From his schooldays at the King's Hospital in the late 1970s, he progressed to senior rugby with Lansdowne the following decade, and played for the first team as late as 1997, aged forty-two.[1] He also had a long stint playing at junior level with Aer Lingus in the 1990s and into the 2000s and was still playing as a fifty-year-old. Nuzum was a ferociously competitive front-row forward who strayed outside the laws of the game occasionally. In 1986, for example, he was suspended for headbutting an opponent.[2] This was as much a feature of front-row forward play at the time as it was any particular malevolence on Nuzum's part.

In his early fifties, Ken Nuzum began showing significant cognitive impairment, and he deteriorated steadily until his death in 2013. His cause of death was CTE (chronic traumatic encephalopathy), a degenerative brain condition common in boxers and American football players.[3] It is impossible to say with certainty that Nuzum's CTE – or anyone's – was caused by sport. But it seems probable that a rugby-playing career of almost thirty years, characterized by abrasiveness and attrition, shortened Nuzum's life. His death was a tragic precursor to a major crisis that would soon engulf the rugby world.

Writing about Ken Nuzum in 2013, Brendan Fanning claimed that this was the 'first time the death of a rugby player had been referred to the Coroner's Court'.[4] This was not quite right. Deaths on the rugby field in Ireland throughout the game's history were rare but not unheard of, and were often followed by inquests. Determining the precise number of such deaths is not possible, as these incidents were not systematically recorded. In any case, injuries sustained in rugby might not have led to death until many years after players retired, not least in the case of brain injuries, as exemplified by Nuzum. But we know for certain that deaths directly attributable to rugby occurred at an average rate of greater than one per decade in the twentieth century.

In October 1913, 22-year-old Charles McIvor, an Irish international who had received the most recent of his seven caps earlier that year, died after sustaining what the press termed 'concussion' in a practice match at College Park in Dublin.[5] Two players died in 1928: one after receiving a kick to the head and the second from a neck injury sustained in a collapsed scrum. The neck injury victim, Brian Hanrahan, was the brother of Irish international Charles, and was playing for Lansdowne in the Leinster Senior Cup when the incident occurred.[6] Another four players died in the 1930s: two from abdominal injuries, one from a blow to the head and another from a neck injury – Patrick Mullen, a sixteen-year-old schoolboy who died in 1933 while playing for Galway Collegians, suffered what was again described as a 'concussion'.[7]

In the decades between the game's Second World War hiatus and the beginning of the 1980s, at least eleven more players died: six as a result of neck or spinal injuries, and five from head injuries.[8] These incidents occurred across all levels of the game, from schoolboys to senior club competition. There were some grim pre-echoes of future crises in some of these incidents. In 1956, for example, Louis Foley died from a head injury sustained while tackling a player in a match in

Dublin. His inquest heard that Foley had been treated for concussion in hospital two years earlier.[9] These deaths on the rugby field were too sporadic to cause any fundamental questioning of the game's safety. It was common for witnesses at an inquest to testify that the death of a player was freakishly accidental, and that the game in which the fatal injury occurred was a clean, sporting one. While newspapers might briefly ruminate on the dangers of the game after a fatality, the prevailing attitude among most observers, it seems, was that rugby was a voluntary activity played by individuals at their own risk.

Some deaths had a greater impact on the public imagination than others. In October 1961, Eddie Lawlor of Limerick club Richmond died of 'general paralysis caused by dislocation of the spine'.[10] He sustained a neck injury during a match at Ennis. The incident was, according to the *Limerick Leader*, 'the most appalling tragedy ever experienced by a Limerick club in the eighty years the game of rugby has been played in Limerick'. Lawlor, who was just twenty years old, was a moulder by trade, and had been the main breadwinner for his family, in which he was the eldest of five children. A committee that included two members of each Limerick rugby club was established to coordinate a compensation appeal for the family.[11] The committee also included a range of local political grandees and senior clergy, and was chaired by the mayor and future government minister, Donogh O'Malley. Rugby was more than just a game in Limerick, and any tragedy on the rugby field was always likely to lead to a strong civic response. Characteristically, the consensus among all witnesses at the inquest, including Eddie Lawlor's parents, was that the game was a clean one and that the whole affair was a tragic accident. The victim, in the days before his death, lying in hospital and paralysed from the neck down, 'made no complaint about the accident', and told his mother that 'it was all in the game'.[12] One solicitor at the inquest pithily summed matters up when he observed that 'in any game of the nature of rugby football the risk of accident was inherent'.[13]

Serious injuries in rugby, then, were greeted with resignation. After a glut of rugby injuries in 1949, for example, an *Irish Independent* reporter observed that 'Rugby is an amateur game, and the authorities here have always shied from anything smacking even slightly of regimentation.'[14] After Omagh's Dan McCurdy died of neck injuries sustained in a match in 1970, former Ireland captain Dr Karl Mullen told the *Sunday Independent* that there was no evidence that rugby was more dangerous than any other sport and that it was 'certainly more safe than riding a bicycle'. An IRFU spokesman claimed that he had no statistical data on rugby-related fatalities and refused to discuss McCurdy's death, claiming it was 'an isolated incident'.[15] The notion of 'player welfare' belonged to the future.

Sporadic concerns about the safety of rugby gave way to more sustained scrutiny from the mid-1970s onwards. The gratuitous violence of the Lions tour to South Africa in 1974 might have added a rich chapter to the macho folklore of the game, but along with the notorious brutality of French teams of the 1970s and other high-profile violent matches, it also raised serious concerns about the safety of rugby. The main focus of concern in Ireland was an apparent increase in serious neck and spinal injuries in rugby matches, particularly at junior and schoolboy level. These injuries often had catastrophic consequences for victims. It seems likely that a small proportion of the apparent upsurge was due to more careful recording. From the 1960s onwards, sufferers of serious spinal injuries in the Republic of Ireland were directed to the National Rehabilitation Centre in Dublin; this meant that cases could be tracked and quantified, and worrying trends could be spotted.

In 1975, the IRFU hosted a major conference on rugby injuries in Dublin. Jack Kyle, then a surgeon based in Zambia, and widely regarded as Ireland's greatest ever player, claimed that the risk of serious neck injuries for players involved in a collapsing scrum was 'Rugby's biggest menace'.[16] This was grimly prophetic. Barely six months later, two players in Northern Ireland were left paralysed after sustaining injuries in separate matches that took place on the same day. The players were admitted to the same ward of the Royal Victoria Hospital in Belfast. One of the two, 24-year-old Gordon Davidson, died a few days later.[17]

The winter of 1979–80 was a particularly dark one: twelve players were admitted to the National Rehabilitation Centre, with four suffering various levels of paralysis (two with injuries sustained in scrums, two in loose play).[18] This was a considerable uptick from the long-term trend: the total number of rugby players admitted with serious neck injuries between 1961 and 1987 was thirty-one.[19] According to the medical director of the centre, Dr Thomas Gregg, 'the rugby authorities and the rugby doctors must decide on some policy on this terrible number of youthful neck fractures'.[20] Added to this was the particularly high-profile retirement of an Ireland international, Rodney O'Donnell, who suffered fractured vertebrae while playing for the Lions in South Africa in 1980. O'Donnell recovered well, but his injury kept rugby in the headlines. After a lull the following season, at least a further six players sustained serious spinal injuries in the Republic between 1981 and 1984.[21] Additionally, between 1979 and 1984, there were seven deaths on the rugby field.[22] Only two of these deaths occurred due to injuries (one spinal and one head), while the remainder were from natural causes. The press tended to emphasize the headline figure, however.

In March 1980, the *Irish Press* carried a front-page story on neck injuries in the game. Dr Gregg, interviewed for the article, stated that 'there is something wrong if boys are coming into us with broken necks and serious paralysis'.[23] In a long piece in the *Irish Times* later that week, Vincent Hogan claimed that 'Rugby violence has been ignored for too long and look at the price. Hundreds of players maimed and paralysed and all in the name of sport. We owe it to those victims to stop this disfigurement of a once beautiful game.'[24] In 1984, Fergal Keane wrote an investigative-style article in the news section of the *Irish Press*, detailing a catalogue of recent serious injuries and deaths in Irish rugby and concluding that 'The indicators are that there is something radically wrong with the game as it is played in this country.'[25]

These were just three of several long articles on the subject, often printed in the news section and coinciding with the schools rugby season.[26] In January 1985, for example, the *Irish Times* printed a feature article under the headline 'Should your child play rugby?' The story carried the grim subheading, 'an accident on the field means a lifetime of paralysis'.[27] The *Irish Independent* carried a 'special report' on spinal injuries in February 1988 in which readers were informed that 25,000 schoolboys played rugby every year. But behind that 'healthy statistic', the author cautioned, 'lurks a new menace for parents', before warning of the 'hidden dangers of the thrilling game'.[28]

The IRFU, reluctant to take any action that might dial down

the physical aspects of the game, tended to view the glut of injuries as a weird anomaly. One IRFU official in 1980 airily claimed that the neck injury situation 'was only a phase'.[29] Other 'rugby sources' described the situation as 'freakish' and 'unprecedented'.[30] There were some reforms, however. The IRFU Charitable Trust was set up in 1978 to offer support to the victims of neck injuries. After the death in 1979 of Tom Fahey from Clonmel, who was left quadriplegic after a match three years earlier, the IRFU introduced a compulsory insurance scheme for clubs. New scrum laws were introduced, and it is likely that the sheer level of public attention focused on the game led to subtle behavioural changes among players and referees. By the early 1990s, the crisis had abated. In 1991, no new seriously injured rugby players had been admitted to the National Rehabilitation Centre in the previous two years.[31] A comprehensive survey of injuries in Ireland published in 1994 found that rule changes in rugby had reduced the danger of scrums and the game was no more dangerous than soccer.[32] Of twelve players who sustained spinal injuries in Irish rugby between 1995 and 2004, just two were injured in scrums.[33]

Spinal injuries, while devastating, were comparatively rare. A more insidious and elusive problem was presented by head injuries. Concussion, first identified as a clinical condition over 1,000 years ago, was studied extensively in boxers throughout the twentieth century. It only came to the forefront of public consciousness, however, in the early 2000s.[34] Since then, global sport has had to contend with what has been termed a 'concussion crisis'.[35] And from around the early 2010s onwards, the risk posed by concussion to the long-term health of rugby union players became a serious focus of attention in places where the game had a significant following.

On the surface, it seems quite remarkable that it took so long for concussion in rugby to be seen as a crisis. The game's authorities had been aware of the dangers of blows to the head for decades. As early as 1965, a British sport medicine expert, J. G. P. Williams, called for concussed players to be removed from play and to be kept out of action for a minimum period.[36] Then, in 1975, as we have seen, the IRFU held a major conference on injuries. Jack Kyle, who had given grim warnings about neck injuries in his presentation, also discussed concussion, telling his audience that 'the rules of rugby should be changed so that a referee can send a player off the field if concussion or head or neck injuries are suspected'.[37] Kyle had personal experience to call on. After making a tackle in a match against Wales in March 1953, he sustained a concussion and played the remainder of the game despite having 'virtually no idea of what was happening for about the next twenty minutes'.[38] Now, in 1975, he described the reluctance of injured players to leave the field as 'the height of rugby madness'.[39]

Another attendee at the Dublin conference was the former Wales international and doctor, J. P. R. Williams. In 1979, he warned that 'there really is no excuse for anyone staying on the field if they cannot remember which day it is'.[40] By then the International Rugby Board had set up a Medical Advisory Committee and had implemented a mandatory three-week stand-down period for players who suffered concussion. The dangers of concussion were further underlined by neuroscientists at major rugby injury conferences held in Bermuda in 1990, Scotland in 1991 and New Zealand in 1992. Representatives of the game's governing bodies attended these events and must have subsequently known, if they chose to listen, that concussion potentially caused permanent damage and that the effects of repeated concussions were cumulative.[41]

Safety measures, if they were to succeed, had a major obstacle to scale: the game's culture and traditions. Any reform might be met with a chorus of club bores dribbling out the tedious assertion that the game had 'gone soft'. More seriously, rugby has always given players incentives to conceal injury. The imperative to 'man up', to tolerate pain and to play through injury, was deeply ingrained in the game's collective psyche; the willingness to put one's 'head where it hurts' was a quality greatly valued by coaches and spectators. When Irish international Mick Quinn lined out for the invitational Wolfhounds team against an Edinburgh Wanderers selection in 1975, he was hailed as the 'hero of the hour' when he scored the winning try. 'Having been off with severe concussion in the first half,' one report stated, Quinn 'came back bravely and played out the game'.[42] In 1978, the Irish international flanker John O'Driscoll suffered a concussion while playing for the Exiles (a team based on London Irish) against Munster. Though he did not remember scoring a try in the match, he refused to leave the field, despite the insistence of four doctors and a medical student who were present. At that point, Dr Mick Molloy, an ex-international himself, summoned O'Driscoll's wife, Kathleen, who successfully convinced her husband to leave the field.[43]

Players often had a cavalier attitude to their own wellbeing. In 2010, Donal Lenihan recalled the case of a Highfield player who, having been concussed in a Munster Senior Cup game in 1990, did not disclose that he had been suffering headaches in the days that followed and insisted he was fit to play the following weekend in a vital game against Young Munster. An alert medic who had been at the cup match the previous week spotted him lining up for the Young Munster match, approached the referee, and declared the player unfit to play, causing 'consternation among the Highfield faithful'.[44] Concealing or downplaying head injuries was a systemic problem. In the 1988–89 season, nine rugby players were admitted to St Vincent's Hospital in Dublin with concussion. Of these, one discharged himself from hospital against medical advice, while five others did not attend follow-up neurology appointments.[45]

The year-long absence from the game, due to a string of concussions, of Irish international Fergus Dunlea in 1989–90 was eye-catching and newsworthy, but looked like an isolated incident and did not, therefore, cause any conspicuous alarm among commentators. Indeed, there was an air of irreverence around Dunlea's injury. When he returned to club rugby in 1990, one newspaper report, under the title 'Heady days here again for Dunlea', claimed that he had been nicknamed 'headbanger' by his teammates.[46]

The pressure to downplay or ignore head injuries existed even at schoolboy level. In the midst of the neck injury crisis of the 1980s, a Dublin physiotherapist complained that

> We get a lot of parents coming into us and enquiring about their sons' injury and putting pressure on the physiotherapists to get their sons back on the field. This is especially the case if their sons are playing for high-profile rugby schools or the family has a whole tradition of rugby.[47]

The motives underlying this attitude were clear. 'The career benefits of rugby can mean anything,' the *Irish Times* pointed out in 1993, 'from the sport's ability to inculcate character in a young person to a member of the old boys' club turning up in the dressing room and asking players if they're interested in a career in accountancy.'[48] So when players, coaches and parents were confronted with the possibility of an enforced three-week absence for a concussion injury, it is hardly surprising that such injuries were concealed.

One of the most visible consequences of the transition to professionalism in rugby was the physical evolution of players, who became heavier, stronger and fitter. Between 1995 and 2015, the average male professional rugby player's weight increased from just over 15 stone (96 kg) to more than 16½ stone (106 kg).[49] In some positions, the shift was startling. The average centre three-quarter (nos. 12 and 13) was more than two stone (14 kg) heavier in 2015 than he was in 1995. This additional physical power, combined with rule changes designed to keep the ball in play for longer, led to more frequent and forceful collisions between players.

Pressure to bulk up naturally was extended to teenage players. As well as lifting weights, players began experimenting with creatine supplements. Creatine is a naturally occurring substance in the body that, when boosted by supplementation, helps users to recover more quickly from intensive training, and can therefore build lean muscle mass. From the mid-1990s to the early 2000s, the alleged use of creatine at schools level caused something akin to a moral panic. 'Rugby has become a quasi weight-lifting sport,' Gerry Thornley wrote in the *Irish Times* in October 1998, 'and worryingly I have it on good authority that school players in the State are taking creatine . . . there are now concerns that creatine can be harmful, especially when taken in large doses'.[50] Thornley did not specify the harms of creatine, but there were recurrent concerns among commentators that it could cause weight gain and liver damage, and that the additional bulk acquired by schoolboys could make the game more dangerous at that level.

The following month IRFU secretary Philip Browne was questioned by the Oireachtas Joint Committee for Tourism and Sport about the use of creatine in rugby, especially in light of rumours that coaches in elite schools were encouraging boys to take it. Browne told the committee that 'We are appalled by people in responsible positions who encourage young people to use this stuff. We must ban it. Legally we must find a way . . . we believe it should be done.'[51] Dr Joe Cummiskey, medical officer to the Olympic Council of Ireland, told the same committee that in his opinion 'creatine will eventually be banned'.[52]

One of the most dogged opponents of creatine use was Tony Ward. On several occasions, the ex-Ireland international used his column in the *Irish Independent* to campaign against its use. In 1998, he told readers that he was 'taken aback' by the number of schoolboys then taking creatine, and claimed that it was 'the clearest form of legalised cheating available'.[53] 'My argument against creatine', he continued, 'is a moral one. For me the beauty of sport, and rugby in particular, has long been its purity.' In light of all this scrutiny, a succession of schools felt compelled to publicly deny that their players used creatine.

To some degree the reaction of journalists, sports officials and the government was understandable. Concern about doping in sport was intense at the time, and the consequences of long-term creatine use were then unknown. But there was already evidence that the effects of creatine may not have warranted the reaction that its use provoked. In December 1998, the International Olympic Committee's Medical Commission refused to ban it. The committee's chair airily told reporters that 'We don't tell people that they can't eat eggs or bread . . .

Creatine is food, and there is no reason to ban it.'[54] A succession of studies in the years that followed found no harmful effects associated with creatine use, culminating in 2007 with the publication of a major review by the International Society of Sports Nutrition which concluded that 'There is no scientific evidence that the short- or long-term use of creatine monohydrate has any detrimental effects on otherwise healthy individuals.'[55]

Creatine consumption was just one facet of the traditional 'win at all costs' attitude in schools rugby. Young players became bigger and stronger than their predecessors. One parent interviewed by the *Sunday Tribune* in 1999 observed that 'The game is faster and more physical than it ever was and there is more emphasis on winning . . . These boys are hyped up and put out on a field. They don't have the maturity to match their weight and size and if this situation continues unchecked it will be accompanied by more and more hurt players.'[56]

All the while, as was later discovered, concussion was quietly doing its evil work on the brains of a generation of players at all levels of the game. The most likely explanation for the silence is quite simple: the persistence of an elaborate conspiracy of concealment among players, coaches, officials and, in some cases, medics. The seriousness of the situation only received sustained public attention starting in the 2010s. In Ireland, there were two high-profile concussion-related retirements in 2010, those of ex-internationals Bernard Jackman and John Fogarty. Both players gave frightening testimony about the effects of repeated blows to the head. Fogarty spoke of severe headaches and mood swings resulting from multiple concussions. Jackman admitted that he had routinely concealed concussion from coaches and medical staff, and argued that the issue was a 'ticking timebomb' and that someone was going to die on the field.

His assertion was tragically prophetic. The following year, a fourteen-year-old schoolboy, Benjamin Robinson, died after taking successive blows to the head while playing for Carrickfergus Grammar School. Though he was checked for concussion three times during the match, he was allowed to continue playing. His death was due to Second Impact Syndrome – a condition caused by consecutive concussions.[57]

We are not reliant on whispers and anecdotes to confirm the suspicion of widespread concealment of concussion among Irish rugby players. During the 2010–11 season, 45 per cent of a sample of 172 elite Irish rugby players reported suffering at least one concussion. Of these, just 47 per cent reported their injury to medical staff. The remaining 53 per cent cited lack of knowledge, unwillingness to withdraw from play, not wishing to let their team down, and, tellingly, thinking that concussion was 'part of the game' as reasons for hiding their injury.[58] Another study from 2010 found that almost three quarters of schoolboy players in Ireland would play an important match while recovering from concussion, and less than a third would voluntarily report suffering concussion symptoms.[59] Among a random sample of male and female players in Ireland in 2016, researchers found that even though 90.8 per cent of players knew they should not continue playing when concussed, 75 per cent of them would continue an important game even if concussed. Of those who had suffered concussion, 39 per cent admitted to having attempted to influence medical assessment, with 78 per cent stating it was 'possible or even quite easy to do so'.[60] This complacency was not confined to players. In 2016, there was an unedifying scene in a Leinster Schools Senior Cup match. The referee, having ordered the substitution of a Gonzaga College player who had sustained a blow to the head, was challenged by the school's medic, who was performing, according to the *Irish Times*, 'a form of HIA [Head Injury Assessment]' on the player.[61] An HIA, where a player is ordered to leave the field to have his or her cognitive state assessed by a medic, was an instrument reserved for the professional game.

The heated exchange, caught on television cameras, prompted an 'internal investigation' by the Leinster Branch, which subsequently issued a statement supporting the referee. As 'the ultimate arbiter of all games played at all levels . . . it is with he/she that any final decision rests with regard to on-field activity and this includes the removal of a player for medical reasons'.[62] The whole incident called into question the application of concussion policies at schools level, not to mention the entire schools rugby culture.

In 2009, Brendan Fanning wrote a startling article in the *Sunday Independent* exposing widespread under-reporting of concussion in Irish rugby. Players, he wrote, continued to play after sustaining blows to the head, often with the 'connivance of coaching and medical staff'.[63] One doctor told Fanning that 'there's under-reporting . . . mainly to do with getting fellas back within the three-week period'.[64] Equally troubling was another article by Fanning the following year in which he found that players were afraid to speak about concussion but admitted widespread under-reporting and deception of medics. 'One player, who is a walking time-bomb, was petrified that he will be identifiable in this article . . . Mostly he is afraid of not being picked.'[65] A doctor who worked in the AIL recalled being pressurized by teams to record concussions as different injuries so that the minimum stand-down period would not be triggered.[66]

World Rugby's answer to under-reporting of concussion was to abandon the three-week stand-down period for professional players in May 2011. From then on, players suffering concussion were obliged to withdraw from play for a minimum of six days, meaning that in some cases they could play the weekend after sustaining their injury. The logic ran that if players were faced with a shorter minimum stand-down period, they might be more willing to disclose symptoms of concussion. There was also a view that the mandatory stand-down period was not medically justified in all cases and that in elite rugby, where professional medical support was always on hand, a more nuanced, case-by-case approach could be taken to return-to-play protocols.

Barry O'Driscoll, a former Irish international, resigned from his role as a medical advisor to World Rugby in protest, claiming that the revised protocol had been introduced for 'commercial reasons'.[67] O'Driscoll was clearly voicing the suspicion that those who employed professional players were worried about getting their money's worth. Putting players back on the field as soon as possible after injury, according to this view, was prioritized over safety. Amid all of this, players allegedly continued to game the protocols, deliberately performing poorly in the preseason baseline tests, or having other players complete their return-to-play cognitive tests.[68] In 2013, the former Scotland international Rory Lamont described the dilemma professional players faced:

> Players can view the baseline test as an obstacle in their way for getting back playing. To achieve an accurate score, you must pay full attention. The conflict of interest is this: the better score you set in the baseline test, the more difficult it will it be to pass the test after concussion. Set a high score

and you might end up missing more games than you would
like . . .[69]

It seems reasonable to question how such practices were feas-
ible without the connivance of club or international personnel.

Concussion was not just a medical or 'commercial' problem, it was also a cultural one. The brute physicality of the
game was an essential part of its appeal to spectators and
the media. The game developed a culture that celebrated
'big hits'. In advance of the Ireland v. France match in 2015,
Bernard Le Roux, a member of the French team, light-
heartedly advised that Ireland out-half Johnny Sexton should
'wear a helmet'.[70] Sexton, by then, had a storied relationship
with concussion. He had been concussed on four occasions
between March and November 2014, and had been stood
down for twelve weeks by a French neurologist after the last
of these incidents (Sexton played his club rugby with Racing
92 in France at the time). Now, three months later, the French
were attempting to gain a psychological edge by playing on
Irish fears for Sexton's wellbeing. 'We should really test him
[Sexton] early on', the French coach, Philippe Saint-André,
told the press.

'The general expectation', that afternoon, according to
Keith Duggan of the *Irish Times*, was that the French would
'instruct Mathieu Bastareaud, their terrifically athletic 19-stone
centre, to come at speed . . . and crash through Sexton'. This
was after former French international Laurent Bénézech told
the press that Bastareaud running at Sexton would be the 'first
way France will use the ball'.[71] Another part of the context
for these comments was an incident in the previous season's
fixture between the two sides when Sexton had been (legally)
knocked out cold by Bastareaud.

'There is something bleak and reductive', Duggan commented, about Bastareaud being called upon to 'lower his shoulder and charge into Ireland's number 10 again and again'. But he also conceded that 'Rugby is a brutally raw contest. That is what makes these afternoons so compelling.'[72] The prospect of a clash between Sexton and Bastareaud was captivating for some, the kind of subplot that the media tends to create around sporting contests. As it happened, Sexton was left with an injured eye after a heavy tackle from Bastareaud, an incident that might have attracted a red card had it happened two years later.

Throughout the 2010s, journalists such as Gerry Thornley, Gavin Cummiskey and Brendan Fanning repeatedly drew attention to the concussion crisis in rugby. In 2015, an award-winning documentary, *Hidden Impact: Concussion in Rugby*, was broadcast on RTÉ. Among a number of contributors was former international Ronan O'Gara, who made the disturbing admission that he played much of the 2003 Rugby World Cup quarter-final with seriously impaired vision, the result of a concussion sustained in the match.[73]

Concussion became more difficult to conceal. Lingering, slow-motion camera shots vividly captured any player dazed or unsteady on their feet. These could be clipped, shared on social media and reach vast audiences quickly. Any gaps in the concussion protocols would therefore be exposed. In June 2022, for example, New Zealand Rugby issued a statement admitting that after a review of match day HIA protocols, Ireland prop Jeremy Loughman was mistakenly allowed to return, despite showing clear symptoms of concussion in a match against the Maori All Blacks in Hamilton. A widely shared and disturbing clip of Loughman attempting, and failing, to get to his feet was a stark indictment of those responsible for player welfare that night.

From 2017, World Rugby began to act decisively, through rule changes, to minimize the sorts of incidents most likely to cause concussion. By then, it was too late for many. As early as 2015, solicitors speculated that there could be legal trouble down the road for the rugby authorities, especially if it came to light that they were aware of the game's dangers and did not introduce reforms in a timely fashion.[74]

Head injuries in rugby had been litigated in the Irish courts as early as 1998, when a rugby player in Cork was awarded IR£125,000 by the High Court after sustaining serious head injuries while playing in 1990. Having taken a blow to the head during a match in March, he returned to play eighteen days later and received another head injury, causing brain damage. He won his case on the basis that he should not have been selected to play less than twenty-one days after the initial injury, as was then mandated by the laws of the game.[75]

Lucas Neville, a former schoolboy at St Michael's in Dublin, was awarded €2.75 million in 2014. He suffered permanent brain damage after sustaining an injury in a match in 2009 that took place seventeen days after he received a blow to the head in training. Again, the mandatory twenty-one days had not been observed.

These cases were harbingers of the great crisis that would engulf the game as the third decade of the twenty-first century dawned. In 2020, a group of former professional rugby players, all diagnosed with early-onset dementia, issued legal proceedings against World Rugby. In 2022, three Irish players, Declan Fitzpatrick, David Corkery and Ben Marshall, sued the provinces they had played for, the IRFU and World Rugby over the lasting effects of head injuries. They were among

250 players in both the UK and Ireland expected to join the lawsuit.[76] By then, the glib phrase 'he puts his head where it hurts', so often uttered to signal the virtue of a courageous player, had disappeared from rugby's lexicon.

12. Rugby country

In 2011, Guinness launched a marketing campaign called 'This is Rugby Country'. A television advert depicted Irish rugby fans in their various places of work: the crew of a fishing trawler, fire brigade staff, farmers, office cleaners, laboratory assistants. The message was clear: rugby in the twenty-first century was an inclusive sport that brought the nation together, irrespective of class.

The claim that Ireland was 'rugby country' drew derision from some commentators. In 2012, the hurler Donal Óg Cusack wrote, 'This is Rugby Country? Not the part of the country I came from anyway. We should be careful or we might be convinced that it is.'[1] In 2019, Philip Lanigan, in the *Irish Daily Mail*, described the campaign as a 'brilliantly devised fiction'.[2] By then, Vodafone, Ireland main sponsors, were running a 'Team of Us' campaign, aiming to convey a similar message to Guinness's, though in a slightly subtler way.

This was all just the exuberance one expects from sponsors, but the idea that rugby had become the national game occasionally cropped up in mainstream media. On RTÉ television's rugby magazine programme *Against the Head* in March 2018, the host Daire O'Brien, reflecting on the game's new-found status in Ireland, told his panel, 'Arguably it's the people's game.' He later added, 'There are people who wouldn't have an opinion on an All-Ireland hurling or football final or a soccer international, but they will have an opinion on and be engaged with this, it's absolutely throughout society.' When RTÉ posted a clip of the discussion on social media, 'The ensuing debate left the Civil War looking like a minor scrap', Mary Hannigan observed in her satirical *Irish Times* column.[3] Later that month, after Ireland secured the Grand Slam, Neil Francis told readers of his *Sunday Independent* column that 'rugby suits the Irish psyche and its attraction and success have more than just caught the imagination. We are now following suit with New Zealand in welcoming it as our national game.'[4]

The question of rugby's closeness to the national pulse bubbled away as a source of debate in the years that followed. In advance of the 2023 Rugby World Cup, Malachy Clerkin wrote a witty article in the *Irish Times* which included the following plea: 'Please, rugby. Don't ruin the Rugby World Cup for the rest of us. The country is genuinely excited for the next seven weeks but the more you claim rugby as the most popular sport in Ireland, the less goodwill you'll find around the place. Do. Not. Do. It.'[5] Though Clerkin did not specify who 'rugby' was, he was gently pushing back against the kind of nebulous hype that the team tended to generate during tournaments, hype that invariably led to backlash on social media.

When Ireland were eliminated from the World Cup at the quarter-final stage, dismay was expressed in newspaper columns at the apparent pleasure taken by some Irish people at the team's demise. Reflecting on the social media reaction, Johnny Watterson told readers of the *Irish Times* that

> The exultation and exuberance that greeted a defeat to New Zealand that had Ireland packing their bags in Paris was something to behold. There were elements of highlighting the school you went to, the fact that mainly former British

colonies play the sport and stuff about Mack Hansen, Jamison Gibson-Park and Bundee Aki not being Irish anyway – the blood-and-soil keyboard ideologues being such a busy bunch.[6]

Rugby's critics had a point. There was, for example, some validity in the idea that a game as elitist as rugby could never be representative of the nation. One of the five pillars of the 'Spirit of Rugby' as outlined in the IRFU's Strategic Plan 2018–23 was 'Inclusivity'. This was the usual paint-by-numbers equality statement that most organizations of any importance committed themselves to, officially at least. The document stated that 'Rugby is a sport of choice for all, it transcends differences of race, gender, religion and sexual orientation.' The absence of social class from this list of social forces that rugby transcends – whether conscious or not – was telling.[7]

In 2017, John O'Sullivan of the *Irish Times* analysed the school backgrounds of the previous one hundred players to have been capped for Ireland (a period that stretched back to 2006), and determined that, of those who were educated in Ireland, 56 per cent had attended fee-paying schools.[8] O'Sullivan failed to note that just 9 per cent of Irish schoolboys attended fee-paying schools in 2006 and this had dropped to 8 per cent by 2017.[9] And if the 56 per cent figure for rugby internationals was lower than it would have been a generation earlier, it is not clear that it represents a fundamental and ongoing shift. When Ireland played their final game of the 2022 Six Nations, every single Irish-born player selected to start, apart from Iain Henderson, had attended a fee-paying school.

A lingering sense of entitlement associated with the schools game was not good for rugby's profile. When the 2020

Leinster Schools Senior Cup final – between Clongowes and Newbridge College – was cancelled due to the Covid-19 pandemic, a petition appeared on change.org demanding that the match should go ahead. The petition, which also favoured the staging of the Junior Cup final, stated:

> All four finalist teams and all those associated with their respective schools are disappointed and outraged. There is no reason whatsoever why these games should not be held behind closed doors to determine a winner . . . This is a matter of great pride for all those involved with the respective schools – not to mention the biggest match of a lot of these players' careers, should they be a sixth-year student. We, therefore, demand the finals to be played at some point in the future.[10]

Johnny Watterson, poking fun at the petition's absurdity, alerted *Irish Times* readers to the comparative triviality of the Schools Cup by listing all the major international sports events that had been cancelled due to Covid-19 restrictions.

One could be forgiven for thinking that the petition was just a tasteless hoax. But this issue was, remarkably, given oxygen in the Oireachtas. In July, a member of the Seanad, Vincent P. Martin, addressed the house pleading for the match to be rescheduled. 'These children, or young adults, gave six years of their lives to this . . . It would be the highlight of their young sporting lives . . .They have worked for six years to get to the promised land and have their moment in the sun. The pandemic has ripped it away from them. It is late but perhaps it is not too late. Could the IRFU look at this again to see if it is possible to put on the match? It would make many families, the teams and supporters so happy if we could defeat the pandemic this way.'[11] The idea that a rugby match between thirty privileged young men could somehow symbolize 'defeating' the pandemic was clearly daft. It was as though he believed these were the only young people denied landmark sporting opportunities on account of the pandemic. Martin made his speech during a month when GAA fields across the country would typically hum with the activity of tens of thousands of children. But those fields, too, had fallen silent.

The idea that rugby was laced with entitlement also featured in commentary on the rape trial in 2018 of Ireland internationals Stuart Olding and Paddy Jackson. Two further men also faced trial, one for indecent exposure and one for perverting the course of justice.

The proceedings attracted vast media coverage and were highly divisive. The complainant was subject to prolonged and arduous cross-examination over eight days, prompting outrage. At the beginning of the cross-examination, Ireland internationals Rory Best and Iain Henderson travelled from Dublin, where Ireland had a day off from preparations for that weekend's match in France, to attend proceedings. The players' presence gave the impression to some that rugby was merely a boys' club closing ranks, and Best, the Ireland captain, became the focus of a considerable public backlash.[12] By then the defendants' group text-message exchanges had been aired in court, revealing a stark undercurrent of misogyny and laddish excess that led to widespread revulsion. In the post-match press conference after victory in Paris, Best told reporters, 'The reason I was there, it's on the record I was called as a character witness, and I was advised that it is important that I got both sides of the story so I could make an informed decision about that.'[13] Of Best's decision, Gavin

Cummiskey of the *Irish Times* later wrote, 'Naivety, loyalty or something else, the decision was always going to be a calculated risk. It backfired spectacularly.'[14] Best subsequently expressed regret for attending. 'I didn't really understand the complexity of the situation', he would write. 'It was incredibly naïve of me.'[15]

After the defendants were acquitted, rallies were held in cities across Ireland in a show of solidarity with the complainant, and there was a picket outside Ravenhill, where several hundred women demanded that Ulster Rugby 'stamp out misogyny'.[16] Jackson and Olding were duly sacked by Ulster Rugby and the IRFU, having been suspended since being charged in the summer of 2017.

The dismissal of the players prompted another backlash. A full-page advert in newspapers, signed 'Real fans standing up for the Ulster men', asserted that Olding and Jackson had been the victims of 'cyber persecution', and that 'a silent majority' wanted the players reinstated.[17] A petition demanding their reinstatement attracted 17,000 signatures.

The journalist Susan McKay, seeking the views of rugby fans in Belfast after the trial,

heard from men who believed in a brotherhood rooted in loyalty. For some it was a physical thing. 'You've put your body on the line for these guys. You've taken injuries. You've got caked in mud together. You've bathed together', said one man. 'And then you get cute wee girls coming up to you.' . . . Some of the men spoke of a 'rugby culture' that included 'good craic' initiations like: 'running about naked or with a toilet roll on your willie, turning up bollock naked in shops . . .'. They spoke of 'girls who liked "sports rodeos"'. They spoke of '"Ulster rugby sluts".'[18]

In the first pre-match press conference after the trial, which came days after the players were sacked, questions on the fallout from the affair were tersely shut down. The Branch, seemingly determined to give a masterclass in bad PR, banned news journalists from attending future press conferences, limiting invitations to sports reporters. Jilly Beattie from the *Daily Mirror* pointed out that 'This story had been naturally running its natural course and news and news consumers were moving on. But Ulster Rugby's decision to ban certain reporters from news conferences delivered a ridiculous, senseless and needless own goal.'[19]

This was not the first time that a criminal trial involving rugby players became a media circus. In 2000, eighteen-year-old Brian Murphy died from injuries sustained after a fight outside Anabel's nightclub in Dublin. When it became apparent that the four young men charged in relation to the death had attended Blackrock College, a predictable media frenzy ensued. The fact that some of the men charged had played for the Blackrock Senior Cup team was noted in most press coverage of the trial, which took place in 2004. Writing in the *Sunday Independent*, which carried four pages of coverage of the trial's outcome, Julia Molony observed that 'southside Dublin has been forced to turn the eye of scrutiny homewards, to examine whether a dark side lurks beneath the genteel accents and polished manners of the private school set'.[20]

An altogether happier symbol of rugby's place in Irish society came from an unexpected source: the GAA. Changes to the GAA's rules signalled a more tolerant attitude to sports the Association's ideologues once derided. The GAA's outright ban on 'foreign' sports had disappeared in 1971. Then, in 2005, the GAA decided to depart from more than a century of tradition by amending Rule 42, thus allowing rugby and soccer fixtures to be staged in Croke Park.

This was no trivial change. Croke Park was a powerfully symbolic sports venue. It was here in November 1920 that Crown forces indiscriminately opened fire on players and spectators at a Gaelic football match, killing fourteen people on a day soon memorialized as Bloody Sunday. Preserving the ground for Gaelic games alone had long been an article of faith for many GAA members. It was as though opening the stadium to sports like rugby and soccer – both crudely referred to as 'Garrison Games' – would have somehow besmirched those killed on Bloody Sunday.

In the second half of the 1990s, a programme of re-development was undertaken at Croke Park that would make the stadium one of the largest in Europe. With the project being part-funded by the government, the GAA came under moral pressure to relax their rules about the playing of non-Gaelic sports at the ground. Some of that pressure came from within. The GAA had always been a deceptively broad church, accommodating both diehards, who saw as sacrilege any accommodation of 'foreign' sports, and moderates, who were much less committed to exclusionary rules. Motions from various counties favouring the opening up of Croke Park to soccer and rugby internationals were submitted to the GAA's annual congress from time to time without success.

The consequences for those who did not observe the rules were harsh. In 1992, Clifden GAA club in County Galway were suspended from the Association after their grounds were used for a Connacht Senior Cup rugby match. When an investigation found that it was club trustees and not officers who had allowed the transgression, the suspension was lifted. In 1994, the An Tóchar club in Wicklow was suspended when officials gave permission to a group of under-11 soccer players to have a game of indoor five-a-side in the local community hall. As the hall was vested in the GAA, An Tóchar had breached Rule 42. The suspension was lifted only when the club resolved not to allow the soccer-playing children – hardly devious agents of British imperialism – to use the facilities thereafter.[21]

All of this made the GAA look small-minded and insular. When Limerick GAA official Noel Drumgoole sought an amendment to Rule 42 that would allow a soccer international to be played in the city's Gaelic Grounds in 1990, it was heavily defeated on the floor at congress. *Irish Independent* reporter Donal Keenan responded scathingly, 'No logic is applied to the arguments against allowing soccer to be played on GAA grounds, while the anti-soccer brigade remains silent when American football, stunt-driving, boxing, and concerts are held.'[22] In 1993, Mooncoin GAA club fell foul of Rule 42 when their efforts to stage a charity soccer match at their grounds were blocked by the Kilkenny County Board. The spurned organizer referred to the rules as 'selfish' and 'silly'. He continued, 'I thought as members of the European Community and about to enter the 21st century, that the GAA would look at it and say we'll move to the next generation.'[23]

Rule 42 had been an occasional source of embarrassment to the GAA. In the aftermath of the Real IRA bomb attack on Omagh in 1998, for example, the GAA's Central Council were forced by their own rulebook to block a fundraising soccer match involving Manchester United from taking place at the town's GAA grounds, Healy Park.[24] Because the GAA's grounds policy was underpinned by written rules, no official had it within their gift to permit soccer or rugby matches in GAA facilities on an *ad hoc* basis. Any changes to these rules required democratic endorsement from the grassroots. And this could only be achieved through a majority vote at the GAA's annual congress.

The IRFU were decidedly more liberal when it came to their facilities. The Union had granted use of Lansdowne Road to many external events and organizations throughout the ground's history. Before they purchased the site in 1932, the IRFU would seek permission from their landlord, Lord Pembroke, to host events other than rugby there. A standing condition seems to have been that no drink should be served at the ground.[25] The Catholic Truth Society held a military tattoo at Lansdowne Road in 1928, the Catholic Emancipation Centenary Committee were welcomed in 1929 and the Eucharistic Congress were accommodated in 1930.[26] One can only imagine the private thoughts of some IRFU committee members as they acceded to these decisions, their noses firmly clenched between their fingertips. But there was a limit to what the Union were willing to tolerate. They declined permission to the Legion of Irish Ex-Servicemen to hold a ladies' soccer match on the ground in 1924, noting that 'we could not give the ground for a ladies match'.[27] The same year, permission was also denied to Sandymount Schools to hold a soccer match on the ground, the Union committee stating that 'we could not give the ground for a "soccer" match'. Soccer, a professional sport, might lower the tone in Ballsbridge, all the more sharply if women played it.

In 1949, the Union received a letter from Albert Freethy, the secretary of Neath RFC – one of the great clubs of the South Wales coalfield – who wondered if his club should grant the request of a local priest to host a Gaelic football match on their grounds. Specifically, Freethy needed assurance that there was no professionalism tolerated in the GAA; he also noted that the Welsh rugby authorities had advised him that the IRFU were not well disposed to Gaelic games. In reply, the IRFU told Freethy, with more than a hint of sanctimony, that

> It is incorrect to state that the IRFU do not look favourably upon Gaelic football, suggesting some prejudice on our part that does not exist. That form of football is quite distinct from Rugby and, so far as we are concerned, both codes can exist side by side in harmony. Accordingly we have no general reason to discourage your club from allowing Gaelic football to be played on its pitch. We would not discriminate unfairly against any amateur game that gives healthy exercise to youth and is properly conducted.[28]

The issue of 'foreign' games being played on GAA grounds was brought to a head by the necessity to redevelop Lansdowne Road in the early years of the twenty-first century. The sight of neo-Nazi England football fans flinging flimsily secured benches from the top tier of the old West Stand during a soccer friendly in 1995 was striking evidence of how rickety the old ground had become. After considering various options for a new multi-purpose stadium in Dublin – including the building of new grounds at Abbotstown, a proposal then seen by many as a vanity project of the Taoiseach, Bertie Ahern – the decision was taken to build a new stadium on the Lansdowne Road site. For the duration of this project, the Ireland rugby and soccer teams would be homeless. The spotlight of public debate was immediately fixed on the GAA.

Amid growing public debate in 2001 about the need for a new national stadium, a motion favouring the amendment of Rule 42 failed to achieve the required two-thirds majority at the GAA's congress by just a single vote.[29] When the

FAI submitted a bid to UEFA to co-host the 2008 European Championship, the government, hoping to bolster this endeavour, attempted to strongarm the GAA into easing Rule 42. The Association, in turn, refused to even discuss the possibility of doing so at their Special Congress in 2002.

By 2005, though, the context had changed. It was one thing to deny the use of Croke Park to a largely pie-in-the-sky bid to host a football tournament – the bid was partly predicated on a new national stadium in Dublin that the government coalition partners, Fianna Fáil and the Progressive Democrats, had not even agreed to build, and were publicly at odds with each other over. It was an entirely different matter to potentially prevent the national soccer and rugby teams from hosting home fixtures in Ireland for several seasons. Indeed, the vision of home internationals in both codes being played abroad was evoked by elements within the GAA campaigning for change.[30] The Association too evolved. By 2005, they had dispensed with Rule 21, which had prevented members of the British Army and the Northern Ireland police from joining the Association. With continued economic progress and a strengthening peace in Northern Ireland, Irish society continued to move away from the rigid conservatism of old. In that context, the GAA's exclusionary rules looked entirely anachronistic.

An *Irish Independent* poll in early 2005 found that eight out of ten Irish people favoured the opening up of Croke Park.[31] The same poll found that more than half of the public would favour the withdrawal of public funding from the GAA if Croke Park remained closed.[32] A month later, the GAA's own marketing committee told the organization that though Croke Park 'exemplifies the best of a new Ireland, there is a distinct danger that attitudes towards its use could depict the GAA in a very negative light . . . old-fashioned, political and redo-lent of an older Ireland'.[33] The matter eventually came before the GAA's congress and, with the energetic support of the Association's president, Seán Kelly, Rule 42 was amended. Specifically, the amendment gave the GAA's Central Council the power to grant the use of Croke Park to soccer and rugby for the duration of the renovation works at Lansdowne Road.

Delegates from the great majority of counties favoured opening Croke Park, but the North was a different story. Here, among nationalists, loyalty to GAA traditions directly related to nationalism was more intense than elsewhere. All six of the Ulster counties north of the border were opposed to amend-ing Rule 42. 'It is our stadium and it should remain exclusive to the GAA', one official stated.[34] The only Southern county to vote against the amendment was Cork, which had a reputa-tion for rebellion to uphold.

And so it was that, on 11 February 2007, the visiting French provided the opposition for Ireland's first match at Croke Park. A couple of weeks later England were the visitors. This was an intensely emotional occasion. Irish players openly wept when singing the national anthem, while 'God Save the Queen' was greeted with respectful silence. Ireland won the match comfortably, and afterwards the country gave itself a pat on the back. The entire occasion was seen as emblematic of a nation growing up, of a decisive break with the enmities of the past. A beaming editorial in the *Irish Independent* told readers that 'The glorious happenings at Croke Park were more than a symptom of the gradual healing that carries us further and further away from the bloody days in these islands. They were an affirmation of the triumph of the human spirits over mean-mindedness.'[35] Though the commentary was perhaps slightly overwrought, it was difficult to gainsay the symbolic power of the event. The only discord came from a few dozen republican protestors who picketed Croke Park. Among them was a young man who carried a placard bearing the slogan 'No to foreign games'. His grasp of irony clearly weak, he was wearing a Glasgow Celtic soccer shirt.

One of the most striking features of the new Ireland that emerged in the early 2000s was the reversal of decades of outward migration. Ireland began to attract migrants in considerable numbers. Irish rugby, like other industries, benefited from the arrival of skilled workers from overseas. This phenomenon was not limited to Ireland. From 1995 onwards, there was a sudden acceleration of player mobility as an international transfer market took shape. A notable pattern was the migration of southern hemisphere players to clubs in Europe.

Scotland – rarely rugby trailblazers – won the Five Nations Championship in 1999 with a team featuring four New Zealanders of Scottish descent: the 'Kilted Kiwis' as they become known. Two of these – John and Martin Leslie – were the sons of former All Black captain Andy Leslie. It seems likely that the Leslie brothers, who were classy enough operators in the northern hemisphere, would have stayed in New Zealand if an All Black call-up was even a remote possibility. There was a suspicion among some that the European nations were becoming havens for southern hemisphere journeymen with little hope of earning selection for the country that they were born in.

Ireland was no exception. Michael Bent, a New Zealand-born prop who was entitled to an Irish passport through his grandmother, landed in Ireland in 2012 and literally made straight for Carton House to join the Ireland rugby squad, which was suffering a shortage of tightheads. Leinster had groped around the international transfer market looking for Ireland-eligible players, and were directed towards Bent by an agent. In a clumsy attempt to assuage potential public concerns about the nature of Bent's selection, the new Ireland squad member was photographed with a hurley and sliotar during his first Ireland training session.[36]

Bent, like the Kilted Kiwis, qualified for his new country by ancestry. But unlike other international sports, there was no requirement in rugby union for international players to have ancestral links with the nation that they represented. This was a longstanding convention in international rugby. Once a player lived in a country for three years (extended to five years from 2020), they became eligible for international selection there, irrespective of ancestry, provided they had not represented their native country at senior level.

In Ireland, this became a matter of public debate from the early 2010s, when the IRFU began actively recruiting young foreign players for the provinces with the view to potentially selecting them for the international team once they had satisfied the residency requirements. In 2010, Munster signed Peter Borlase, a prop from New Zealand. That summer Borlase told reporters that he was signing as a 'special project player'.[37] (This seems to have been the first use of a term later shortened to 'project player'.) He was given a two-year contract, and Munster had an option for a third – after which he would be Irish-qualified. But Borlase made hardly any impact and Munster did not exercise their option for a third season.

There was never any intention to flood the provinces with foreign-born players. From 2012, the IRFU introduced a 'four plus one' policy: the provinces were permitted a maximum of five non-Irish players each, at least one of whom had to be uncapped at international level (and thus eligible to play for Ireland after three years). There were also strict limitations on the number of non-Irish players permitted in each position. Richardt Strauss, a hooker from South Africa, has sometimes been described as the first project player to represent Ireland – he was capped seventeen times, starting in 2012. But he joined Leinster on a one-year contract in 2009, apparently before the programme had been conceived, and nothing was made of Strauss's potential future eligibility for Ireland when he signed. By late 2010, however, he was demonstrating his class, and journalists routinely referred to him as a 'project player'.

This provoked a minor nativist backlash from commentators. A very loosely articulated sense that the policy somehow undermined the value of international caps was accompanied by the argument that young Irish-born players might have their progress stymied by mercenary imports. Of the prospect of Borlase and Strauss gaining Irish caps, John O'Brien, in the *Sunday Independent* in 2010, wrote, 'It is hard to escape the feeling that something precious will be lost the day that happens.'[38]

Players such as C. J. Stander and Bundee Aki exemplified what critics of the residency criteria were concerned about. Stander, who did not speak English well when he came to Ireland in 2012, had been told by South African coaches that he was too small to play for his native country. Aki, a New Zealander of Samoan heritage, had hinted that the comparatively generous salary on offer in Ireland had encouraged him to move to Connacht in 2014. These players were only doing what other ambitious players did: pursuing international rugby and trying to make a decent living. But some critics seemed to find these motives suspect in players who didn't come from Ireland.

Neil Francis, writing in the *Irish Independent* in 2017, made Aki the main focus of a broadside against 'project players':

> He will play for Ireland this November – he will be able to do so because he could hop on an airplane and fly 18,000 kilometres to a place he had never really heard of, stay there for 36 months and get to play international rugby – a level of rugby which he had no chance of playing at in New Zealand. We seem to be quite happy to accommodate him in his quest to play international [sic] for 'somebody'. . . We watch in glib fascination as the IRFU hand out jerseys which represent our island to well-paid tourists – some of whom know the words of 'Amhrán na bhFiann' and some who don't.[39]

In some cases, players who qualified for Ireland through ancestry came from similar distances, and were similarly unfamiliar with the national anthem; but those eligible through ancestry did not receive the same level of scrutiny as those who, having been born abroad, were picked for Ireland after only three years with a province. Little was made, for example, of the selection for Ireland in the 2020s of Kieran Treadwell and Billy Burns, both of whom played at underage level for England. Indeed, Burns's brother Freddie played for England at senior level, winning five caps.

Ireland's selection of 'project players' drew criticism from elsewhere. In advance of the 2023 World Cup quarter-final, the rugby journalist Gregor Paul wrote in the *New Zealand Herald* that 'The label on the All Blacks' . . . opponents says Ireland, but it would be more accurate if it said "assembled and finished in Ireland".' He claimed that a third of the team had been developed in the southern hemisphere, including the supposedly South African Josh van der Flier.[40] This would have been news to van der Flier, who was born and raised in Ireland. Paul's article was a genre-defining exhibition of hypocrisy. The New Zealand World Cup squad included three Tongan-born players, a Samoan and a Fijian. The All Blacks had been asset-stripping the Pacific Islands for decades, and some of New Zealand's greatest players had but the most tenuous links with the country. The scintillating full-back and 1987 World Cup winner John Gallagher grew up in London to Irish parents. His only connection with New Zealand was the relatively short period of his young adulthood that he spent there. He was capped for Ireland 'A' (the second-choice XV) towards the end of a glittering career. By any orthodox measure, Ireland had a greater claim over Gallagher than New Zealand.

The point here is that Ireland, in selecting players on residency grounds, were following the rules of international rugby and were in good company. Literally every other major rugby-playing country had done it. By the time the 2023 Rugby World Cup came around, three of Ireland's six backs had qualified on residency grounds and a fourth – Mack Hansen, who played for Australia at underage level – qualified through his Irish mother. By then, commentators seemed less exercised about the issue. The positive contribution of 'project players' was now obvious. A powerful illustration of this came at Twickenham in 2018, where Ireland arrived for their final championship match of the season looking to secure the Grand Slam. In the twenty-fourth minute, Aki's footwork and pace carved open the English defence before he delivered a brilliant inside pass to the onrushing Stander to score Ireland's second try in a comprehensive win. It is highly unlikely that questions about Aki's and Stander's Irishness featured prominently in conversations among celebrating Irish fans that night.

In any case, Irishness in a rugby sense was always a protean, shape-shifting affair, and Ireland had a long history of selecting players who were not Irish. In the pre-independence period, several Englishmen who, through professional or educational commitments, lived in Ireland for a time, ended up wearing the green jersey. Basil Maclear, one of Ireland's greatest pre-war players and World Rugby Hall of Fame inductee, was English plain and simple. He was deemed not good enough to play for his native country, but a military posting to County Cork gave Maclear the opportunity to gain selection for Munster and then Ireland, with whom he earned eleven caps. Now, in the twenty-first century, players such as Stander and Aki showed an earnest commitment, not just to the Irish shirt, but to life in Ireland and to the communities they became part of.

Rugby, there seems little doubt, occupied a more prominent place in Irish life in the twenty-first century than ever before. This was borne out by television viewing figures. In 2022, four of the ten most viewed television programmes in the Republic of Ireland were Six Nations fixtures.[41] In 2023, Ireland's World Cup quarter-final drew a television audience of close to 1.5 million and 78 per cent of those watching television in Ireland at that time were tuned into the match.[42]

This upward trend commenced in the early 2000s. Viewers were not only treated to the action on the field but enjoyed colourful analysis as well. RTÉ put together a panel of analysts to rival their legendary soccer equivalent. The host, Tom McGurk, was a suave, slightly irreverent journalist from Northern Ireland. He was joined by an eccentric Corkman, George Hook, who came to broadcasting late having been, by his own admission, a highly unsuccessful businessman.

His fellow analyst was a New Zealander, Brent Pope. Calm, amiable and fair-minded, Pope was the perfect foil for Hook's cantankerous shtick. For some, television viewing figures proved nothing. When Ireland's Six Nations fixture against France in 2018 was the most watched sporting event in Ireland that year, one noisy critic reasoned that 'rather than highlight rugby's popularity, it pointed to its fickle, bandwagoning nature'.[43] In this view, evidence of rugby's popularity served only as proof of its unpopularity.

Bandwagon-jumping is less an intrinsic feature of Irish rugby than it is a completely normal human tendency. Even if there was some truth to this criticism of Ireland's relationship with rugby, the more salient fact is that the provinces and the national team had made the game an exhilarating bandwagon to mount: something that would have seemed fairly unlikely for most of the game's history here. The genius of Irish rugby was that once a player pulled on the green jersey or a fan donned a green and white scarf, the 'Ireland' that he or she represented or supported was at once both a shared national idea and a matter of personal conviction.

Select bibliography

Archival sources

Irish Rugby Football Union

IRFU Committee Minutes
Miscellaneous letters

Munster Branch IRFU

Munster Branch Committee Minutes

National Archives of Ireland

Department of the Taoiseach
Department of Foreign Affairs
Office of the President of Ireland

Blackrock College Archives

College register
College ledgers
Community journal

University College Dublin Archives

Leinster Branch records

Cork City Archives

Cork Constitution Football Club minutes

Bureau of Military History

Witness statement, Dr Patrick O'Sullivan
Witness statement, Francis O'Duffy

Newspapers and periodicals

An Phoblacht
Belfast News Letter
Belfast Telegraph
Bell's Life
Belvederian, The
Blue, White and Blue
Castleknock College Chronicle
Church of Ireland Gazette
Clare Champion
Connacht Sentinel
Cork Constitution
Cork Daily Herald
Cork Examiner
Cork Weekly Examiner
Daily Telegraph
Derry Journal
Donegal News
Drogheda Argus
Dublin Daily Express
Dublin Evening Telegraph

Dundalk Democrat
Dundee Evening Telegraph
Evening Echo
Evening Herald
Evening Press
Field, The
Freeman's Journal
Frontier Sentinel
Guardian
Hampshire Advertiser and Southampton Times
Independent (London)
Ireland's Saturday Night
Irish Christian Advocate
Irish Examiner
Irish Independent
Irish News
Irish People
Irish Press
Irish Times
Kerry News
Kerry Sentinel
Kildare Observer
Limerick Chronicle
Limerick Leader
Meath Chronicle
Munster News
Nationalist and Leinster Times
Northern Whig
Our School Times
Roscommon Messenger
Rugby Ireland
Saunders News-Letter and Daily Advertiser

Scottish Referee
Skibbereen Eagle
Sligo Chronicle
Sport
Sporting Life
St Andrew's College Magazine
Strabane Chronicle
Sunday Business Post
Sunday Independent
Sunday Life
Sunday Press
Sunday Tribune
Sunday World
Tallaght Echo
Ulster Examiner
United Ireland
United Irishman
Warder and Dublin Weekly Mail
Weekly Irish Times
Young Ireland

Official publications and works of reference

Shaun Boylan, 'Barrington, Sir Charles Burton', *Dictionary of Irish Biography*
Census of Ireland 1891: General Report
Cheltenham College Register, 1841–1889
Terry Clavin, 'Doyle, Mick', *Dictionary of Irish Biography*
Pauric J. Dempsey and Shaun Boylan, 'Arnott, Sir John', *Dictionary of Irish Biography*
Department of Education, Statistical Bulletin, July 2021

Irish Civil Records
Linde Lunney, 'Foster, Alexander Roulston', *Dictionary of Irish Biography*
Desmond McCabe, 'Galbraith, Joseph Allen', *Dictionary of Irish Biography*
Liam O'Callaghan, 'Kyle, Jack', *Dictionary of Irish Biography*
Turlough O'Riordan, 'Bulger, Lawrence Quinlivan', *Dictionary of
    Irish Biography*
Parliamentary Debates Dáil Éireann
*Return of Number of Roman Catholic Students on books of Trinity College,
    Dublin, July 1877*, House of Commons Papers, no. 449
Jim Shanahan, 'Peter, Richard Milliken', *Dictionary of Irish Biography*

Journal articles/book chapters

Douglas Booth, 'Hitting apartheid for six? The politics of the
    South African sports boycott', *Journal of Contemporary History*,
    vol. 38, no. 3 (2003), pp. 477–93
T. W. Buford, R. B. Kreider, J. R. Stout, M. Greenwood, B. Campbell,
    M. Spano, T. Ziegenfuss, H. Lopez, J. Landis and J. Antonio,
    'International Society of Sports Nutrition position stand: cre-
    atine supplementation and exercise', *Journal of the International
    Society of Sports Nutrition*, vol. 4, no. 1 (2007), pp. 1–8
Mike Cronin, 'Playing away from home: identity in Northern
    Ireland and the experience of Derry City Football Club', *National
    Identities*, vol. 2, no. 1 (2000), pp. 65–79
———, '"Trinity mysteries": responding to a chaotic reading of
    Irish history', *International Journal of the History of Sport*, vol. 28,
    no. 18 (2011), pp. 2753–60
S. E. Delahunty, E. Delahunt, B. Condon, D. Toomey and C. Blake,
    'Prevalence of and attitudes about concussion in Irish schools'
    rugby union players', *Journal of School Health*, vol. 85, no. 1 (2015),
    pp. 17–26

M. Fraas, G. F. Coughlan, E. C. Hart and C. McCarthy, 'Concussion history and reporting rates in elite Irish rugby union players', *Physical Therapy in Sport*, vol. 15, no. 3 (2014), pp. 136–42

Marcus Free, '"Smart, clued-in guys": Irish rugby players as sporting celebrities in post-Celtic Tiger Irish media', *International Journal of Media & Cultural Politics*, vol. 14, no. 2 (2018), pp. 215–32

J. Gibney, 'PALS – The Irish at Gallipoli', *History Ireland*, vol. 23, no. 3 (2015), pp. 50–51

N. E. Hill, S. Rilstone, M. J. Stacey, D. Amiras, S. Chew, D. Flatman and N. S. Oliver, 'Changes in northern hemisphere male international rugby union players' body mass and height between 1955 and 2015', *BMJ Open Sport & Exercise Medicine*, vol. 4 (2018) https:// bmjopensem.bmj.com/content/bmjosem/4/1/e000459.full.pdf

H. A. Hinkson, 'Education in Ireland, Catholic and Protestant', *Westminster Review* (July 1895), pp. 80–87

Martin Johnes, 'A Prince, a King, and a referendum: rugby, politics, and nationhood in Wales, 1969–1979', *Journal of British Studies*, vol. 47, no. 1 (2008), pp. 129–48

T. Lodge, 'An "boks amach": the Irish Anti-Apartheid Movement', *History Ireland*, vol. 14, no. 4 (2006), pp. 35–9

E. Morris, '"God Save the King" versus "The Soldier's Song": the 1929 Trinity College national anthem dispute and the politics of the Irish Free State', *Irish Historical Studies*, vol. 31, no. 121 (1998), pp. 72–90

W. J. Mullaly, 'Concussion', *American Journal of Medicine*, vol. 130, no. 8 (2017), pp. 885–92

Liam O'Callaghan, 'Rugby football and identity politics in Free State Ireland', *Éire–Ireland*, vol. 48, no. 1 (2013), pp. 148–67

——, 'Irish rugby and the First World War', *Sport in Society*, vol. 19, no. 1 (2016), pp. 95–109

E. O'Connell and M. G. Molloy, 'Concussion in rugby: knowledge and attitudes of players', *Irish Journal of Medical Science*, no. 185

(2016), pp. 521–8

Vic Rigby and Liam O'Callaghan, 'The Riddle of Ravenhill', in M. Ní Fhuartháin and D. M. Doyle (eds.), *Ordinary Irish Life: Music, Sport and Culture* (Newbridge, Irish Academic Press, 2013), pp. 98–113

Paul Rouse, 'The politics of culture and sport in Ireland: a history of the GAA ban on foreign games, 1884–1971. Part one: 1884–1921', *International Journal of the History of Sport*, vol. 10, no. 3 (1993), pp. 333–60

J. M. Ryan and R. McQuillan, 'A survey of rugby injuries attending an accident & emergency department', *Irish Medical Journal*, vol. 85, no. 2 (1992), pp. 72–3

M. J. Shelly, J. S. Butler, M. Timlin, M. G. Walsh, A. R. Poynton and J. M. O'Byrne, 'Spinal injuries in Irish rugby: a ten-year review', *Journal of Bone and Joint Surgery*, vol. 88, no. 6 (2006), pp. 771–5

M. A. Stokes, J. A. McKeever, R. F. McQuillan and N. J. O'Higgins, 'A season of football injuries', *Irish Journal of Medical Science*, vol. 163 no. 6 (1994), pp. 290–93

Jason Tuck, 'Making sense of emerald commotion: rugby union, national identity and Ireland', *Identities: Global Studies in Culture and Power*, vol. 10, no. 4 (2003), pp. 495–515

Books

Rory Best, *My Autobiography* (London, Hodder & Stoughton, 2020)

Fergus Campbell, *The Irish Establishment 1879–1914* (Oxford, OUP, 2009)

Tony Collins, *Rugby's Great Split: Class, Culture and the Origins of Rugby League Football* (London, Frank Cass, 1998)

————, *A Social History of English Rugby Union* (Abingdon, Routledge, 2009)

————, *The Oval World: A Global History of Rugby* (London, Bloomsbury, 2015)

————, *How Football Began: A Global History of How the World's Football Codes were Born* (Abingdon, Routledge, 2019)

Ali Donnelly, *Scrum Queens: The Story of Women's Rugby* (Chichester, Pitch Publishing, 2022)

David Doolin, *A History of Rugby in Leinster* (Newbridge, Merrion Press, 2023)

Mick Doyle, *Doyler* (Dublin, Gill and Macmillan, 1991)

Tom English, *No Borders: Playing Rugby for Ireland* (Edinburgh, Polaris, 2015)

Brendan Fanning, *From There to Here: Irish Rugby in the Professional Era* (Dublin, Gill and Macmillan, 2007)

P. P. Fry, *The North of Ireland Cricket and Football Club 1859–1959* (Belfast, Thomas Brough, Cox and Dunn, 1959)

T. Gibson and J. Davies (eds.), *Rugby Medicine* (Oxford, Blackwell, 1991)

Henry Hanna, *The Pals at Suvla Bay: Being the Record of 'D' Company of the 7th Royal Dublin Fusiliers* (Dublin, E. Ponsonby, 1916)

W. J. McBride and P. Bills, *Willie John: The Story of My Life* (London, Piatkus, 2004)

Richard McElligott, *Forging a Kingdom: The GAA in Kerry, 1884–1934* (Cork, Collins Press, 2013)

Fr W. Maher, *A History of St Mary's College, Rathmines, Dublin 1890–1990* (Dublin, Paraclete Press, 1994)

Dominic Malcolm, *The Concussion Crisis in Sport* (Abingdon, Routledge, 2020)

J. A. Mangan, *Athleticism in the Victorian and Edwardian Public School: The Emergence and Consolidation of an Educational Ideology* (Cambridge, CUP, 1981)

The Rev. F. Marshall et al., *Football: The Rugby Union Game* (London, Paris and Melbourne, Cassell & Company, 1892)

Liam O'Callaghan, *Rugby in Munster: A Social and Cultural History* (Cork, Cork University Press, 2011)

R. M. Peter, *Irish Football Annual* (1880; repr. Newtownards, Ulster Historical Association, 1999)

Paul Rouse, *Sport and Ireland: A History* (Oxford, OUP, 2015)

————, *The Hurlers: The First All-Ireland Championship and the Making of Modern Hurling* (Dublin, Penguin Ireland, 2018)

David Smith and Gareth Williams, *Fields of Praise: The Official History of the Welsh Rugby Union 1881–1981* (Cardiff, University of Wales Press, 1980)

Edmund Van Esbeck, *One Hundred Years of Irish Rugby: The Official History of the Irish Rugby Union* (Dublin, Gill and Macmillan, 1974)

Trevor West (ed.), *Dublin University Football Club, 1854–2004: 150 Years of Trinity Rugby* (Bray, Wordwell, 2003)

Internet and audio-visual

CAIN: Sutton index of deaths, https://cain.ulster.ac.uk/sutton/chron/1987.html

Michael Dwyer, 'Mike Ryan', in his Tipperary Athletes series, http://tipperaryathletics.com/forms/2021/Tipperary%20Athlete%20--%20Mike%20Ryan.pdf

Hidden Impact: Concussion in Rugby (dir. A. McCarthy, Wildfire Films, 2015)

IRFU Strategic Plan 2018–23, https://d19fc3vdoojo3m.cloudfront.net/irfu/wp-content/uploads/2018/12/19161726/IRFU_Strategic_Plan_2018-2023.pdf

RTÉ Archives, https://www.rte.ie/archives/2015/0522/703076-womens-rugby-in-ireland/

RTÉ Century Ireland project, https://www.rte.ie/centuryireland/index.php/articles/wicklow-train-tragedy

References

Prologue: shoulder to shoulder

1 *Belfast Telegraph*, 25 March 1995.

2 *Irish Times*, 5 December 1998.

3 *Sunday World*, 28 January 1996.

4 *Irish Independent*, 26 May 1987.

5 *Irish Press*, 26 May 1987.

6 *Cork Examiner*, 30 May 1987.

7 CAIN: Sutton index of deaths. https://cain.ulster.ac.uk/sutton/chron/1987.html.

8 *Irish Times*, 5 June 1987.

9 *Evening Herald*, 29 May 1987.

10 *Sunday Press*, 31 May 1987.

11 *Irish Press*, 22 October 1991.

12 *Belfast Telegraph*, 22 February 1982.

13 *Irish Times*, 6 February 1984.

14 *Belfast News Letter*, 27 October 1980.

15 *Belfast Telegraph*, 9 February 1988.

16 Ibid., 27 January 1993.

17 Ibid., 30 January 1993.

18 Ibid., 28 January 1993.

19 *Irish Press*, 23 March 1990.

20 Martin Johnes, 'A Prince, a King, and a referendum: rugby, politics, and nationhood in Wales, 1969–1979', *Journal of British Studies*, vol. 47, no. 1 (2008), pp. 129–48.

21 *Irish Press*, 4 March 1994.

22 *Belfast Telegraph*, 27 January 1995.

23 *Evening Herald*, 12 February 1995.

24 *Irish Times*, 31 January 2015.

25 *Evening Herald*, 27 March 1998.

26 *Irish Times*, 29 October 1999.

27 *Sunday Independent*, 18 February 1996.

28 *Limerick Leader*, 22 December 1997.

29 *Limerick Chronicle*, 5 October 1999.

30 See, for example, *Belfast Telegraph*, 14 April 1995.

31 *Irish Times*, 12 February 1997.

32 *Sunday Independent*, 17 September 2006.

33 *Belfast Telegraph*, 4 July 2008.

34 *Irish Times*, 21 December 2021, 12 March 2022.

35 *Sunday Tribune*, 31 May 1987.

1. Tom Brown's game in Ireland

1 https://www.dufc.ie/. Accessed 13 December 2021.

2 Tony Collins, *How Football Began: A Global History of How the World's Football Codes were Born* (Abingdon, Routledge, 2019), p. 21.

3 Tony Collins, *The Oval World: A Global History of Rugby* (London, Bloomsbury, 2015), p. 32.

4 Collins, *How Football Began*, p. 8.

5 *Irish Times*, 5 July 1890.

6 Trevor West (ed.), *Dublin University Football Club, 1854–2004: 150 Years of Trinity Rugby* (Bray, Wordwell, 2003), p. 15.

7 Ibid., p. 15.

8 Ibid., p. 15.

9 Ibid., p. 14.

10 *The Field*, 18 January 1862.

11 *Dublin Daily Express*, 2 December 1865.

12 Tony Collins, *A Social History of English Rugby Union* (Abingdon, Routledge, 2009), p. vii.

13 Ibid., pp. 11–12.

14 Richard McElligott, *Forging a Kingdom: The GAA in Kerry, 1884–1934*, (Cork, Collins Press, 2013), pp. 20–21; Liam O'Callaghan, *Rugby in Munster: A Social and Cultural History* (Cork, Cork University Press, 2011), pp. 18–24.

15 *Irish Times*, 10 June 1865.

16 Ibid., 28 November 1953.

17 *Saunders News-Letter and Daily Advertiser*, 22 November 1856.

18 *Dublin Daily Express*, 17 February 1857.

19 *Irish Times*, 6 December 1860.

20 Ibid., 19 November 1867.

21 Ibid., 21 October 1872.

22 Ibid., 28 October 1867.

23 Ibid., 20 October 1868.

24 Collins, *English Rugby Union*, p. 134.

25 *Irish Times*, 23 April 1867.

26 Ibid., 16 April 1867.

27 *Warder and Dublin Weekly Mail*, 20 April 1867.

28 *Irish Times*, 20 October 1868.

29 Ibid.

30 Shaun Boylan, 'Barrington, Sir Charles Burton', *Dictionary of Irish Biography*.

31 *Hampshire Advertiser and Southampton Times*, 10 February 1940.

2. 'Against the World'

1 Edmund Van Esbeck, *One Hundred Years of Irish Rugby: The Official History of the Irish Rugby Union* (Dublin, Gill and Macmillan, 1974), p. 21.

2 *Freeman's Journal*, 30 December 1875.

3 *Sligo Chronicle*, 2 January 1875.

4 *Bell's Life*, 30 January 1875.

5 P. P. Fry, *The North of Ireland Cricket and Football Club 1859–1959*

(Belfast, Thomas Brough, Cox and Dunn, 1959), p. 15.

6 *Belfast News Letter*, 11 January 1869.

7 Ibid., 13 February 1869.

8 Ibid., 17 November 1869.

9 *Dublin Daily Express*, 16 December 1871.

10 *Sport*, 11 February 1882. McCarthy gave a similar account in Rev. F. Marshall et al., *Football: The Rugby Union Game* (London, Paris and Melbourne, Cassell & Company, 1892), p. 227.

11 IRFU Minutes, 12 October 1875, 24 October 1878, 4 November 1878.

12 *Bell's Life*, 28 March 1874.

13 Ibid., 30 January 1875.

14 *Belfast News Letter*, 5 February 1875.

15 *Bell's Life*, 30 January 1875.

16 *Sport*, 11 February 1882.

17 Marshall et al., *Football*, p. 229.

18 *The Field*, 20 February 1875.

19 *Ulster Examiner*, 20 February 1877.

20 *Cork Constitution*, 27 February 1878.

21 *Freeman's Journal*, 9 March 1878.

22 IRFU Minutes, 24 October 1878.

23 Ibid., 25 November 1878.

24 Ibid., 20 November 1878, 11 June 1879.

25 *Sport*, 4 February 1882.

26 Ibid., 9 March 1889.

27 IRFU Minutes, n.d. List of affiliated clubs 1884–85.

28 Author's database of Irish rugby internationals.

29 *Return of Number of Roman Catholic Students on Books of Trinity College, Dublin, July 1877*, House of Commons Papers, no. 449; *Census of Ireland 1891: General Report*, p. 65.

30 H. A. Hinkson, 'Education in Ireland, Catholic and Protestant', *Westminster Review* (July 1895), p. 85.

31 Mike Cronin, '"Trinity mysteries": responding to a chaotic reading of Irish history', *International Journal of the History of Sport*, vol. 28, no. 18 (2011), p. 2756

32 *Sport*, 14 October 1882.

33 IRFU Minutes, 19 March 1875.

34 Jim Shanahan, 'Peter, Richard Milliken', *Dictionary of Irish Biography*, http://dib.ie/biography/peter-richard-milliken-a7294.

35 *Irish Times*, 4 January 1873, 17 April 1920.

36 Ibid., 14 November 1874.

37 A potted history is offered in ibid., 9 October 1954.

38 R. M. Peter, *Irish Football Annual* (Dublin Steam Printing Co., 1880; repr. Newtownards, Ulster Historical Association, 1999), p. 49.

39 Desmond McCabe, 'Galbraith, Joseph Allen', *Dictionary of Irish Biography*, https://www.dib.ie/index.php/biography/galbraith-joseph-allen-a3401.

40 *Irish Times*, 18 March 1876.

41 Pauric J. Dempsey and Shaun Boylan, 'Arnott, Sir John', *Dictionary of Irish Biography*, https://www.dib.ie/biography/arnott-sir-john-a0228, accessed 28 June 2018; *Cheltenham College Register 1841–1889*.

42 J. A. Mangan's study remains the best analysis of this phenomenon. See J. A. Mangan, *Athleticism in the Victorian and Edwardian Public School: The Emergence and Consolidation of an Educational Ideology* (Cambridge, CUP, 1981).

43 *Irish Times*, 27 March 1880; *Waterford Standard*, 10 April 1880.

44 *Irish Times*, 28 October 1975.

45 Ibid., 29 January 1876, 7 February 1876.

46 *Bell's Life*, 4 December 1875.

47 *Irish Times*, 20 April 1898.

48 Ibid., 15 March 1902.

49 *Cork Examiner*, 26 July 1915.

50 *Sport*, 1 December 1888.

51 Ibid., 8 December 1888.

3. The old school tie

1 *Church of Ireland Gazette*, 20 March 1908.
2 Ibid.
3 Ibid.
4 Turlough O'Riordan, 'Bulger, Lawrence Quinlivan ('Larry')', *Dictionary of Irish Biography*, https://www.dib.ie/biography/bulger-lawrence-quinlivan-larry-a9796.
5 *Sport*, 8 October 1921.
6 Peter, *Irish Football Annual*, p. 62.
7 *Dublin Daily Express*, 1 November 1862.
8 *Blue, White and Blue* (March 1885).
9 *Our School Times*, 2 March 1874.
10 Ibid., 1 July 1872.
11 Ibid., 1 October 1872.
12 Ibid., 1 July 1874.
13 Ibid., 2 December 1872.
14 *Northern Whig*, 27 January 1876.
15 *Irish Christian Advocate*, 10 July 1891.
16 IRFU Minutes, 4 October 1876.
17 *Blue, White and Blue* (June 1892).
18 Fergus Campbell, *The Irish Establishment 1879–1914*, p. 79.
19 Ibid., p. 76.
20 Blackrock College Archives, community journal, 4 March 1887.
21 Ibid., 19 March 1889.
22 *The Belvederian* (Summer 1909).
23 Ibid. (1917).
24 Fr W. Maher, *A History of St Mary's College, Rathmines, Dublin 1890–1990* (Dublin, Paraclete Press, 1994), pp. 45–6.
25 *Castleknock College Chronicle* (June 1898).
26 Ibid., (June 1913).
27 Ibid.
28 *Cork Examiner*, 21 August 1888.

29 *The Collegian* (1931).

30 *The Belvederian* (Summer 1909).

31 Ibid. (1910).

32 *Cork Examiner*, 12 March 1938.

33 *The Belvederian* (Summer 1922).

34 As in, for example, *Blue, White and Blue* (March 1883).

35 Ibid. (June 1883).

36 Ibid. (November 1885).

37 Blackrock College Archives, community journal, 18 December 1885.

38 *The Belvederian* (Summer 1909).

39 Tony Collins, *Rugby's Great Split: Class, Culture and the Origins of Rugby League Football* (London, Frank Cass, 1998), pp. 49–50.

40 *Sport*, 12 November 1887.

41 Ibid.

42 Ibid., 9 October 1886.

43 *Irish Independent*, 2 February 1903.

44 Ibid., 7 February 1903.

45 Collins, *English Rugby Union*, p. 41.

46 *Sport*, 25 March 1899.

47 *Scottish Referee*, 20 March 1899.

48 Collins, *English Rugby Union*, p. 39.

49 *Church of Ireland Gazette*, 20 March 1908.

50 *Sport*, 24 December 1898.

4. The 'foreign' game?

1 *Sport*, 16 October 1886.

2 Ibid., 26 February 1887.

3 *Munster News*, 1 December 1886.

4 *Sport*, 10 December 1887.

5 Ibid., 17 February 1887.

6 Ibid., 23 February 1889.

7 Ibid., 26 February 1887.

8 *Munster News*, 23 November 1887.

9 Ibid., 3 December 1887.

10 Ibid., 13 January 1886.

11 *United Ireland*, 13 February 1886.

12 *United Irishman*, 20 October 1900.

13 *Young Ireland*, 3 May 1919.

14 Paul Rouse, *The Hurlers: The First All-Ireland Championship and the Making of Modern Hurling* (Dublin, Penguin Ireland, 2018), p. 40.

15 *Munster News*, 2 October 1886.

16 Ibid., 27 November 1886.

17 Ibid., 27 July 1887.

18 *Cork Constitution*, 28 December 1887.

19 *Freeman's Journal*, 18 September 1883.

20 *United Ireland*, 24 January 1885.

21 *Freeman's Journal*, 2 November 1885.

22 Ibid.

23 *United Ireland*, 31 October 1885, 13 March 1885.

24 O'Callaghan, *Rugby in Munster*, p. 82.

25 *Freeman's Journal*, 8 March 1886.

26 Ibid.

27 *Sport*, 10 April 1886.

28 *Cork Examiner*, 8 March 1886.

29 Collins, *How Football Began*, pp. 102–3.

30 *Sport*, 4 December 1886.

31 *Cork Constitution*, 1 March 1890; *Cork Daily Herald*, 10 June 1891; *Sport*, 5 April 1890.

32 *Irish Independent*, 14 January 1893.

33 *Cork Examiner*, 23 November 1892.

34 All three appear on the team list of Pembroke rugby club in February 1893. See *Cork Constitution*, 3 February 1893.

35 This was, in fact, the 1892 final. It was then common for

All-Ireland finals to be played in a different year to the championship season.

36 *Cork Daily Herald*, 14 October 1893.

37 Ibid., 25 November 1895.

38 *Evening Herald*, 18 July 1896.

39 *Cork Examiner*, 31 January 1888.

40 Ibid., 15 February 1888.

41 *Sport*, 25 February 1888.

42 Ibid., 19 March 1898; *Cork Examiner*, 3 March 1948.

43 *Sport*, 4 February 1899.

44 *Irish People*, 14 October 1899.

45 *Kerry News*, 29 November 1898.

46 *Sporting Life*, 24 January 1899.

47 Paul Rouse, 'The politics of culture and sport in Ireland: a history of the GAA ban on foreign games 1884–1971. Part one: 1884–1921', *International Journal of the History of Sport*, vol. 10, no. 3 (1993), pp. 333–60.

48 *Kerry Sentinel*, 18 December 1901.

49 *Dundalk Democrat*, 18 December 1909.

50 He appears on various contemporary Cork County team lists. See, for example, *Sunday Independent*, 18 November 1906.

51 *Cork Constitution*, 24 November 1892.

52 *Skibbereen Eagle*, 26 October 1889.

53 *Church of Ireland Gazette*, 28 June 1907.

54 Ibid., 30 March 1908.

55 Marshall et al., *Football*, p. 222.

56 *Sport*, 27 March 1926; *United Ireland*, 3 January 1885; O'Callaghan, *Rugby in Munster*, p. 85.

57 *Cork Examiner*, 9 February 1887.

58 *Dublin Evening Telegraph*, 6 February 1899.

59 *United Ireland*, 21 March 1896.

60 *Sport*, 12 February 1887.

61 Ibid., 17 December 1887.

62 *Kerry Sentinel,* 18 December 1901.

63 *Sport,* 3 February 1900.

64 Michael Dwyer, 'Mike Ryan' in his Tipperary Athletes series, http://tipperaryathletics.com/forms/2021/Tipperary%20 Athlete%20--%20Mike%20Ryan.pdf.

65 *Cork Daily Herald,* 13 February 1899.

66 *Irish Independent,* 4 December 1909.

67 O'Callaghan, *Rugby in Munster,* pp. 94–5.

5. Patriotic games

1 *Irish Times,* 10 February 1917.

2 Irish Civil Records (online).

3 Henry Hanna, *The Pals at Suvla Bay: Being the Record of 'D' Company of the 7th Royal Dublin Fusiliers* (Dublin, E. Ponsonby, 1916; repr. Uckfield, Naval and Military Press, 2015), p. 216.

4 RTÉ Century Ireland project, https://www.rte.ie/century ireland/index.php/articles/wicklow-train-tragedy.

5 *Irish Times,* 5 September 1914.

6 Collins, *English Rugby Union,* p. 50.

7 *St Andrew's College Magazine* (June 1906).

8 *Irish Times,* 1 December 1915.

9 Ibid., 23 December 1915.

10 Liam O'Callaghan, 'Irish rugby and the First World War', *Sport in Society,* vol. 19, no. 1 (2016), pp. 95–109.

11 *Northern Whig,* 23 December 1913.

12 *Belfast Telegraph,* 31 December 1913.

13 Ibid., 23 December 1913.

14 *Northern Whig,* 23 December 1913.

15 *Strabane Chronicle,* 3 January 1914.

16 *Belfast News Letter,* 21 January 1914.

17 *Northern Whig,* 21 January 1914.

18 *Belfast News Letter*, 19 January 1914.

19 Ibid., 8 June 1921.

20 *Irish Times*, 27 August 1960.

21 O'Callaghan, 'Irish rugby and the First World War'.

22 *St Andrew's College Magazine* (June 1917).

23 *Castleknock Chronicle*, vol. XXVI (1911); vol. XXXI (1916).

24 O'Callaghan, 'Irish rugby and the First World War'.

25 J. Gibney, 'PALS — The Irish at Gallipoli', *History Ireland*, vol. 23, no. 3 (2015), p. 50.

26 O'Callaghan, 'Irish rugby and the First World War'.

27 *Kildare Observer*, 19 September 1914.

28 *Evening Herald*, 17 September 1914.

29 *Irish Times*, 26 March 1915.

30 West (ed.), *Dublin University Football Club*, p. 28.

31 *Irish Times*, 11 May 1915.

32 *Dublin Daily Express*, 15 November 1906.

33 *Clare Champion*, 4 May 1957.

34 IRFU M/065 VC minutes, 18 July 1915, 21 December 1915, 5 April 1916, IRFU M065.

35 Ibid., 11 October 1916.

36 *The Belvederian* (1919).

37 Ibid. (1918).

38 Ibid. (1921).

39 Ibid. (Summer 1922).

40 Bureau of Military History, witness statement, Dr Patrick O'Sullivan; *Evening Herald*, 16 March 1914; additional biographical information from Blackrock College Archives, college register.

41 *Cork Examiner*, 1 December 1915.

42 *Irish Independent*, 23 January 1947.

43 *Limerick Leader*, 6 July 1942.

44 *Sport*, 10 January 1914; Munster Branch Committee Minutes, 6 October 1938.

45 *Limerick Leader*, 5 January 1934.
46 Bureau of Military History, witness statement, Francis O'Duffy.
47 *Belfast News Letter*, 5 November 1923.
48 IRFU minutes, 21 February 1919, 6 October 1920, 6 March 1925.

6. 'The rugby game has no boundaries'

1 *Irish Times*, 12 March 1927.
2 *Sport*, 19 March 1927.
3 *Drogheda Argus*, 2 April 1927.
4 Cork Constitution Football Club minutes, 28 March 1924, CCAA/SP/CC/1/1.
5 Ibid., 7 May 1924, CCAA/SP/CC/1/1.
6 Blackrock College Archives, community journal, 15 March 1925.
7 *Belfast News Letter*, 31 October 1927.
8 IRFU Minutes, 10 January 1931.
9 Ibid., 25 May 1926, 15 June 1926.
10 Jeffares to O'Brien, 2 March 1929, IRFU Archives, F062.
11 Jeffares to O'Brien, n.d. 1946, IRFU Archives, F0178/3.
12 IRFU Minutes, 19 March 1929.
13 Ibid., 25 September 1929; religions derived from 1911 Census.
14 IRFU Minutes, 25 September 1929.
15 Ibid.
16 Munster Branch Committee Minutes, 10 October 1929.
17 Ibid., 15 December 1929.
18 Ibid., 14 November 1929.
19 *Kildare Observer*, 12 January 1929.
20 *Roscommon Messenger*, 7 December 1929.
21 IRFU Minutes, 25 November 1929, 6 December 1929.
22 Ibid., 25 November 1929.
23 O'Callaghan, *Rugby in Munster*, pp. 100–104.
24 *Sport*, 21 April 1928.

25 Ibid., 1 March 1930.

26 IRFU Minutes, 25 June 1926.

27 Munster Branch Committee Minutes, 27 April 1933.

28 Daly to Jeffares, 2 February 1932, IRFU Archives.

29 IRFU Minutes, 30 September 1927.

30 Ibid., 29 November 1940.

31 *An Phoblacht*, 6 November 1925.

32 O'Callaghan, *Rugby in Munster*, p. 171.

33 Notes of meeting between Cosgrave and Connacht Branch, NAI TAOIS/S2950.

34 McGilligan to Clarke, 5 February 1932, IRFU Archives.

35 Liam O'Callaghan, 'Rugby football and identity politics in Free State Ireland', *Éire–Ireland*, vol. 48, no. 1 (2013), p. 152.

36 Ibid.

37 Notes for Minister, n.d. April 1952, NAI DFA/5/340/12/132/1.

38 General file: Attendance at non-Gaelic matches, 10 February 1940, NAI PRES 2005/3/116.

39 General file: Rugby matches, 14 November 1938, NAI PRES 2005/3/116.

40 Minute from the Irish Minister at Canberra, 17 August 1950, NAI DFA/6/415/4/1.

41 Ibid., 2 August 1950, NAI DFA/6/415/4/1.

42 Ibid., 29 May 1950, NAI DFA/6/415/4/1.

43 Ibid.

44 E. Morris, '"God Save the King" versus "The Soldier's Song": the 1929 Trinity College national anthem dispute and the politics of the Irish Free State', *Irish Historical Studies*, vol. 31, no. 121 (1998), pp. 72–90.

45 Ibid, p. 77.

46 *Frontier Sentinel*, 15 June 1929.

47 *Belfast News Letter*, 1 March 1929.

48 *Dundee Evening Telegraph*, 16 April 1923.

49 *Irish Times*, 2 January 1925.

50 Letter from Seán Murphy (for Joseph P. Walshe) to Count Gerald O'Kelly de Gallagh (Paris) (1489/458), Documents on Irish Foreign Policy, vol. 3, no. 493, NAI DFA GR 1489.

51 Ibid. Letter from Count Gerald O'Kelly de Gallagh to Joseph P. Walshe (Dublin) (52/D/31).

52 *Belfast News-Letter*, 29 February 1929.

53 *Irish Press*, 10 February 1947.

54 See, for example, *Edinburgh Evening News*, 17 February 1934.

55 International Rugby football matches. Attendance of the President, 23 February 1948, 27 February 1948, NAI PRES/1/ P2943.

56 Jeffares to Glynn, 11 March 1953, IRFU Archives, F101/2.

57 Jason Tuck, 'Making sense of emerald commotion: rugby union, national identity and Ireland', *Identities: Global Studies in Culture and Power*, vol. 10, no. 4 (2003), p. 510.

58 Irish Rugby Union, 5 February 1953, NAI PRES/2005/3/116.

59 Glynn to Jeffares, 9 February 1953, IRFU Archives, F101/2.

60 Jeffares to Glynn, 11 February 1953, IRFU Archives, F101/2.

61 *Irish Times*, 29 January 1953.

62 *Connacht Sentinel*, 27 January 1953.

63 *Irish Weekly and Ulster Examiner*, 7 March 1953.

64 *Derry Journal*, 23 February 1953.

65 Vic Rigby and Liam O'Callaghan, 'The Riddle of Ravenhill', in M. Ní Fhuartháin and D. M. Doyle (eds.), *Ordinary Irish Life: Music, Sport and Culture* (Newbridge, Irish Academic Press, 2013), pp. 98–113.

66 *Irish Times*, 28 May 2015.

67 Ibid., 28 October 1955, 29 June 1968.

68 Ibid., 29 June 1968.

69 *Belfast News Letter*, 27 February 1967.

70 *Irish Times*, 15 February 1947.

71 Quoted in *Evening Herald*, 15 March 1948.

72 Liam O'Callaghan, 'Kyle, Jack', *Dictionary of Irish Biography*, https://www.dib.ie/biography/kyle-jack-a10172.

73 Linde Lunney, 'Foster, Alexander Roulston', *Dictionary of Irish Biography*, https://www.dib.ie/biography/foster-alexander-roulston-alec-a9798.

74 *Independent* (London), 8 January 2010.

7. Political football

1 *Belfast Telegraph*, 5 January 1970.

2 Ibid., 6 January 1970.

3 *Irish Times*, 9 January 1970.

4 *Irish Independent*, 26 November 1969.

5 *Belfast Telegraph*, 27 November 1969.

6 Ibid., 28 November 1969.

7 *Irish Press*, 9 January 1970.

8 *Evening Herald*, 7 January 1970.

9 *Belfast Telegraph*, 11 November 1969.

10 *Irish Times*, 27 January 1965.

11 *Belfast Telegraph*, 17 October 1963.

12 Ibid., 7 February 1964.

13 Ibid., 20 November 1982.

14 Ibid., 10 April 1979.

15 *Irish News*, 25 January 2020.

16 Mike Cronin, 'Playing away from home: identity in Northern Ireland and the experience of Derry City football club', *National Identities*, vol. 2, no. 1 (2000), pp. 65–79.

17 *Irish Press*, 13 March 1950.

18 *Derry Journal*, 13 March 1950.

19 *Belfast Telegraph*, 13 March 1950.

20 Cremin to Jeffares, 21 November 1951, NAI JUS/8/975.

21 Hogan to Coyne, 22 November 1951, NAI JUS/8/975.

22 Anti-Partition League leaflet, n.d. 1951, NAI JUS/8/975.

23 Garda report, 12 December 1951, NAI JUS/8/975.

24 *Belfast News Letter*, 2 November 1971.

25 Ibid., 5 February 1972.

26 Munster Branch Committee Minutes, 3 February 1972.

27 *Belfast News Letter*, 3 February 1972.

28 Ibid., 17 February 1972.

29 Annual meeting of the Council of the Branch, 25 May 1972. Leinster Branch IRFU records, UCD Archives.

30 *Belfast News Letter*, 18 February 1972.

31 Munster Branch Committee Minutes, 15 June 1972.

32 *Belfast Telegraph*, 18 November 1972.

33 Annual meeting of the Council of the Branch, 31 May 1973, Leinster Branch IRFU records, UCD Archives.

34 *Sunday Independent*, 7 January 1973.

35 *Irish Times*, 10 February 1973.

36 Ibid., 12 February 1973.

37 *Belfast Telegraph*, 12 February 1973.

38 *Irish Examiner*, 6 April 2012.

39 *Sunday Tribune*, 3 January 1988.

40 *Belfast News Letter*, 23 April 1998.

41 *Belfast Telegraph*, 15 May 1996.

42 Collins, *Oval World*, pp. 53, 134, 461.

43 Ganly to Walsh, 1 April 1981, NAI TAOIS/2009/135/686.

44 Parliamentary Debates Dáil Éireann, vol. 214, no. 5 (18 February 1965).

45 Douglas Booth, 'Hitting apartheid for six? The politics of the South African sports boycott', *Journal of Contemporary History*, vol. 38, no. 3 (2003), pp. 477–93.

46 Opening address of Michael O'Kennedy to conference on relations between the EEC and South Africa, NAI TAOIS/2009/135/888.

47 Tom Lodge, 'An "boks amach": the Irish Anti-Apartheid Movement', *History Ireland*, vol. 14, no. 4 (2006), pp. 35–9.

48 Department of Foreign Affairs public statement, NAI TAOIS/2009/135/888.

49 Note of information for the Taoiseach, n. d., September 1979, NAI TAOIS/2009/135/888.

50 Killannin to Lynch, 5 September 1979; Killannin to Montgomery, 5 September 1979, NAI TAOIS/2009/135/888.

51 *Belfast Telegraph*, 11 September 1979.

52 Government statement, 18 September 1979, NAI TAOIS/2009/135/888.

53 Kirwan to Fitzgerald, 15 October 1979, NAI TAOIS/2009/135/888.

54 *Belfast Telegraph*, 31 October 1979.

55 Parliamentary Debates Dáil Éireann, vol. 325, no. 5 (10 December 1980).

56 *Belfast Telegraph*, 5 January 1981.

57 Ibid., 3 January 1981.

58 Asmal to Haughey, 2 March 1981, NAI TAOIS/2011/127/932.

59 Aide memoire, ICTU, 24 April 1981, NAI TAOIS/2011/127/932.

60 Memo: The IRFU Rugby Tour to South Africa – Reactions and Effects, n. d. 1981 NAI TAOIS/2011/127/932.

61 Implications of proposed rugby tour of South Africa for Ireland, NAI TAOIS/2011/127/932.

62 Ganly to Haughey, 1 May 1981, NAI TAOIS/2011/127/932.

63 Government statement, 4 May 1981, NAI TAOIS/2011/127/932.

64 Memo: The IRFU Rugby Tour to South Africa – Reactions and Effects, n.d. 1981, NAI TAOIS/2011/127/932.

65 W. J. McBride and P. Bills, *Willie John: The Story of My Life* (London, Piatkus, 2004), p. 164.

66 Ibid., p. 243.

67 *Irish Times*, 14 April 2020.

68 *Daily Mirror*, 31 January 1981.

69 Barrington to O'Grady, 14 November 1981, NAI TAOIS/ 2011/127/932.

70 *Irish Independent*, 20 September 1989.

71 Much of this paragraph is based on IRFU public statement, 18 September 1989, NAI DFA/2022/23/6341.

72 Ibid.

8. Amateurism: decline and fall

1 *Irish Times*, 12 August 1997.

2 *The People*, 8 October 1967.

3 *Irish Times*, 20 September 1966, 9 November 1966.

4 Collins, *Oval World*, p. 435.

5 *Irish Press*, 28 April 1964.

6 Collins, *Oval World*, p. 158.

7 *Irish Times*, 7 October 1969.

8 Ibid., 22 January 1969.

9 Ibid., 21 January 1969.

10 *Irish Independent*, 15 March 1969.

11 *Cork Examiner*, 2 October 1964.

12 Munster Branch Committee Minutes, 1 October 1965.

13 *Irish Times*, 15 December 1987.

14 *Belfast Telegraph*, 23 April 1989.

15 *Irish Times*, 13 May 1987.

16 Collins, *Oval World*, p. 315.

17 Results taken from espn.com .

18 Leinster Branch Irish Rugby Football Union, Honorary Secretary's Report, 1991–92, Leinster Branch IRFU records, UCD Archives.

19 Ibid.

20 Munster Branch Committee Minutes, 11 November 1976.

21 Ibid., 18 October 1973.

22 *Irish Times*, 7 June 1983.

23 Ibid., 24 August 1985.

24 Ibid., 17 January 1987.

25 Ibid., 5 February 1987.

26 Ibid., 6 June 1987.

27 *Sunday Independent*, 8 December 1991; Brendan Fanning, *From There to Here: Irish Rugby in the Professional Era* (Dublin, Gill and Macmillan, 2007), pp. xi–xv.

28 *Irish Independent*, 10 December 1991.

29 *Irish Times*, 6 November 1924.

30 Leinster Branch Irish Rugby Football Union, Honorary Secretary's Report, 1990–91, Leinster Branch IRFU records, UCD Archives.

31 Tuck, 'Making sense of emerald commotion', pp. 495–515.

32 *Ireland's Saturday Night*, 16 May 1987.

33 *Sunday Independent*, 19 January 1995.

34 Ibid., 29 January 1995.

35 Mike Doyle, *Doyler* (Dublin, Gill and Macmillan, 1991).

36 Terry Clavin, 'Doyle, Mick', *Dictionary of Irish Biography*, www.dib.ie.

37 *Sunday Independent*, 12 February 1995.

38 Ibid., 10 September 1995.

39 *Irish Times*, 17 May 1995.

40 *Sunday Independent*, 3 September 1995.

41 *Irish Times*, 1 September 1995.

42 Munster Branch Committee Minutes, 6 March 1973.

43 Leinster Branch Irish Rugby Football Union, Honorary Secretary's Report, 1991–92, Leinster Branch IRFU records, UCD Archives.

44 *Sunday Independent*, 7 October 1990.

9. Four proud provinces

1 *Sunday Tribune*, 5 November 1995.
2 O'Callaghan, *Rugby in Munster*, p. 220.
3 *Irish Times*, 1 January 1996; *Irish Independent*, 18 March 1996.
4 Fanning, *From There to Here*, pp. 58–83.
5 *Irish Times*, 12 November 1997.
6 *Evening Herald*, 26 April 1997.
7 *Irish Times*, 30 January 1999.
8 Ibid., 1 February 1999.
9 O'Callaghan, *Rugby in Munster*, p. 213.
10 Ibid., p. 224.
11 C. Houlihan, 'State of the Heart', *Rugby Ireland*, vol. 3, no. 7 (June 2002).
12 *Irish Examiner*, 8 January 2000, 23 July 2004.
13 Ibid., 21 June 2007.
14 *Evening Press*, 23 November 1978.
15 *Irish Times*, 23 September 2008.
16 Leinster Branch Irish Rugby Football Union, Honorary Secretary's Report, 1989–90, Leinster Branch IRFU records, UCD Archives.
17 Ibid.
18 Leinster Branch Irish Rugby Football Union, Honorary Secretary's Report, 1992–93, Leinster Branch IRFU records, UCD Archives.
19 Minutes of Executive Committee Meeting, 10 March 1992, Leinster Branch IRFU records, UCD Archives.
20 Leinster Branch Irish Rugby Football Union, Honorary Secretary's Report, 1994–95, Leinster Branch IRFU records, UCD Archives.
21 *Irish Times*, 11 January 2016.
22 *Irish Independent*, 26 November 2008.
23 *Irish Times*, 31 January 2006.

24 Ibid., 28 February 2004.

25 Ibid., 13 February 2020.

26 Ibid., 31 January 1998.

27 Ibid., 18 January 2020.

28 *Daily Telegraph*, 31 March 2018.

29 *Irish Independent*, 14 January 2018.

30 Marcus Free. '"Smart, clued-in guys": Irish rugby players as sporting celebrities in post-Celtic Tiger Irish media', *International Journal of Media & Cultural Politics*, vol. 14, no. 2 (2018), pp. 215–32.

31 *Irish Times*, 21 August 2023.

32 IRFU Minutes, 17 December 1937.

33 Ibid., 1 December 1933.

34 Fanning, *From There to Here*, pp. 167–82.

10. The man's game?

1 *Irish Independent*, 7 January 1994.

2 *Sport*, 3 October 1885.

3 Ibid., 20 February 1926.

4 *Irish Times*, 27 February 1979.

5 *Sunday Press*, 16 March 1986.

6 *Sunday Independent*, 25 June 1995.

7 *Evening Herald*, 9 October 1993.

8 *Sunday Independent*, 30 September 2007.

9 Ali Donnelly, *Scrum Queens: The Story of Women's Rugby* (Chichester, Pitch Publishing, 2022), chapters 1–3.

10 RTÉ Archives, https://www.rte.ie/archives/2015/0522/703076-womens-rugby-in-ireland/.

11 *Irish Press*, 26 January 1978.

12 *Evening Press*, 7 October 1983.

13 *Irish Press*, 28 December 1972.

14 *Sunday Life*, 6 November 1988.

15 *Ireland's Saturday Night*, 14 September 1991.

16 *Tallaght Echo*, 4 April 1985.

17 *Evening Echo*, 12 January 1986.

18 Ibid., 30 April 1986.

19 *Evening Press*, 1 October 1990.

20 Ibid., 4 June 1990.

21 *Belfast Telegraph*, 12 February 1994.

22 *Irish Press*, 24 November 1992.

23 Ibid., 10 October 1993.

24 *Ireland's Saturday Night*, 12 February 1994.

25 *Irish Times*, 12 January 1994.

26 *Evening Herald*, 3 February 1997.

27 *Irish Times*, 15 May 2000.

28 *Limerick Leader*, 16 February 2013.

29 Donnelly, *Scrum Queens*, p. 109.

30 *Evening Herald*, 3 August 2006.

31 *Irish Times*, 16 March 2013.

32 *Donegal News*, 15 March 2013.

33 *Irish Times*, 17 December 2021.

34 https://www.rte.ie/sport/rugby/2021/1109/1258850-pressure-mounts-on-womens-rugby-director-anthony-eddy/.

35 *Irish Independent*, 21 September 2021.

36 Donnelly, *Scrum Queens*, pp. 212–15.

37 *Irish Times*, 6 March 2014.

38 *Irish Times*, 17 September 2018.

39 https://www.the42.ie/irfu-womens-contracts-2-5904555-Oct2022/.

40 https://www.bbc.co.uk/sport/rugby-union/63417538.

41 *Daily Telegraph*, 13 April 2023.

42 *Nationalist and Leinster Times*, 20 February 1998.

43 *Belfast Telegraph*, 9 September 2000.

44 *Evening Herald*, 27 October 2006.

45 https://ulster.rugby/content/ulster-u18-girls-squad-named-for-interpro-series.

11. Putting his head where it hurts

1 *Sunday Tribune*, 17 April 1997.
2 *Irish Independent*, 21 January 1987.
3 Ibid., 29 September 2022.
4 Ibid.
5 *Irish Times*, 20 October 1913.
6 *Belfast News Letter*, 5 March 1928, 11 December 1928.
7 *Irish Times*, 19 April 1930; *Connacht Tribune*, 25 February 1933; *Cork Examiner*, 27 March 1935; *Weekly Irish Times*, 21 January 1939.
8 *Irish Times*, 14 November 1956; *Weekly Irish Times*, 21 January 1939; *Belfast Telegraph*, 11 November 1948; *Meath Chronicle*, 14 March 1953; *Nationalist and Leinster Times*, 31 October 1959; *Evening Herald*, 17 November 1960; *Irish Press*, 18 November 1960; *Limerick Leader*, 4 November 1961; *Belfast News Letter*, 9 November 1970; *Cork Weekly Examiner*, 8 April 1971; *Irish Independent*, 15 November 1975; *Irish Press*, 29 January 1980.
9 *Irish Times*, 14 November 1956.
10 *Clare Champion*, 21 October 1961.
11 *Limerick Leader*, 4 November 1961.
12 *Clare Champion*, 21 October 1961.
13 Ibid.
14 *Irish Independent*, 22 November 1949.
15 *Sunday Independent*, 13 December 1970.
16 *Belfast Telegraph*, 23 April 1975.
17 *Irish Independent*, 15 November 1975.
18 *Evening Press*, 12 March 1980; *Evening Herald*, 28 March 1980.
19 *Irish Press*, 22 February 1988.
20 *Evening Herald*, 28 March 1980.

21 *Irish Press*, 16 April 1984; *Evening Herald*, 29 September 1984.

22 *Evening Press*, 18 April 1984.

23 *Irish Press*, 12 March 1980.

24 *Irish Times*, 18 March 1980.

25 *Irish Press*, 18 April 1984.

26 *Irish Times*, 4 January 1985.

27 Ibid.

28 *Irish Independent*, 22 February 1988.

29 *Evening Press*, 12 March 1980.

30 *Irish Press*, 1 May 1980.

31 *Evening Herald*, 23 August 1991.

32 M. A. Stokes, J. A. McKeever, R. F. McQuillan and N. J. O'Higgins, 'A season of football injuries', *Irish Journal of Medical Science*, vol. 163, no. 6 (1994), pp. 290–93.

33 M. J. Shelly, J. S. Butler, M. Timlin, et al., 'Spinal injuries in Irish rugby: a ten-year review', *Journal of Bone and Joint Surgery*, vol. 88, no. 6 (2006), pp. 771–5.

34 W. J. Mullaly, 'Concussion', *American Journal of Medicine*, vol. 130, no. 8 (2017), pp. 885–92.

35 Dominic Malcolm, *The Concussion Crisis in Sport* (Abingdon, Routledge, 2020).

36 *Irish Times*, 19 October 1965.

37 *Belfast Telegraph*, 23 April 1975.

38 *Irish Times*, 16 March 1953.

39 *Belfast Telegraph*, 23 April 1975.

40 *Irish Times*, 18 March 1980.

41 T. Gibson and J. Davies (eds.), *Rugby Medicine* (Oxford, Blackwell, 1991).

42 *Irish Times*, 22 September 1975.

43 *Irish Independent*, 26 September 1978.

44 *Irish Examiner*, 20 November 2010.

45 J. M. Ryan and R. McQuillan, 'A survey of rugby injuries

attending an accident & emergency department', *Irish Medical Journal*, vol. 85, no. 2 (1992), pp. 72–3.

46 *Irish Independent*, 4 December 1990.

47 Ibid., 22 February 1988.

48 *Irish Times*, 25 October 1993.

49 N. E. Hill, S. Rilstone, M. J. Stacey, et al., 'Changes in northern hemisphere male international rugby union players' body mass and height between 1955 and 2015', *BMJ Open Sport & Exercise Medicine*, vol. 4 (2018), https://bmjopensem.bmj.com/content/bmjosem/4/1/e000459.full.pdf.

50 *Irish Times*, 10 October 1998.

51 Ibid., 13 November 1998.

52 Ibid.

53 *Irish Independent*, 17 November 1998.

54 *Independent* (London), 15 December 1998.

55 T. W. Buford, R. B. Kreider, J. R. Stout, et al., 'International Society of Sports Nutrition position stand: creatine supplementation and exercise', *Journal of the International Society of Sports Nutrition*, vol. 4, no. 1 (2007), pp. 1–8.

56 *Sunday Tribune*, 21 March 1999.

57 *Irish Times*, 18 December 2013.

58 M. Fraas, G. F. Coughlan, E. C. Hart and C. McCarthy, 'Concussion history and reporting rates in elite Irish rugby union players', *Physical Therapy in Sport*, vol. 15, no. 3 (2014), pp. 136–42.

59 S. E. Delahunty, E. Delahunt, B. Condon, et al., 'Prevalence of and attitudes about concussion in Irish schools' rugby union players', *Journal of School Health*, vol. 85, no. 1 (2015), pp. 17–26.

60 E. O'Connell and M. G. Molloy, 'Concussion in rugby: knowledge and attitudes of players', *Irish Journal of Medical Science*, vol. 185 (2016), pp. 521–8.

61 *Irish Times*, 26 February 2016.

62 Ibid., 12 February 2016, 10 March 2016.
63 *Sunday Independent*, 5 April 2009.
64 Ibid.
65 *Sunday Independent*, 23 May 2010.
66 *Irish Times*, 16 September 2015.
67 Ibid., 11 February 2021.
68 Ibid., 3 June 2011.
69 http://en.espn.co.uk/scrum/rugby/story/208943.html.
70 *Irish Times*, 14 February 2015.
71 Ibid.
72 Ibid.
73 *Hidden Impact: Concussion in Rugby* (dir. A. McCarthy, Wildfire Films, 2015).
74 *Irish Times*, 23 February 2015.
75 *Irish Independent*, 27 February 1998.
76 *Irish Times*, 29 September 2022.

12. Rugby country

1 *Irish Examiner*, 12 July 2012.
2 *Irish Daily Mail*, 22 October 2019.
3 *Irish Times*, 7 March 2018.
4 *Sunday Independent*, 25 March 2018.
5 *Irish Times*, 8 September 2023.
6 Ibid., 17 October 2023.
7 IRFU Strategic Plan 2018–23, https://d19fc3vdoojo3m.cloud-front.net/irfu/wp-content/uploads/2018/12/19161726/IRFU_Strategic_Plan_2018-2023.pdf.
8 *Irish Times*, 9 February 2017.
9 Department of Education, Statistical Bulletin, July 2021, https://www.gov.ie/pdf/?file=https://assets.gov.ie/139883/8cc02789-a453-4abd-8940-b6195377909f.pdf#page=null.
10 *Irish Times*, 23 March 2020.

11 Parliamentary Debates Seanad Éireann, vol. 270, no. 11 (31 July 2020).

12 *Irish Times*, 29 March 2018.

13 Ibid., 22 May 2020.

14 Ibid.

15 Rory Best, *My Autobiography* (London, Hodder & Stoughton, 2020), p. 246.

16 *Guardian*, 4 December 2018.

17 *Belfast Telegraph*, 11 April 2018.

18 *Guardian*, 4 December 2018.

19 *Irish Times*, 27 April 2018.

20 *Sunday Independent*, 29 February 2004.

21 *Irish Press*, 1 April 1994.

22 *Irish Independent*, 2 February 1990.

23 *Evening Echo*, 4 March 1993.

24 *Evening Herald*, 31 March 2000.

25 IRFU Minutes, 7 May 1924, 13 July 1925, 5 November 1928.

26 Ibid., 11 January 1929, 29 August 1930.

27 Ibid., 1 April 1924.

28 Jeffares to Freethy, 17 February 1949, IRFU Archives F0178/5.

29 *Irish Times*, 14 April 2001.

30 Ibid., 18 May 2020.

31 *Irish Independent*, 26 February 2005.

32 Ibid., 26 February 2005.

33 *Irish Independent*, 15 March 2005.

34 Ibid., 12 March 2005.

35 Ibid., 26 February 2007.

36 *Irish Times*, 30 October 2012.

37 *Limerick Leader*, 21 August 2010.

38 *Sunday Independent*, 28 October 2010.

39 *Irish Independent*, 26 October 2017.

40 *New Zealand Herald*, 10 October 2023.

41 https://www.tamireland.ie/top-50-tv-programmes-2022/.
42 *Irish Times*, 16 October 2023.
43 *Sunday Business Post*, 1 March 2019.

Acknowledgements

This book lived in my head for years, and might have continued to do so were it not for the encouragement of my friend Niall Carson. Over a coffee with Niall on Smithdown Road, Liverpool, in the summer of 2021, he convinced me that the vague notion I had of writing this book should become a concrete plan. I will always be grateful to him for this nudge, which I needed at that point.

For close to two decades I have benefited from the unrivalled support and intellectual generosity of Mike Cronin and Tony Collins. Their advice and encouragement – including on this project – have given me confidence and assurance throughout my career. Mike took time out of his busy schedule to read draft work, while Tony helped me to clarify my thoughts on rugby's idiosyncratic relationship with amateurism and the strange bonds of loyalty that developed historically among rugby officials across the world.

Historians cannot make bricks without straw. In that regard, I owe a debt of gratitude to those who have facilitated access to archival sources. At the IRFU, Declan Meade was a generous and gregarious host. Many years ago, the late John Coleman was very helpful in facilitating access to the Munster Branch records. Jessica Cunningham at Blackrock College is in charge of a superb collection of records. Dr Cunningham was unfailingly generous in responding to my several requests. The staff at UCD Archives, at a time when the facility was undergoing renovation, were courteous and helpful when I visited their temporary reading room. Paul Rouse helped me to gain access to the Leinster Branch records, while David Doolin very kindly shared his excellent research on Leinster rugby. John Cussen of Newcastle West made time to share insights about his family's long connection with Blackrock College and with rugby.

My research trips to Dublin were all the more productive thanks to the hospitality of David and Marie Doyle. The friendship and generosity of David – my long-time collaborator – and of his wife, Marie, went well beyond any reasonable expectations I could have had.

At Liverpool Hope University, I have been fortunate to work in an atmosphere that fosters collegiality and academic freedom. My thanks to many colleagues from over the years. Professor Atulya Nagar and Professor Omid Khaiyat have provided practical support to the research that underpinned this book. Caroline Wakefield, a wonderful colleague and friend, has provided bountiful support and encouragement, as have Neil Ferguson, Simon Kawycz and Liam Owens. I would also like to acknowledge the lasting friendship of my former colleagues Victor Merriman, Mark Mc Auley, Joel Rookwood and Brian Desmond.

In Ireland, the friendship of Aaron Buckley, Eoin McCormack, Lorcan McCormack and Ronan Goggin has endured my long stay in Liverpool.

I would like to thank the team at Penguin Sandycove, particularly Brendan Barrington. As an editor, Brendan is a first-rate advocate for the reader. His probing and challenging comments have improved the text immeasurably.

As ever, my greatest debts are to those closest to me. I am fortunate that I grew up in a very supportive household. I owe a debt of gratitude to my parents, brother and sister that

ACKNOWLEDGEMENTS

I can never repay. My brother, Ruairí, read some early drafts, offering the perspective of an astute rugby fan. In Cork, I have shared great times with my mother-in-law and sister-in-law. Their kindness and hospitality mean a lot to me. Finally, none of this would have been possible without the love, support and patience of my wife, Susan Murphy. She has lived alongside this project from the start, and has been incredibly stoic in the face of my absences, both physical and mental. This book is humbly dedicated to her.

Index

Abraham, Myley 58
Adams, Gerry 169
Adidas 7, 159
Aer Lingus 145, 200
Against the Head (rugby magazine programme) 220–21
Agnew, Paddy 130
Ahern, Bertie 230
Aherne, Tom 76, 82
Aki, Bundee 222, 235, 236, 237, 238
All-Ireland League (AIL) 149, 161, 165, 166, 170–71, 183, 214
amateurism 58–63, 103, 117, 124, 128, 144–5, 147
  broken-time payments and 59
  decline and fall of/turn to professionalism 149–66
  greatest Irish national team of amateur era 124
  Ireland and Scotland view themselves as allies in battle to defend 61–2
  Ireland viewed by rugby world as sternest defenders of 58
  moral framework of 58–9
  rugby league origins and 20, 59, 62, 151, 154, 155
  working-class players and 58–61

'Amhrán na bhFiann' (anthem) 2, 3, 4, 5, 6, 9–10, 11, 12, 13, 115, 116–17, 118, 119, 122, 136, 236
An Phoblacht 111
An Tóchar 227–8
Anderson, Henry 104, 180–81
Anderson, Willie 191
anthems 1–13, 41, 56, 110, 115–22, 123, 232, 236
Anti-Partition League 131
Argentina (men's national rugby union team) 11
Arigho, Jack 105
Arlington School 49
Arnold, Thomas 20–21
Arnott, David 40–42
Arnott, John 40
Arravale Rovers 76
Asmal, Kader 140
Australia (men's national rugby union team) 5, 147, 152, 156, 160, 237

Ballyseedy massacre (1923) 97
Bandon 75
Barbarians 137, 140, 141
Barrington, Sir Charles Burton 16–19, 25–8, 30
Barrington, Sir Croker 16